TRAVELS IN
ALASKA

Alpenglow on Summit of Mount Muir, Harrison Fiord, Prince William Sound

John Muir

Travels in Alaska

Introduction by Edward Hoagland

THE MODERN LIBRARY

NEW YORK

2002 Modern Library Paperback Edition

LIBRARY OF CONGRESS CATALOGING-IN-PUBLICATION DATA
Muir, John, 1838–1914
Travels in Alaska / John Muir: introduction by Edward Hoagland.—
Modern Library pbk. ed.
p.   cm.
Originally published: Boston: Houghton Mifflin Co., 1915.
1. Muir, John, 1838–1914—Journeys—Alaska.   2. Alaska—Description
and travel.   3. Naturalists—United States—Biography.   I. Title.
ISBN 0-375-76049-0
QH31.M9 A3 2002
508.798'092—dc21
[B]   2002072247

Modern Library website address: www.modernlibrary.com

Printed in the United States of America

2   4   6   8   9   7   5   3

JOHN MUIR

John Muir was born on April 21, 1838, in Dunbar, Scotland, the third of eight children of Daniel Muir and Anne Gilrye Muir. In 1849, the Muir family immigrated to the United States and settled on a farm near Portage, Wisconsin. As the eldest son, Muir labored unremittingly on the family farm, where his affection for the wilderness and his interest in science and literature took root. In 1860, Muir's inventiveness in the design of machines led to an exhibit at the state fair in Madison; the acclaim his inventions received resulted in numerous job offers and Muir's acceptance at the University of Wisconsin.

Although Muir never received a degree (he left after three years), he studied geology and botany, discovered Emerson and Thoreau, and began to develop a conception of the natural world independent of his father's stricter religious one. Still, it would be several years before Muir would make the study and preservation of the wilderness his life's work.

In September 1867, his sight restored after a serious eye injury, Muir set out on what was to become a 1,000-mile walk from Indiana to Florida. He then traveled to California, arriving in San Francisco in March 1868, and walked for six weeks across the state until he arrived at the Sierra Nevada mountains, where he would spend much of the next ten years exploring the place he called the "Range of Light."

Journals from these excursions would be collected in book form in *My First Summer in the Sierra* (1911) and *A Thousand-Mile Walk to the Gulf* (1916). But Muir's earliest published writings appeared as magazine articles on Sierra geology and the glacial origin of the Yosemite Valley. He would go on to publish nearly one hundred essays and articles in newspapers and magazines such as the *San Francisco Bulletin, Overland Monthly,* and *Scribner's Monthly.* Admirers of Muir's work like Ralph Waldo Emerson and President Theodore Roosevelt were known to have met Muir and to have been touched by his passion for the wilderness.

In 1879, Muir made his first of many trips to Alaska, where he discovered Glacier Bay. The following year, Muir married Louise Strentzel, the daughter of a wealthy fruit rancher, and moved to Martinez, California. Muir spent much of his time managing the Strentzel ranch and raising his daughters, Wanda and Helen. In 1888, Muir's wife sold parcels of the family estate to allow Muir more time for his Sierra studies.

Soon after, Muir met Robert Underwood Johnson, associate editor of *The Century Magazine,* who encouraged him to write two articles on the need to protect the wilderness of the Yosemite Valley. These articles appeared in *The Century* in the fall of 1890. Wilderness preservation, thanks to Muir's literary zeal and Johnson's lobbying efforts, received more publicity than ever before; their efforts paid off and Yosemite was designated a national park. In 1892, Muir, Johnson, and others founded the Sierra Club, and Muir served as its president until his death in 1914.

Another fruitful result of Muir's friendship with Johnson was the publication of Muir's first book, *The Mountains of California.* Published in 1894, *The Mountains of California* was an instant success and continued Muir's "education of his countrymen in the advantages of wild country." Muir would continue to write on behalf of the wilderness, and he published, among other books, *Our National Parks* (1901), *The Yosemite* (1912), *The Story of My Boyhood and Youth* (1913), and *Travels in Alaska* (1915). Though Muir was crucial to the designation of Sequoia, Mount Rainier, the Petrified Forest, and the Grand Canyon as national parks, he lost his last preservationist battle over the damming of the Hetch Hetchy Valley in Yosemite. Nonetheless, he would set a national environmental movement in motion that continues today.

John Muir died of pneumonia in January 1914 while visiting one of his daughters in California. Muir's legacy is vast and includes Muir Glacier in Alaska, and in California the John Muir Trail, the John Muir Historic Site in Martinez, and Muir Woods National Monument.

CONTENTS

TRAVELS IN ALASKA

PART III. THE TRIP OF 1890

ILLUSTRATIONS

Except as otherwise indicated the illustrations are from photographs by Herbert W. Gleason.

INTRODUCTION

Edward Hoagland

John Muir (1838–1914), being diligent first and a dreamer second, wore many hats. So although he was a visionary—a founder of the Sierra Club and savior of Yosemite National Park—we do have quite a wonderfully meticulous record of the progress of his visions. In middle age and on the brink of his belated marriage, after considerable wandering in the Great Lakes and Appalachian wildernesses as a rattled and anguished but indefatigable young man, and then more definitively in California's High Sierra as an amateur botanist and geologist, he went almost inevitably to Alaska. Where else would an American rhapsodist of wild places ultimately go? Joy, in fact, was his currency, though he didn't know it at the time. He thought that in such scenic mightiness he was studying glaciers: and he did do some original work on them. But a century and a quarter later, we are reading his account because there in the glorious fiords, "the great fresh unblighted, unredeemed wilderness," he is at our elbow, nudging us along, prompting us to understand that heaven is on earth—*is* the Earth—and rapture is the sensible response wherever a clear line of sight remains.

Thoreau's more famous agenda, back East in Massachusetts sixty years before *Travels in Alaska* was finished, had been to try to alter the way that people lived, both with regard to nature and each other. Thus, wilderness figured as rather a minor factor in *Walden*'s ruminations. The godhead could be located much nearer home, in a backlot pond ("earth's eye"), as well as in a mountain massif. At one point elsewhere Thoreau advocated that every township should preserve one square mile in a natural state. Hardly a wilderness but sufficient—you didn't need to roam the frontier in order to find it.

Muir, although he carried a volume of Thoreau's essays on his first trip to Alaska, seems to have expected that you did, and we are the beneficiaries because he exerted his string-bean frame so strenuously to search. The journal jottings from which he fashioned most of his books, often decades later, were originally the product of scientific more than literary ambition, but otherwise were hymns of praise. He lived for Emersonian Transcendentalism perhaps more single-mindedly than even Emerson or Thoreau—who were involved in the Abolition movement and other controversies, such as women's rights and the injustice of the Mexican War, and the contemporary intellectual currents that they lectured on for a livelihood—an activity that the shyer Muir didn't begin to take to until later in life, and then only as a polemicist for the cause of preservation.

Muir was up in mountains that would have flabbergasted the Massachusetts men—mountains of a pelagic scale that dwarfed the White Mountains or Mount Katahdin. There is no disjunction, however, between their concepts of nature except that the New Englanders more fully comprehended that human nature is a part of nature and were more interested in it. Muir, awestruck by the cathedral, kept gazing up into the nave, whereas Thoreau had a habit of noticing and quarreling with the conduct of the parishioners. And until lately, when we have become a bit panicky at the disappearance of wild landscapes nearly everywhere and what we call "the natural world," Muir was scanted as a marginal, a johnny-one-note figure. A few decades ago, it was hard to find an eastern literary person who had even heard of him, and although I *had*, my appreciation of his love of radiance, his seize-the-day impetuosity, yet tireless exactitude—so calm, except about life's gleeful dimensions—has grown by leaps and bounds. Despite extraordinary feats of derring-do, he didn't climb to conquer nature but to witness and to savor it, testing not his braggadocio but his faith: which is more interesting.

Thoreau (1817–62) himself had required at least half a century posthumously to gather much attention, although pantheism is a big-tent religion. It was especially exalting for a self-taught observer like Muir because God does indeed "reside in the details." Canoeing in the outwash of huge glaciers was geology sprung alive. Like Bach on Sunday, he found that he was delineating the anatomy, the raiments, of joy. Nobody is against natural grandeur; monotheists accept the premise that God did that too. And Alaska itself is a big tent, perennially compelling as a "last" wilderness. But it was the tumult Muir reveled in that scares most of us. He was elastic and enlivened out-of-doors, rising as if on a thermal, or like a fish freed from an aquarium. This era before the Klondike Gold Rush brought in crowds of settlers, and almost thirty years before Mount McKinley was first climbed, exhilarated instead of intimidating him.

Jack London would preempt Muir's rapturous interpretations of Alaska for decades to come with his tales of nature red in tooth and claw—just as now we tend to neglect London for Muir. Both were Californians; both had had brutalized childhoods (Muir's in Scotland, his birthplace, and in Wisconsin), which made them rolling stones and ardent romantics: London's religion was socialism. And both wrote immortal dog stories based on real animals— Buck, the brave, wolfish hero of *The Call of the Wild,* and Stickeen, of *Stickeen,* the intuitive, intrepid border-collie mix who accompanied Muir on several hairy Alaskan ice-field adventures near the Stikine River. But London (1876–1916) died at forty, burned out, disillusioned, whereas Muir ripened into a seventy-six-year-old celebrity replete with loving daughters and grandchildren and a roster of national accomplishments. He knew that having influenced two presidents, Roosevelt and Taft, toward preservationist action was of lasting significance and that his magazine articles had been battle-tested. But he probably never recognized that his books, as books, would have real staying power, too. Otherwise he wouldn't have written *My First Summer in the Sierra* at the end of his life from forty-year-old notes, dictated his autobiography, *The Story of My Boyhood and Youth,* to the millionaire railroadman Edward Harriman's secretary, only at Harriman's insistence, and postponed the completion of *Travels in Alaska* (a better book) until pneumonia beat him to the punch and another sympathetic secretary had to do the final editing.

Just as, like Thoreau and Emerson, he didn't foresee the furnace of destruction, ever-accelerating industrially and technologically, that would afflict nature worldwide, Muir was not in a position to imagine how rare his experiences and especially his frequent bouts of virtual ecstasy would strike and register with us—"dancing down" the mountains, sun-beaten, trackless mountains themselves "made divine." Because of Charles Darwin, Rudyard Kipling, the Brothers Grimm, and the cutthroat competition of free enterprise, a nature portrayed like London's as red in tooth and claw was no surprise to most people, but for nature conveyed as glee we had to remember writers like Ivan Turgenev and W. H. Hudson, or the *Odyssey* and the biblical *Song of Songs.* In a burstingly utilitarian, expansive country it had been considered countereconomic, "backward" like a primitive shaman, to conceive of nature as rapturous and therefore potentially precious. *That* was for the Indians, who had been decimated and swept aside in the march of progress. Yet Muir's longevity isn't just because he was on the right-thinking side of a farsighted struggle. So were George Perkins Marsh (1801–82), his precursor protoconservationist, and others who have since disappeared from the debate. Muir loved the world—loved Creation—so much that we, being part of it, can warm to him almost physiologically as we read along. Dire prophecies don't work as well on us as rhapsodies. Muir was a rather shaky, chilly, wounded individual in person, like many nature writers who are seeking a balm for their injuries. But he loved the calving, thunderous glaciers, the "fountaining" snowfields way high up among the peaks that were their source, and the rainy maritime clouds that replenished these. The green waves and white spindrift shone in a fitful sunlight that was refracted amazingly, prismatically through the stunning planes of ice—blue and red—as the weather revolved around his thirty-six-foot Tlingit dugout canoe, with an occasional seal hunter bobbing by in a smaller craft offering them a fresh salmon for ten cents.

The joy he felt was hard to ascribe simply to Evolution's provision for survival tools. I've been to the mouth and watershed of the Stikine myself during the middle 1960s, when it still seemed somewhat *the way the world was made,* as I kept murmuring to myself, watching seals surfacing in the tangled currents, the salmon running, the eagles posted profusely in the trees, the swimming otters, beavers, bears, and teeming rafts of river birds. I goggled and grinned—mainly at the dashing, wheeling mobs of waterbirds, the sudden sandbars and piled-up drift logs challenging our boat, the river's jumbo, roaring rush and backwash sloughs, under the snowy, high horizons—never having seen such dimensions of gush and ebullience before. Words were so fragile by comparison that Muir must have thought them inadequate to the task of conveying everything he had witnessed on these herculean trips. But not knowing how frangible the wilderness itself would prove to be, he couldn't guess how valuable his experiences, even partially preserved, would come to seem.

In this valedictory bouquet to the magic of life, presented in his middle seventies—when, more confidently, he plucked some of the high points of his memories—Muir censored his personal reactions less timorously and betrayed more intimacy with his companions than in lone-wolf books like *A Thousand-Mile Walk to the Gulf, My First Summer in the Sierra,* and *The Mountains of California,* that retrieve earlier history. In Alaska, in his forties, he had felt much more empathy with the Tlingits than he ever had with California's shattered "Digger" Indians, while in his thirties. And to the Tlingits he was a "Boston man," their term for American whites because the first Americans they had met had been whalers out of Massachusetts, as distinct from the Russian fur seal hunters who initially laid claim to Alaska. So by this amusing bit of irony, which Muir must have perceived, he was at last linked with his heroes in Concord, Thoreau and Emerson.

Yet because of the magnetism of the landscapes he gravitated toward, which were biblical in scale and "innocence" and ballasted his jitters, he is unique. Unique, as well, because interstitial to his effusions of frank and genuine inspiration (such as the great British explorers seldom indulged in) were the kind of close, specific observations that a man of science would demand of his notes, which keeps them intriguing for us. We wind through these drenched and bristly islands with a man as spartan as but less judgmental of the early gold rushers than Thoreau would have been, and more interested, in any case, in "the plant people," "the little ones as well as the trees," than in the human ones, even the Indians, while the clouds are "fondling" the mountains. "Standing here," he says near Cape Fanshaw, "one learns that the world, though made, is yet being made; that this is still the morning of creation." Which echoes *Walden*'s celebrated ending: "There is more day to dawn. The sun is but a morning star."

Not a caroming radical fixated on brute force, like Jack London, or a spiky contrarian like Thoreau, Muir was a practical, canny Scotsman grounded in exactitude but bathing in a splendidly self-effacing joy. He had been to the Nile and Amazon, to China, Siberia, and India by the time he finally put his nose to the grindstone and wrote this fragmentary book, and wasn't tempted to gussy it polemically. He wished to steep it in the exuberance he felt, and sustains the narrative thrust and the timbre of his superlatives more convincingly than in earlier books. Love was the wellspring of all his work, but these memories were doubly intense and central. He was truly a coureur de bois, a "runner of the woods," a sort of Franciscan Daniel Boone, who upbraided his Indian companions when they shot more than one deer (he himself ate bread, rice, and beans) and rocked the canoe to spoil their aim when they tried for a duck.

Transcendentalism, located between Puritanism and Pragmaticism in America's philosophical development, has an enduring appeal, and Muir lived it as an exemplary avatar. Though his mind was narrower than Thoreau's, his life, stretching much longer, was broadened somewhat further than Thoreau's with reams of new experiences and new acquaintances, and then took on an avuncular docent's role for hikes and overnighters with members of the Sierra Club. (Indeed, it might be argued that Thoreau, after the disappointment of *Walden*'s failure to find much of a readership, became increasingly Muir-like in his focus upon natural history, until he died of tuberculosis at forty-four.) For both of them, heaven was the here and now, with daily intimations of divinity. And this exhilaration is what gradually lifted Muir out of the category of regional California writer, such as Bret Harte, in which he once languished. He had possessed a marked charisma, for those who knew him, and a bully pulpit in magazines like *The Overland Monthly* and *The Atlantic Monthly* for hortatory purposes. But the high-pitched extravagance of this Alaska account, with a waterfall of observations accompanying it, about the Stikine and Taku rivers and Sum Dum Bay and Glacier Bay, is not arguing a point. It is a riff and a testament, when he was at death's door, of days back in paradise, hasty-paced because his stay was limited. He had had to leave his calling there and go and get married (the next year, again, for the birth of his first baby) and breathe the nitrogen of ordinary life instead of pure oxygen. He was dutiful enough, but we have other writers who have chronicled domesticity and scarcely any who have gone up unravished rivers to the meadows, rock, and ice of origination. As more and more of us grow aghast at what we have done to the world we started with, Muir's reverence and devotion will seem keenly germane, and our regret may be transmuted into a fight for the future.

—

EDWARD HOAGLAND is the author of *Notes from the Century Before*, available as a paperback in the Modern Library Exploration series, and nearly twenty other books, several of which have been nominated for the National Book Award, the American Book Award, and the National Book Critics Circle Award. He lives in Bennington, Vermont.

PART ONE

THE TRIP OF
1879

CHAPTER I

PUGET SOUND AND
BRITISH COLUMBIA

After eleven years of study and exploration in the Sierra Nevada of California and the mountain-ranges of the Great Basin, studying in particular their glaciers, forests, and wild life, above all their ancient glaciers and the influence they exerted in sculpturing the rocks over which they passed with tremendous pressure, making new landscapes, scenery, and beauty which so mysteriously influence every human being, and to some extent all life, I was anxious to gain some knowledge of the regions to the northward, about Puget Sound and Alaska. With this grand object in view I left San Francisco in May, 1879, on the steamer Dakota, without any definite plan, as with the exception of a few of the Oregon peaks and their forests all the wild north was new to me.

To the mountaineer a sea voyage is a grand, inspiring, restful change. For forests and plains with their flowers and fruits we have new scenery, new life of every sort; water hills and dales in eternal visible motion for rock waves, types of permanence.

It was curious to note how suddenly the eager countenances of the passengers were darkened as soon as the good ship passed through the Golden Gate and began to heave on the waves of the open ocean. The crowded deck was speedily deserted on account of seasickness. It seemed strange that nearly every one afflicted should be more or less ashamed.

Next morning a strong wind was blowing, and the sea was gray and white, with long breaking waves, across which the Dakota was racing half-buried in spray. Very few of the passengers were on deck to enjoy the wild scenery. Every wave seemed to be making enthusiastic, eager haste to the shore, with long, irised tresses streaming from its tops, some of its outer fringes borne away in scud to refresh the wind, all the rolling, pitching, flying water exulting in the beauty of rainbow light. Gulls and albatrosses, strong, glad life in the midst of the stormy beauty, skimmed the waves against the wind, seemingly without effort, oftentimes flying nearly a mile without a single wing-beat, gracefully swaying from side to side and tracing the curves of the briny water hills with the finest precision, now and then just grazing the highest.

And yonder, glistening amid the irised spray, is a still more striking revelation of warm life in the so-called howling waste,—a half-dozen whales, their broad backs like glaciated bosses of granite heaving aloft in near view, spouting lustily, drawing a long breath, and plunging down home in colossal health and comfort. A merry school of porpoises, a square mile of them, suddenly appear, tossing themselves into the air in abounding strength and hilarity, adding foam to the waves and making all the wilderness wilder. One cannot but feel sympathy with and be proud of these brave neighbors, fellow citizens in the commonwealth of the world, making a living like the rest of us. Our good ship also seemed like a thing of life, its great iron heart beating on through calm and storm, a truly noble spectacle. But think of the hearts of these whales, beating warm against the sea, day and night, through dark and light, on and on for centuries; how the red blood must rush and gurgle in and out, bucketfuls, barrelfuls at a beat!

The cloud colors of one of the four sunsets enjoyed on the voyage were remarkably pure and rich in tone. There was a well-defined range of cumuli a few degrees above the horizon, and a massive, dark-gray rain-cloud above it, from which depended long, bent fringes overlapping the lower cumuli and partially veiling them; and from time to time sunbeams poured through narrow openings and painted the exposed bosses and fringes in ripe yellow tones, which, with the reflections on the water, made magnificent pictures. The scenery of the ocean, however sublime in vast expanse, seems far less beautiful to us dry-shod animals than that of the land seen only in comparatively small patches; but when we contemplate the whole globe as one great dewdrop, striped and dotted with continents and islands, flying through space with other stars all singing and shining together as one, the whole universe appears as an infinite storm of beauty.

The California coast-hills and cliffs look bare and uninviting as seen from the ship, the magnificent forests keeping well back out of sight beyond the reach of the sea winds; those of Oregon and Washington are in some places clad with conifers nearly down to the shore; even the little detached islets, so marked a feature to the northward, are mostly tree-crowned. Up through the Straits of Juan de Fuca the forests, sheltered from the ocean gales and favored with abundant rains, flourish in marvelous luxuriance on the glacier-sculptured mountains of the Olympic Range.

We arrived in Esquimault Harbor, three miles from Victoria, on the evening of the fourth day, and drove to the town through a magnificent forest of Douglas spruce,—with an undergrowth in open spots of oak, madrone, hazel, dogwood, alder, spiræa, willow, and wild rose,—and around many an upswelling *moutonné* rock, freshly glaciated and furred with yellow mosses and lichens.

Victoria, the capital of British Columbia, was in 1879 a small old-fashioned English town on the south end of Vancouver Island. It was said to contain about six thousand inhabitants. The government buildings and some of the business blocks were noticeable, but the attention of the traveler was more worthily attracted to the neat cottage homes found here, embowered in the freshest and floweriest climbing roses and honeysuckles conceivable. Californians may well be proud of their home roses loading sunny verandas, climbing to the tops of the roofs and falling over the gables in white and red cascades. But here, with so much bland fog and dew and gentle laving rain, a still finer development of some of the commonest garden plants is reached. English honeysuckle seems to have found here a most congenial home. Still more beautiful were the wild roses, blooming in wonderful luxuriance along the woodland paths, with corollas two and three inches wide. This rose and three species of spiræa fairly filled the air with fragrance after showers; and how brightly then did the red dogwood berries shine amid the green leaves beneath trees two hundred and fifty feet high.

Strange to say, all of this exuberant forest and flower vegetation was growing upon fresh moraine material scarcely at all moved or in any way modified by post-glacial agents. In the town gardens and orchards, peaches and apples fell upon glacial-polished rocks, and the streets were graded in moraine gravel; and I observed scratched and grooved rock bosses as unweathered and telling as those of the High Sierra of California eight thousand feet or more above sea-level. The Victoria Harbor is plainly glacial in origin, eroded from the solid; and the rock islets that rise here and there in it are unchanged to any appreciable extent by all the waves that have broken over them since first they came to light toward the close of the glacial period. The shores also of the harbor are strikingly grooved and scratched and in every way as glacial in all their characteristics as those of new-born glacial lakes. That the domain of the sea is being slowly extended over the land by incessant wave-action is well known; but in this freshly glaciated region the shores have been so short a time exposed to wave-action that they are scarcely at all wasted. The extension of the sea affected by its own action in post-glacial times is probably less than the millionth part of that affected by glacial action during the last glacier period. The direction of the flow of the ice-sheet to which all the main features of this wonderful region are due was in general southward.

From this quiet little English town I made many short excursions—up the coast to Nanaimo, to Burrard Inlet, now the terminus of the Canadian Pacific Railroad, to Puget Sound, up Fraser River to New Westminster and Yale at the head of navigation, charmed everywhere with the wild, new-born scenery. The most interesting of these and the most difficult to leave was the Puget Sound region, famous the world over for the wonderful forests of gigantic trees about its shores. It is an arm and many-fingered hand of the sea, reaching southward from the Straits of Juan de Fuca about a hundred miles into the heart of one of the noblest coniferous forests on the face of the globe. All its scenery is wonderful— broad river-like reaches sweeping in beautiful curves around bays and capes and jutting promontories, opening here and there into smooth, blue, lake-like expanses dotted with islands and feathered with tall, spiry evergreens, their beauty doubled on the bright mirror-water.

Sailing from Victoria, the Olympic Mountains are seen right ahead, rising in bold relief against the sky, with jagged crests and peaks from six to eight thousand feet high,—small residual glaciers and ragged snow-fields beneath them in wide amphitheatres opening down through the forest-filled valleys. These valleys mark the courses of the Olympic glaciers at the period of their greatest extension, when they poured their tribute into that portion of the great northern ice-sheet that overswept Vancouver Island and filled the strait between it and the mainland.

On the way up to Olympia, then a hopeful little town situated at the end of one of the longest fingers of the Sound, one is often reminded of Lake Tahoe, the scenery of the widest expanses is so lake-like in the clearness and stillness of the water and the luxuriance of the surrounding forests. Doubling cape after cape, passing uncounted islands, new combinations break on the view in endless variety, sufficient to satisfy the lover of wild beauty through a whole life. When the clouds come down, blotting out everything, one feels as if at sea; again lifting a little, some islet may be seen standing alone with the tops of its trees dipping out of sight in gray misty fringes; then the ranks of spruce and cedar bounding the water's edge come to view; and when at length the whole sky is clear the colossal cone of Mt. Rainier may be seen in spotless white, looking down over the dark woods from a distance of fifty or sixty miles, but so high and massive and so sharply outlined, it seems to be just back of a strip of woods only a few miles wide.

Mt. Rainier, or Tahoma (the Indian name), is the noblest of the volcanic cones extending from Lassen Butte and Mt. Shasta along the Cascade Range to Mt. Baker. One of the most telling views of it hereabouts is obtained near Tacoma. From a bluff back of the town it was revealed in all its glory, laden with glaciers and snow down to the forested foothills around its finely curved base. Up to this time (1879) it had been ascended but once. From observations made on the summit with a single aneroid barometer, it was estimated to be about 14,500 feet high. Mt. Baker, to the northward, is about 10,700 feet high, a noble mountain. So also are Mt. Adams, Mt. St. Helens, and Mt. Hood. The latter, overlooking the town of Portland, is perhaps the best known. Rainier, about the same height as Shasta, surpasses them all in massive icy grandeur,—the most majestic solitary mountain I had ever yet beheld. How eagerly I gazed and longed to climb it and study its history only the mountaineer may know, but I was compelled to turn away and bide my time.

The species forming the bulk of the woods here is the Douglas spruce (*Pseudotsuga douglasii*), one of the greatest of the western giants. A specimen that I measured near Olympia was about three hundred feet in height and twelve feet in diameter four feet above the ground. It is a widely distributed tree, extending northward through British Columbia, southward through Oregon and California, and eastward to the Rocky Mountains. The timber is used for ship-building, spars, piles, and the framework of houses, bridges, etc. In the California lumber markets it is known as "Oregon pine." In Utah, where it is common on the Wahsatch Mountains, it is called "red pine." In California, on the western slope of the Sierra Nevada, it forms, in company with the yellow pine, sugar pine, and incense cedar, a pretty well-defined belt at a height of from three to six thousand feet above the sea; but it is only in Oregon and Washington, especially in this Puget Sound region, that it reaches its very grandest development,—tall, straight, and strong, growing down close to tide-water.

All the towns of the Sound had a hopeful, thrifty aspect. Port Townsend, picturesquely located on a grassy bluff, was the port of clearance for vessels sailing to foreign parts. Seattle was famed for its coal-mines, and claimed to be the coming town of the North Pacific Coast. So also did its rival, Tacoma, which had been selected as the terminus of the much-talked-of Northern Pacific Railway. Several coal-veins of astonishing thickness were discovered the winter before on the Carbon River, to the east of Tacoma, one of them said to be no less than twenty-one feet, another twenty feet, another fourteen, with many smaller ones, the aggregate thickness of all the veins being upwards of a hundred feet. Large deposits of magnetic iron ore and brown hematite, together with limestone, had been discovered in advantageous proximity to the coal, making a bright outlook for the Sound region in general in connection with its railroad hopes, its unrivaled timber resources, and its far-reaching geographical relations.

After spending a few weeks in the Puget Sound region with a friend from San Francisco, we engaged passage on the little mail steamer California, at Portland, Oregon, for Alaska. The sail down the broad lower reaches of the Columbia and across its foamy bar, around Cape Flattery, and up the Juan de Fuca Strait, was delightful; and after calling again at Victoria and Port Townsend we got fairly off for icy Alaska.

CHAPTER II

Alexander Archipelago and the Home I Found in Alaska

To the lover of pure wildness Alaska is one of the most wonderful countries in the world. No excursion that I know of may be made into any other American wilderness where so marvelous an abundance of noble, new-born scenery is so charmingly brought to view as on the trip through the Alexander Archipelago to Fort Wrangell and Sitka. Gazing from the deck of the steamer, one is borne smoothly over calm blue waters, through the midst of countless forest-clad islands. The ordinary discomforts of a sea voyage are not felt, for nearly all the whole long way is on inland waters that are about as waveless as rivers and lakes. So numerous are the islands that they seem to have been sown broadcast; long tapering vistas between the largest of them open in every direction.

Day after day in the fine weather we enjoyed, we seemed to float in true fairyland, each succeeding view seeming more and more beautiful, the one we chanced to have before us the most surprisingly beautiful of all. Never before this had I been embosomed in scenery so hopelessly beyond description. To sketch picturesque bits, definitely bounded, is comparatively easy—a lake in the woods, a glacier meadow, or a cascade in its dell; or even a grand master view of mountains beheld from some commanding outlook after climbing from height to height above the forests. These may be attempted, and more or less telling pictures made of them; but in these coast landscapes there is such indefinite, on-leading expansiveness, such a multitude of features without apparent redundance, their lines graduating delicately into one another in endless succession, while the whole is so fine, so tender, so ethereal, that all penwork seems hopelessly unavailing. Tracing shining ways through fiord and sound, past forests and waterfalls, islands and mountains and far azure headlands, it seems as if surely we must at length reach the very paradise of the poets, the abode of the blessed.

Some idea of the wealth of this scenery may be gained from the fact that the coast-line of Alaska is about twenty-six thousand miles long, more than twice as long as all the rest of the United States. The islands of the Alexander Archipelago, with the straits, channels, canals, sounds, passages, and fiords, form an intricate web of land and water embroidery sixty or seventy miles wide, fringing the lofty icy chain of coast mountains from Puget Sound to Cook Inlet; and, with infinite variety, the general pattern is harmonious throughout its whole extent of nearly a thousand miles. Here you glide into a narrow channel hemmed in by mountain walls, forested down to the water's edge, where there is no distant view, and your attention is concentrated on the objects close about you—the crowded spires of the spruces and hemlocks rising higher and higher on the steep green slopes; stripes of paler green where winter avalanches have cleared away the trees, allowing grasses and willows to spring up; zigzags of cascades appearing and disappearing among the bushes and trees; short, steep glens with brawling streams hidden beneath alder and dogwood, seen only where they emerge on the brown algæ of the shore; and retreating hollows, with lingering snow-banks marking the fountains of ancient glaciers. The steamer is often so near the shore that you may distinctly see the cones clustered on the tops of the trees, and the ferns and bushes at their feet.

But new scenes are brought to view with magical rapidity. Rounding some bossy cape, the eye is called away into far-reaching

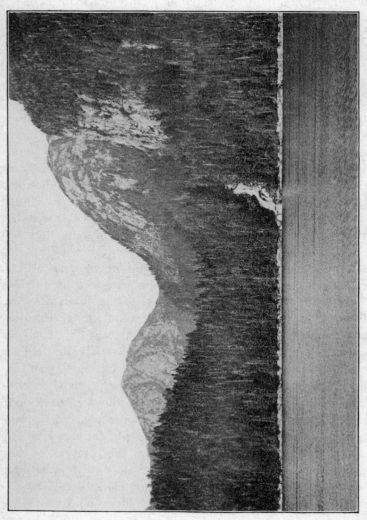

Hanging Valley and Waterfall, Fraser Reach

vistas, bounded on either hand by headlands in charming array, one dipping gracefully beyond another and growing fainter and more ethereal in the distance. The tranquil channel stretching river-like between, may be stirred here and there by the silvery plashing of upspringing salmon, or by flocks of white gulls floating like waterlilies among the sun spangles; while mellow, tempered sunshine is streaming over all, blending sky, land, and water in pale, misty blue. Then, while you are dreamily gazing into the depths of this leafy ocean lane, the little steamer, seeming hardly larger than a duck, turning into some passage not visible until the moment of entering it, glides into a wide expanse—a sound filled with islands, sprinkled and clustered in forms and compositions such as nature alone can invent; some of them so small the trees growing on them seem like single handfuls culled from the neighboring woods and set in the water to keep them fresh, while here and there at wide intervals you may notice bare rocks just above the water, mere dots punctuating grand, outswelling sentences of islands.

The variety we find, both as to the contours and the collocation of the islands, is due chiefly to differences in the structure and composition of their rocks, and the unequal glacial denudation different portions of the coast were subjected to. This influence must have been especially heavy toward the end of the glacial period, when the main ice-sheet began to break up into separate glaciers. Moreover, the mountains of the larger islands nourished local glaciers, some of them of considerable size, which sculptured their summits and sides, forming in some cases wide cirques with cañons or valleys leading down from them into the channels and sounds. These causes have produced much of the bewildering variety of which nature is so fond, but none the less will the studious observer see the underlying harmony—the general trend of the islands in the direction of the flow of the main ice-mantle from the mountains of the Coast Range, more or less varied by subordinate foothill ridges and mountains. Furthermore, all the islands, great and small, as well as the headlands and promontories of the mainland, are seen to have a rounded, over-rubbed appearance produced by the over-sweeping ice-flood during the period of greatest glacial abundance.

The canals, channels, straits, passages, sounds, etc., are subordinate to the same glacial conditions in their forms, trends, and extent as those which determined the forms, trends, and distribution of the land-masses, their basins being the parts of the pre-glacial margin of the continent, eroded to varying depths below sea-level, and into which, of course, the ocean waters flowed as the ice was melted out of them. Had the general glacial denudation been much less, these ocean ways over which we are sailing would have been valleys and cañons and lakes; and the islands rounded hills and ridges, landscapes with undulating features like those found above sea-level wherever the rocks and glacial conditions are similar. In general, the island-bound channels are like rivers, not only in separate reaches as seen from the deck of a vessel, but continuously so for hundreds of miles in the case of the longest of them. The tide-currents, the fresh driftwood, the inflowing streams, and the luxuriant foliage of the out-leaning trees on the shores make this resemblance all the more complete. The largest islands look like part of the mainland in any view to be had of them from the ship, but far the greater number are small, and appreciable as islands, scores of them being less than a mile long. These the eye easily takes in and revels in their beauty with ever fresh delight. In their relations to each other the individual members of a group have evidently been derived from the same general rock-mass, yet they never seem broken or abridged in any way as to their contour lines, however abruptly they may dip their sides. Viewed one by one, they seem detached beauties, like extracts from a poem, while, from the completeness of their lines and the way that their trees are arranged, each seems a finished stanza in itself. Contemplating the arrangement of the trees on these small islands, a distinct impression is produced of their having been sorted and harmonized as to size like a well-balanced bouquet. On some of the smaller tufted islets a group of tapering spruces is planted in the middle, and two smaller groups that evidently correspond with each other are planted on the ends at about equal distances from the central group; or the whole appears as one group with marked fringing trees that match each other spreading around the sides, like flowers leaning outward against the rim of a vase. These harmonious tree relations are so constant that they evidently are the result of design, as much so as the arrangement of the feathers of birds or the scales of fishes.

Thus perfectly beautiful are these blessed evergreen islands, and their beauty is the beauty of youth, for though the freshness of their verdure must be ascribed to the bland moisture with which they are bathed from warm ocean-currents, the very existence of the islands, their features, finish, and peculiar distribution, are all immediately referable to ice-action during the great glacial winter just now drawing to a close.

—

We arrived at Wrangell July 14, and after a short stop of a few hours went on to Sitka and returned on the 20th to Wrangell, the most inhospitable place at first sight I had ever seen. The little steamer that had been my home in the wonderful trip through the archipelago, after taking the mail, departed on her return to Portland, and as I watched her gliding out of sight in the dismal blurring rain, I felt strangely lonesome. The friend that had accompanied me thus far now left for his home in San Francisco, with two other interesting travelers who had made the trip for health and scenery, while my fellow passengers, the missionaries, went direct to the Presbyterian home in the old fort. There was nothing like a tavern or lodging-house in the village, nor could I find any place in the stumpy, rocky, boggy ground about it that looked dry enough to camp on until I could find a way into the wilderness to begin my studies. Every place within a mile or two of the town seemed strangely shelterless and inhospitable, for all the trees had long ago been felled for building-timber and firewood. At the worst, I thought, I could build a bark hut on a hill back of the village, where something like a forest loomed dimly through the draggled clouds.

I had already seen some of the high glacier-bearing mountains in distant views from the steamer, and was anxious to reach them. A

Lowe Inlet, British Columbia

few whites of the village, with whom I entered into conversation, warned me that the Indians were a bad lot, not to be trusted, that the woods were well-nigh impenetrable, and that I could go nowhere without a canoe. On the other hand, these natural difficulties made the grand wild country all the more attractive, and I determined to get into the heart of it somehow or other with a bag of hardtack, trusting to my usual good luck. My present difficulty was in finding a first base camp. My only hope was on the hill. When I was strolling past the old fort I happened to meet one of the missionaries, who kindly asked me where I was going to take up my quarters.

"I don't know," I replied. "I have not been able to find quarters of any sort. The top of that little hill over there seems the only possible place."

He then explained that every room in the mission house was full, but he thought I might obtain leave to spread my blanket in a carpenter-shop belonging to the mission. Thanking him, I ran down to the sloppy wharf for my little bundle of baggage, laid it on the shop floor, and felt glad and snug among the dry, sweet-smelling shavings.

The carpenter was at work on a new Presbyterian mission building, and when he came in I explained that Dr. Jackson* had suggested that I might be allowed to sleep on the floor, and after I assured him that I would not touch his tools or be in his way, he goodnaturedly gave me the freedom of the shop and also of his small private side room where I would find a wash-basin.

I was here only one night, however, for Mr. Vanderbilt, a merchant, who with his family occupied the best house in the fort, hearing that one of the late arrivals, whose business none seemed to know, was compelled to sleep in the carpenter-shop, paid me a good-Samaritan visit and after a few explanatory words on my glacier and forest studies, with fine hospitality offered me a room and a place at his table. Here I found a real home, with freedom to go on all sorts of excursions as opportunity offered. Annie

---

* Dr. Sheldon Jackson, 1834–1909, became Superintendent of Presbyterian Missions in Alaska in 1877, and United States General Agent of Education in 1885. [W. F. B.]

Vanderbilt, a little doctor of divinity two years old, ruled the household with love sermons and kept it warm.

Mr. Vanderbilt introduced me to prospectors and traders and some of the most influential of the Indians. I visited the mission school and the home for Indian girls kept by Mrs. MacFarland, and made short excursions to the nearby forests and streams, and studied the rate of growth of the different species of trees and their age, counting the annual rings on stumps in the large clearings made by the military when the fort was occupied, causing wondering speculation among the Wrangell folk, as was reported by Mr. Vanderbilt.

"What can the fellow be up to?" they inquired. "He seems to spend most of his time among stumps and weeds. I saw him the other day on his knees, looking at a stump as if he expected to find gold in it. He seems to have no serious object whatever."

One night when a heavy rainstorm was blowing I unwittingly caused a lot of wondering excitement among the whites as well as the superstitious Indians. Being anxious to see how the Alaska trees behave in storms and hear the songs they sing, I stole quietly away through the gray drenching blast to the hill back of the town, without being observed. Night was falling when I set out and it was pitch dark when I reached the top. The glad, rejoicing storm in glorious voice was singing through the woods, noble compensation for mere body discomfort. But I wanted a fire, a big one, to see as well as hear how the storm and trees were behaving. After long, patient groping I found a little dry punk in a hollow trunk and carefully stored it beside my matchbox and an inch or two of candle in an inside pocket that the rain had not yet reached; then, wiping some dead twigs and whittling them into thin shavings, stored them with the punk. I then made a little conical bark hut about a foot high, and, carefully leaning over it and sheltering it as much as possible from the driving rain, I wiped and stored a lot of dead twigs, lighted the candle, and set it in the hut, carefully added pinches of punk and shavings, and at length got a little blaze, by the light of which I gradually added larger shavings, then twigs all set on end astride the inner flame, making the little hut higher and wider. Soon I had light enough to enable me to select the best dead branches and large sections of bark, which were set on end, gradually increasing the height and corresponding light of the hut fire. A considerable area was thus well lighted, from which I gathered abundance of wood, and kept adding to the fire until it had a strong, hot heart and sent up a pillar of flame thirty or forty feet high, illuminating a wide circle in spite of the rain, and casting a red glare into the flying clouds. Of all the thousands of camp-fires I have elsewhere built none was just like this one, rejoicing in triumphant strength and beauty in the heart of the rain-laden gale. It was wonderful,— the illumined rain and clouds mingled together and the trees glowing against the jet background, the colors of the mossy, lichened trunks with sparkling streams pouring down the furrows of the bark, and the gray-bearded old patriarchs bowing low and chanting in passionate worship!

My fire was in all its glory about midnight, and, having made a bark shed to shelter me from the rain and partially dry my clothing, I had nothing to do but look and listen and join the trees in their hymns and prayers.

Neither the great white heart of the fire nor the quivering enthusiastic flames shooting aloft like auroral lances could be seen from the village on account of the trees in front of it and its being back a little way over the brow of the hill; but the light in the clouds made a great show, a portentous sign in the stormy heavens unlike anything ever before seen or heard of in Wrangell. Some wakeful Indians, happening to see it about midnight, in great alarm aroused the Collector of Customs and begged him to go to the missionaries and get them to pray away the frightful omen, and inquired anxiously whether white men had ever seen anything like that sky-fire, which instead of being quenched by the rain was burning brighter and brighter. The Collector said he had heard of such strange fires, and this one he thought might perhaps be what the white man called a "volcano, or an *ignis fatuus.*" When Mr. Young was called from his bed to pray, he, too, confoundedly astonished and at a loss for any sort of explanation, confessed that he had never seen anything like it in the sky or anywhere else in such cold wet weather, but that it was probably some sort of spontaneous combustion "that the white man called St. Elmo's fire, or Will-of-the-wisp." These explanations, though not convincingly clear, perhaps served to veil their own astonishment and in some measure to diminish the superstitious fears of the natives; but from what I heard, the few whites who happened to see the strange light wondered about as wildly as the Indians.

I have enjoyed thousands of camp-fires in all sorts of weather and places, warm-hearted, short-flamed, friendly little beauties glowing in the dark on open spots in high Sierra gardens, daisies and lilies circled about them, gazing like enchanted children; and large fires in silver fir forests, with spires of flame towering like the trees about them, and sending up multitudes of starry sparks to enrich the sky; and still greater fires on the mountains in winter, changing camp climate to summer, and making the frosty snow look like beds of white flowers, and oftentimes mingling their swarms of swift-flying sparks with falling snow-crystals when the clouds were in bloom. But this Wrangell camp-fire, my first in Alaska, I shall always remember for its triumphant storm-defying grandeur, and the wondrous beauty of the psalm-singing, lichen-painted trees which it brought to light.

CHAPTER III

WRANGELL ISLAND AND
ALASKA SUMMERS

Wrangell Island is about fourteen miles long, separated from the mainland by a narrow channel or fiord, and trending in the direction of the flow of the ancient ice-sheet. Like all its neighbors, it is densely forested down to the water's edge with trees that never seem to have suffered from thirst or fire or the axe of the lumberman in all their long century lives. Beneath soft, shady clouds, with abundance of rain, they flourish in wonderful strength and beauty to a good old age, while the many warm days, half cloudy, half clear, and the little groups of pure sun-days enable them to ripen their cones and send myriads of seeds flying every autumn to insure the permanence of the forests and feed the multitude of animals.

The Wrangell village was a rough place. No mining hamlet in the placer gulches of California, nor any backwoods village I ever saw, approached it in picturesque, devil-may-care *abandon*. It was a lawless draggle of wooden huts and houses, built in crooked lines, wrangling around the boggy shore of the island for a mile or so in the general form of the letter S, without the slightest subordination to the points of the compass or to building laws of any kind. Stumps and logs, like precious monuments, adorned its two streets, each stump and log, on account of the moist climate, moss-grown and tufted with grass and bushes, but muddy on the sides below the limit of the bog-line. The ground in general was an oozy, mossy bog on a foundation of jagged rocks, full of concealed pit-holes. These picturesque rock, bog, and stump obstructions, however, were not so very much in the way, for there were no wagons or carriages there. There was not a horse on the island. The domestic animals were represented by chickens, a lonely cow, a few sheep, and hogs of a breed well calculated to deepen and complicate the mud of the streets.

Most of the permanent residents of Wrangell were engaged in trade. Some little trade was carried on in fish and furs, but most of the quickening business of the place was derived from the Cassiar gold-mines, some two hundred and fifty or three hundred miles inland, by way of the Stickeen River and Dease Lake. Two stern-wheel steamers plied on the river between Wrangell and Telegraph Creek at the head of navigation, a hundred and fifty miles from Wrangell, carrying freight and passengers and connecting with pack-trains for the mines. These placer mines, on tributaries of the Mackenzie River, were discovered in the year 1874. About eighteen hundred miners and prospectors were said to have passed through Wrangell that season of 1879, about half of them being Chinamen. Nearly a third of this whole number set out from here in the month of February, traveling on the Stickeen River, which usually remains safely frozen until toward the end of April. The main body of the miners, however, went up on the steamers in May and June. On account of the severe winters they were all compelled to leave the mines the end of September. Perhaps about two thirds of them passed the winter in Portland and Victoria and the towns of Puget Sound. The rest remained here in Wrangell, dozing away the long winter as best they could.

Indians, mostly of the Stickeen tribe, occupied the two ends of the town, the whites, of whom there were about forty or fifty, the middle portion; but there was no determinate line of demarcation, the dwellings of the Indians being mostly as large and solidly built of logs and planks as those of the whites. Some of them were adorned with tall totem poles.

The fort was a quadrangular stockade with a dozen block and frame buildings located upon rising ground just back of the business part of the town. It was built by our Government shortly after the purchase of Alaska, and was abandoned in 1872, reoccupied by the military in 1875, and finally abandoned and sold to private parties in 1877. In the fort and about it there were a few good, clean homes, which shone all the more brightly in their sombre surroundings. The ground occupied by the fort, by being carefully leveled and drained was dry, though formerly a portion of the general swamp, showing how easily the whole town could have been improved. But in spite of disorder and squalor, shaded with clouds, washed and wiped by rain and sea winds, it was triumphantly salubrious through all the seasons. And though the houses seemed to rest uneasily among the miry rocks and stumps, squirming at all angles as if they had been tossed and twisted by earthquake shocks, and showing but little more relation to one another than may be observed among moraine boulders, Wrangell was a tranquil place. I never heard a noisy brawl in the streets, or a clap of thunder, and the waves seldom spoke much above a whisper along the beach. In summer the rain comes straight down, steamy and tepid. The clouds are usually united, filling the sky, not racing along in threatening ranks suggesting energy of an overbearing destructive kind, but forming a bland, mild, laving bath. The cloudless days are calm, pearl-gray, and brooding in tone, inclining to rest and peace; the islands seem to drowse and float on the glassy water, and in the woods scarce a leaf stirs.

The very brightest of Wrangell days are not what Californians would call bright. The tempered sunshine sifting through the moist atmosphere makes no dazzling glare, and the town, like the landscape, rests beneath a hazy, hushing, Indian-summerish spell. On the longest days the sun rises about three o'clock, but it is daybreak at midnight. The cocks crowed when they woke, without reference to the dawn, for it is never quite dark; there were only a few full-grown roosters in Wrangell, half a dozen or so, to awaken the town and give it a civilized character. After sunrise a few languid smoke-columns might be seen, telling the first stir of the people. Soon an

Indian or two might be noticed here and there at the doors of their barn-like cabins, and a merchant getting ready for trade; but scarcely a sound was heard, only a dull, muffled stir gradually deepening. There were only two white babies in the town, so far as I saw, and as for Indian babies, they woke and ate and made no crying sound. Later you might hear the croaking of ravens, and the strokes of an axe on firewood. About eight or nine o'clock the town was awake, Indians, mostly women and children, began to gather on the front platforms of the half-dozen stores, sitting carelessly on their blankets, every other face hideously blackened, a naked circle around the eyes, and perhaps a spot on the cheek-bone and the nose where the smut has been rubbed off. Some of the little children were also blackened, and none were over-clad, their light and airy costume consisting of a calico shirt reaching only to the waist. Boys eight or ten years old sometimes had an additional garment, —a pair of castaway miner's overalls wide enough and ragged enough for extravagant ventilation. The larger girls and young women were arrayed in showy calico, and wore jaunty straw hats, gorgeously ribboned, and glowed among the blackened and blanketed old crones like scarlet tanagers in a flock of blackbirds. The women, seated on the steps and platform of the traders' shops, could hardly be called loafers, for they had berries to sell, basketfuls of huckleberries, large yellow salmon-berries, and bog raspberries that looked wondrous fresh and clean amid the surrounding squalor. After patiently waiting for purchasers until hungry, they ate what they could not sell, and went away to gather more.

Yonder you see a canoe gliding out from the shore, containing perhaps a man, a woman, and a child or two, all paddling together in natural, easy rhythm. They are going to catch a fish, no difficult matter, and when this is done their day's work is done. Another party puts out to capture bits of driftwood, for it is easier to procure fuel in this way than to drag it down from the outskirts of the woods through rocks and bushes. As the day advances, a fleet of canoes may be seen along the shore, all fashioned alike, high and long beak-like prows and sterns, with lines as fine as those of the breast of a duck. What the mustang is to the Mexican *vaquero*, the canoe is to these coast Indians. They skim along the shores to fish and hunt and trade, or merely to visit their neighbors, for they are sociable, and have family pride remarkably well developed, meeting often to inquire after each other's health, attend potlatches and dances, and gossip concerning coming marriages, births, deaths, etc. Others seem to sail for the pure pleasure of the thing, their canoes decorated with handfuls of the tall purple epilobium.

Yonder goes a whole family, grandparents and all, making a direct course for some favorite stream and camp-ground. They are going to gather berries, as the baskets tell. Never before in all my travels, north or south, had I found so lavish an abundance of berries as here. The woods and meadows are full of them, both on the lowlands and mountains—huckleberries of many species, salmon-berries, black-berries, raspberries, with service-berries on dry open places, and cranberries in the bogs, sufficient for every bird, beast, and human being in the territory and thousands of tons to spare. The huckle-berries are especially abundant. A species that grows well up on the mountains is the best and largest, a half-inch and more in diameter and delicious in flavor. These grow on bushes three or four inches to a foot high. The berries of the commonest species are smaller and grow almost everywhere on the low grounds on bushes from three to six or seven feet high. This is the species on which the Indians depend most for food, gathering them in large quantities, beating them into a paste, pressing the paste into cakes about an inch thick, and drying them over a slow fire to enrich their winter stores. Salmon-berries and service-berries are preserved in the same way.

A little excursion to one of the best huckleberry-fields adjacent to Wrangell, under the direction of the Collector of Customs, to which I was invited, I greatly enjoyed. There were nine Indians in the party, mostly women and children going to gather huckleberries. As soon as we had arrived at the chosen camp-ground on the bank of a trout stream, all ran into the bushes and began eating berries before anything in the way of camp-making was done, laughing and chattering in natural animal enjoyment. The Collector went up the stream to examine a meadow at its head with reference to the quantity of hay it might yield for his cow, fishing by the way. All the

Indian Canoes

Indians except the two eldest boys who joined the Collector, remained among the berries.

The fishermen had rather poor luck, owing, they said, to the
sunny brightness of the day, a complaint seldom heard in this climate. They got good exercise, however, jumping from boulder to
boulder in the brawling stream, running along slippery logs and
through the bushes that fringe the bank, casting here and there into
swirling pools at the foot of cascades, imitating the tempting little
skips and whirls of flies so well known to fishing parsons, but perhaps still better known to Indian boys. At the lake-basin the
Collector, after he had surveyed his hay-meadow, went around it to
the inlet of the lake with his brown pair of attendants to try their
luck, while I botanized in the delightful flora which called to mind
the cool sphagnum and carex bogs of Wisconsin and Canada. Here
I found many of my old favorites the heathworts—kalmia, pyrola,
chiogenes, huckleberry, cranberry, etc. On the margin of the
meadow darling linnæa was in its glory; purple panicled grasses in
full flower reached over my head, and some of the carices and ferns
were almost as tall. Here, too, on the edge of the woods I found the
wild apple tree, the first I had seen in Alaska. The Indians gather
the fruit, small and sour as it is, to flavor their fat salmon. I never
saw a richer bog and meadow growth anywhere. The principal
forest-trees are hemlock, spruce, and Nootka cypress, with a few
pines (*P. contorta*) on the margin of the meadow, some of them
nearly a hundred feet high, draped with gray usnea, the bark also
gray with scale lichens.

We met all the berry-pickers at the lake, excepting only a small
girl and the camp-keeper. In their bright colors they made a lively
picture among the quivering bushes, keeping up a low pleasant
chanting as if the day and the place and the berries were according
to their own hearts. The children carried small baskets, holding two
or three quarts; the women two large ones swung over their shoulders. In the afternoon, when the baskets were full, all started back
to the camp-ground, where the canoe was left. We parted at the
lake, I choosing to follow quietly the stream through the woods. I
was the first to arrive at camp. The rest of the party came in shortly

afterwards, singing and humming like heavy-laden bees. It was interesting to note how kindly they held out handfuls of the best berries to the little girl, who welcomed them all in succession with smiles and merry words that I did not understand. But there was no mistaking the kindliness and serene good nature.

While I was at Wrangell the chiefs and head men of the Stickeen tribe got up a grand dinner and entertainment in honor of their distinguished visitors, three doctors of divinity and their wives, fellow passengers on the steamer with me, whose object was to organize the Presbyterian church. To both the dinner and dances I was invited, was adopted by the Stickeen tribe, and given an Indian name (Ancoutahan) said to mean adopted chief. I was inclined to regard this honor as being unlikely to have any practical value, but I was assured by Mr. Vanderbilt, Mr. Young, and others that it would be a great safeguard while I was on my travels among the different tribes of the archipelago. For travelers without an Indian name might be killed and robbed without the offender being called to account as long as the crime was kept secret from the whites; but, being adopted by the Stickeens, no one belonging to the other tribes would dare attack me, knowing that the Stickeens would hold them responsible.

The dinner-tables were tastefully decorated with flowers, and the food and general arrangements were in good taste, but there was no trace of Indian dishes. It was mostly imported canned stuff served Boston fashion. After the dinner we assembled in Chief Shakes's large block-house and were entertained with lively examples of their dances and amusements, carried on with great spirit, making a very novel barbarous durbar. The dances seemed to me wonderfully like those of the American Indians in general, a monotonous stamping accompanied by hand-clapping, head-jerking, and explosive grunts kept in time to grim drum-beats. The chief dancer and leader scattered great quantities of downy feathers like a snowstorm as blessings on everybody, while all chanted, "Hee-ee-ah-ah, hee-ee-ah-ah," jumping up and down until all were bathed in perspiration.

After the dancing excellent imitations were given of the gait, gestures, and behavior of several animals under different circumstances—walking, hunting, capturing, and devouring their prey, etc. While all were quietly seated, waiting to see what next was going to happen, the door of the big house was suddenly thrown open and in bounced a bear, so true to life in form and gestures we were all startled, though it was only a bear-skin nicely fitted on a man who was intimately acquainted with the animals and knew how to imitate them. The bear shuffled down into the middle of the floor and made the motion of jumping into a stream and catching a wooden salmon that was ready for him, carrying it out on to the bank, throwing his head around to listen and see if any one was coming, then tearing it to pieces, jerking his head from side to side, looking and listening in fear of hunters' rifles. Besides the bear dance, there were porpoise and deer dances with one of the party imitating the animals by stuffed specimens with an Indian inside, and the movements were so accurately imitated that they seemed the real thing.

These animal plays were followed by serious speeches, interpreted by an Indian woman: "Dear Brothers and Sisters, this is the way we used to dance. We liked it long ago when we were blind, we always danced this way, but now we are not blind. The Good Lord has taken pity upon us and sent his son, Jesus Christ, to tell us what to do. We have danced to-day only to show you how blind we were to like to dance in this foolish way. We will not dance any more."

Another speech was interpreted as follows: " 'Dear Brothers and Sisters,' the chief says, 'this is the way we used to dance and play. We do not wish to do so any more. We will give away all the dance dresses you have seen us wearing, though we value them very highly.' He says he feels much honored to have so many white brothers and sisters at our dinner and plays."

Several short explanatory remarks were made all through the exercises by Chief Shakes, presiding with grave dignity. The last of his speeches concluded thus: "Dear Brothers and Sisters, we have been long, long in the dark. You have led us into strong guiding light and taught us the right way to live and the right way to die. I thank you for myself and all my people, and I give you my heart."

At the close of the amusements there was a potlatch when robes made of the skins of deer, wild sheep, marmots, and sables were distributed, and many of the fantastic head-dresses that had been worn by Shamans. One of these fell to my share.

The floor of the house was strewn with fresh hemlock boughs, bunches of showy wild flowers adorned the walls, and the hearth was filled with huckleberry branches and epilobium. Altogether it was a wonderful show.

———

I have found southeastern Alaska a good, healthy country to live in. The climate of the islands and shores of the mainland is remarkably bland and temperate and free from extremes of either heat or cold throughout the year. It is rainy, however,—so much so that hay-making will hardly ever be extensively engaged in here, whatever the future may show in the way of the development of mines, forests, and fisheries. This rainy weather, however, is of good quality, the best of the kind I ever experienced, mild in temperature, mostly gentle in its fall, filling the fountains of the rivers and keeping the whole land fresh and fruitful, while anything more delightful than the shining weather in the midst of the rain, the great round sun-days of July and August, may hardly be found anywhere, north or south. An Alaska summer day is a day without night. In the Far North, at Point Barrow, the sun does not set for weeks, and even here in southeastern Alaska it is only a few degrees below the horizon at its lowest point, and the topmost colors of the sunset blend with those of the sunrise, leaving no gap of darkness between. Midnight is only a low noon, the middle point of the gloaming. The thin clouds that are almost always present are then colored yellow and red, making a striking advertisement of the sun's progress beneath the horizon. The day opens slowly. The low arc of light steals around to the northeastward with gradual increase of height and span and intensity of tone; and when at length the sun appears, it is without much of that stirring, impressive pomp, of flashing, awakening, triumphant energy, suggestive of the Bible imagery, a bridegroom coming out of his chamber and rejoicing like a strong man to run a race. The red clouds with yellow edges dissolve in hazy dimness; the islands, with grayish-white ruffs of mist about them, cast ill-defined shadows on the glistening waters, and the whole down-bending firmament becomes pearl-gray. For three or four hours after sunrise there is nothing especially impressive in the landscape. The sun, though seemingly unclouded, may almost be looked in the face, and the islands and mountains, with their wealth of woods and snow and varied beauty of architecture, seem comparatively sleepy and uncommunicative.

As the day advances toward high noon, the sun-flood streaming through the damp atmosphere lights the water levels and the sky to glowing silver. Brightly play the ripples about the bushy edges of the islands and on the plume-shaped streaks between them, ruffled by gentle passing wind-currents. The warm air throbs and makes itself felt as a life-giving, energizing ocean, embracing all the landscape, quickening the imagination, and bringing to mind the life and motion about us—the tides, the rivers, the flood of light streaming through the satiny sky; the marvelous abundance of fishes feeding in the lower ocean; the misty flocks of insects in the air; wild sheep and goats on a thousand grassy ridges; beaver and mink far back on many a rushing stream; Indians floating and basking along the shores; leaves and crystals drinking the sunbeams; and glaciers on the mountains, making valleys and basins for new rivers and lakes and fertile beds of soil.

Through the afternoon, all the way down to the sunset, the day grows in beauty. The light seems to thicken and become yet more generously fruitful without losing its soft mellow brightness. Everything seems to settle into conscious repose. The winds breathe gently or are wholly at rest. The few clouds visible are downy and luminous and combed out fine on the edges. Gulls here and there, winnowing the air on easy wing, are brought into striking relief; and every stroke of the paddles of Indian hunters in their canoes is told by a quick, glancing flash. Bird choirs in the grove are scarce heard as they sweeten the brooding stillness; and the sky, land, and water meet and blend in one inseparable scene of enchantment. Then comes the sunset with its purple and gold, not a narrow arch on the horizon, but oftentimes filling all the sky. The level cloud-bars usually present are fired on the edges, and the spaces of clear sky between them are greenish-yellow or pale amber, while the orderly flocks of small overlapping clouds, often seen higher up, are mostly touched with crimson like the out-leaning sprays of maple-groves in the beginning of an Eastern Indian Summer. Soft, mellow purple flushes the sky to the zenith and fills the air, fairly steeping and transfiguring the islands and making all the water look like wine. After the sun goes down, the glowing gold vanishes, but because it descends on a curve nearly in the same plane with the horizon, the glowing portion of the display lasts much longer than in more southern latitudes, while the upper colors with gradually lessening intensity of tone sweep around to the north, gradually increase to the eastward, and unite with those of the morning.

The most extravagantly colored of all the sunsets I have yet seen in Alaska was one I enjoyed on the voyage from Portland to Wrangell, when we were in the midst of one of the most thickly is-landed parts of the Alexander Archipelago. The day had been showery, but late in the afternoon the clouds melted away from the west, all save a few that settled down in narrow level bars near the horizon. The evening was calm and the sunset colors came on grad-ually, increasing in extent and richness of tone by slow degrees as if requiring more time than usual to ripen. At a height of about thirty degrees there was a heavy cloud-bank, deeply reddened on its lower edge and the projecting parts of its face. Below this were three horizontal belts of purple edged with gold, while a vividly defined, spreading fan of flame streamed upward across the purple bars and faded in a feather edge of dull red. But beautiful and im-pressive as was this painting on the sky, the most novel and exciting effect was in the body of the atmosphere itself, which, laden with moisture, became one mass of color—a fine translucent purple haze in which the islands with softened outlines seemed to float, while a dense red ring lay around the base of each of them as a fit-ting border. The peaks, too, in the distance, and the snow-fields and glaciers and fleecy rolls of mist that lay in the hollows, were flushed with a deep, rosy alpenglow of ineffable loveliness. Everything near and far, even the ship, was comprehended in the glorious picture and the general color effect. The mission divines we had aboard seemed then to be truly divine as they gazed transfigured in the celestial glory. So also seemed our bluff, storm-fighting old captain, and his tarry sailors and all.

About one third of the summer days I spent in the Wrangell region were cloudy with very little or no rain, one third decidedly rainy, and one third clear. According to a record kept here of a hundred and forty-seven days beginning May 17 of that year, there were sixty-five on which rain fell, forty-three cloudy with no rain, and thirty-nine clear. In June rain fell on eighteen days, in July eight days, in August fifteen days, in September twenty days. But on some of these days there was only a few minutes' rain, light showers scarce enough to count, while as a general thing the rain fell so gently and the temperature was so mild, very few of them could be called stormy or dismal; even the bleakest, most bedraggled of them all usually had a flush of late or early color to cheer them, or some white illumination about the noon hours. I never before saw so much rain fall with so little noise. None of the summer winds make roaring storms, and thunder is seldom heard. I heard none at all. This wet, misty weather seems perfectly healthful. There is no mildew in the houses, as far as I have seen, or any tendency toward mouldiness in nooks hidden from the sun; and neither among the people nor the plants do we find anything flabby or dropsical.

In September clear days were rare, more than three fourths of them were either decidedly cloudy or rainy, and the rains of this month were, with one wild exception, only moderately heavy, and the clouds between showers drooped and crawled in a ragged, unsettled way without betraying hints of violence such as one often sees in the gestures of mountain storm-clouds.

July was the brightest month of the summer, with fourteen days of sunshine, six of them in uninterrupted succession, with a temperature at 7 A.M. of about 60°, at 12 M., 70°. The average 7 A.M. temperature for June was 54.3°; the average 7 A.M. temperature for July was 55.3°; at 12 M. the average temperature was 61.45°; the average

7 A.M. temperature for August was 54.12°; 12 M., 61.48°; the average 7 A.M. temperature for September was 52.14°; and 12 M., 56.12°.

The highest temperature observed here during the summer was seventy-six degrees. The most remarkable characteristic of this summer weather, even the brightest of it, is the velvet softness of the atmosphere. On the mountains of California, throughout the greater part of the year, the presence of an atmosphere is hardly recognized, and the thin, white, bodiless light of the morning comes to the peaks and glaciers as a pure spiritual essence, the most impressive of all the terrestrial manifestations of God. The clearest of Alaskan air is always appreciably substantial, so much so that it would seem as if one might test its quality by rubbing it between the thumb and finger. I never before saw summer days so white and so full of subdued lustre.

The winter storms, up to the end of December when I left Wrangell, were mostly rain at a temperature of thirty-five or forty degrees, with strong winds which sometimes roughly lash the shores and carry scud far into the woods. The long nights are then gloomy enough and the value of snug homes with crackling yellow cedar fires may be finely appreciated. Snow falls frequently, but never to any great depth or to lie long. It is said that only once since the settlement of Fort Wrangell has the ground been covered to a depth of four feet. The mercury seldom falls more than five or six degrees below the freezing-point, unless the wind blows steadily from the mainland. Back from the coast, however, beyond the mountains, the winter months are very cold. On the Stickeen River at Glenora, less than a thousand feet above the level of the sea, a temperature of from thirty to forty degrees below zero is not uncommon.

CHAPTER IV

THE STICKEEN RIVER

The most interesting of the short excursions we made from Fort Wrangell was the one up the Stickeen River to the head of steam navigation. From Mt. St. Elias the coast range extends in a broad, lofty chain beyond the southern boundary of the territory, gashed by stupendous cañons, each of which carries a lively river, though most of them are comparatively short, as their highest sources lie in the icy solitudes of the range within forty or fifty miles of the coast. A few, however, of these foaming, roaring streams—the Alsek, Chilcat, Chilcoot, Taku, Stickeen, and perhaps others—head beyond the range with some of the southwest branches of the Mackenzie and Yukon.

The largest side branches of the main-trunk cañons of all these mountain streams are still occupied by glaciers which descend in showy ranks, their massy, bulging snouts lying back a little distance in the shadows of the walls, or pushing forward among the cottonwoods that line the banks of the rivers, or even stretching all the way across the main cañons, compelling the rivers to find a channel beneath them.

The Stickeen was, perhaps, the best known of the rivers that cross the Coast Range, because it was the best way to the Mackenzie River

Cassiar gold-mines. It is about three hundred and fifty miles long, and is navigable for small steamers a hundred and fifty miles to Glenora, and sometimes to Telegraph Creek, fifteen miles farther. It first pursues a westerly course through grassy plains darkened here and there with groves of spruce and pine; then, curving southward and receiving numerous tributaries from the north, it enters the Coast Range, and sweeps across it through a magnificent cañon three thousand to five thousand feet deep, and more than a hundred miles long. The majestic cliffs and mountains forming the cañon-walls display endless variety of form and sculpture, and are wonderfully adorned and enlivened with glaciers and waterfalls, while throughout almost its whole extent the floor is a flowery landscape garden, like Yosemite. The most striking features are the glaciers, hanging over the cliffs, descending the side cañons and pushing forward to the river, greatly enhancing the wild beauty of all the others.

Gliding along the swift-flowing river, the views change with bewildering rapidity. Wonderful, too, are the changes dependent on the seasons and the weather. In spring, when the snow is melting fast, you enjoy the countless rejoicing waterfalls; the gentle breathing of warm winds; the colors of the young leaves and flowers when the bees are busy and wafts of fragrance are drifting hither and thither from miles of wild roses, clover, and honeysuckle; the swaths of birch and willow on the lower slopes following the melting of the winter avalanche snow-banks; the bossy cumuli swelling in white and purple piles above the highest peaks; gray rain-clouds wreathing the outstanding brows and battlements of the walls; and the breaking-forth of the sun after the rain; the shining of the leaves and streams and crystal architecture of the glaciers; the rising of fresh fragrance; the song of the happy birds; and the serene color-grandeur of the morning and evening sky. In summer you find the groves and gardens in full dress; glaciers melting rapidly under sunshine and rain; waterfalls in all their glory; the river rejoicing in its strength; young birds trying their wings; bears enjoying salmon and berries; all the life of the cañon brimming full like the streams. In autumn comes rest, as if the year's work were done. The rich hazy sunshine streaming over the cliffs calls forth the last

of the gentians and goldenrods; the groves and thickets and meadows bloom again as their leaves change to red and yellow petals; the
rocks also, and the glaciers, seem to bloom like the plants in the
mellow golden light. And so goes the song, change succeeding
change in sublime harmony through all the wonderful seasons and
weather.

———

My first trip up the river was made in the spring with the missionary party soon after our arrival at Wrangell. We left Wrangell in the
afternoon and anchored for the night above the river delta, and
started up the river early next morning when the heights above the
"Big Stickeen" Glacier and the smooth domes and copings and
arches of solid snow along the tops of the cañon walls were glowing in the early beams. We arrived before noon at the old trading-
post called "Buck's" in front of the Stickeen Glacier, and remained
long enough to allow the few passengers who wished a nearer view
to cross the river to the terminal moraine. The sunbeams streaming
through the ice pinnacles along its terminal wall produced a wonderful glory of color, and the broad, sparkling crystal prairie and
the distant snowy fountains were wonderfully attractive and made
me pray for opportunity to explore them.

Of the many glaciers, a hundred or more, that adorn the walls of
the great Stickeen River Cañon, this is the largest. It draws its
sources from snowy mountains within fifteen or twenty miles of the
coast, pours through a comparatively narrow cañon about two miles
in width in a magnificent cascade, and expands in a broad fan five or
six miles in width, separated from the Stickeen River by its broad
terminal moraine, fringed with spruces and willows. Around the
beautifully drawn curve of the moraine the Stickeen River flows,
having evidently been shoved by the glacier out of its direct course.
On the opposite side of the cañon another somewhat smaller glacier, which now terminates four or five miles from the river, was
once united front to front with the greater glacier, though at first
both were tributaries of the main Stickeen Glacier which once
filled the whole grand cañon. After the main trunk cañon was
melted out, its side branches, drawing their sources from a height of

three or four to five or six thousand feet, were cut off, and of course became separate glaciers, occupying cirques and branch cañons along the tops and sides of the walls. The Indians have a tradition that the river used to run through a tunnel under the united fronts of the two large tributary glaciers mentioned above, which entered the main cañon from either side; and that on one occasion an Indian, anxious to get rid of his wife, had her sent adrift in a canoe down through the ice tunnel, expecting that she would trouble him no more. But to his surprise she floated through under the ice in safety. All the evidence connected with the present appearance of these two glaciers indicates that they were united and formed a dam across the river after the smaller tributaries had been melted off and had receded to a greater or lesser height above the valley floor.

The big Stickeen Glacier is hardly out of sight ere you come upon another that pours a majestic crystal flood through the evergreens, while almost every hollow and tributary cañon contains a smaller one, the size, of course, varying with the extent of the area drained. Some are like mere snow-banks; others, with the blue ice apparent, depend in massive bulging curves and swells, and graduate into the river-like forms that maze through the lower forested regions and are so striking and beautiful that they are admired even by the passing miners with gold-dust in their eyes.

Thirty-five miles above the Big Stickeen Glacier is the "Dirt Glacier," the second in size. Its outlet is a fine stream, abounding in trout. On the opposite side of the river there is a group of five glaciers, one of them descending to within a hundred feet of the river.

Near Glenora, on the northeastern flank of the main Coast Range, just below a narrow gorge called "The Cañon," terraces first make their appearance, where great quantities of moraine material have been swept through the flood-choked gorge and of course outspread and deposited on the first open levels below. Here, too, occurs a marked change in climate and consequently in forests and general appearance of the face of the country. On account of destructive fires the woods are younger and are composed of smaller trees about a foot to eighteen inches in diameter and seventy-five feet high, mostly two-leaved pines which hold their seeds for several years after they are ripe. The woods here are without a trace of those deep accumulations of mosses, leaves, and decaying trunks which make so damp and unclearable a mass in the coast forests. Whole mountain-sides are covered with gray moss and lichens where the forest has been utterly destroyed. The river-bank cottonwoods are also smaller, and the birch and contorta pines mingle freely with the coast hemlock and spruce. The birch is common on the lower slopes and is very effective, its round, leafy, pale-green head contrasting with the dark, narrow spires of the conifers and giving a striking character to the forest. The "tamarac pine" or black pine, as the variety of *P. contorta* is called here, is yellowish-green, in marked contrast with the dark lichen-draped spruce which grows above the pine at a height of about two thousand feet, in groves and belts where it has escaped fire and snow avalanches. There is another handsome spruce hereabouts, *Picea alba*, very slender and graceful in habit, drooping at the top like a mountain hemlock. I saw fine specimens a hundred and twenty-five feet high on deep bottom land a few miles below Glenora. The tops of some of them were almost covered with dense clusters of yellow and brown cones.

We reached the old Hudson's Bay trading-post at Glenora about one o'clock, and the captain informed me that he would stop here until the next morning, when he would make an early start for Wrangell.

At a distance of about seven or eight miles to the northeastward of the landing, there is an outstanding group of mountains crowning a spur from the main chain of the Coast Range, whose highest point rises about eight thousand feet above the level of the sea; and as Glenora is only a thousand feet above the sea, the height to be overcome in climbing this peak is about seven thousand feet. Though the time was short I determined to climb it, because of the advantageous position it occupied for general views of the peaks and glaciers of the east side of the great range.

Although it was now twenty minutes past three and the days were getting short, I thought that by rapid climbing I could reach the summit before sunset, in time to get a general view and a few pencil sketches, and make my way back to the steamer in the night. Mr. Young, one of the missionaries, asked permission to accompany me, saying that he was a good walker and climber and would not delay me or cause any trouble. I strongly advised him not to go, explaining that it involved a walk, coming and going, of fourteen or sixteen miles, and a climb through brush and boulders of seven thousand feet, a fair day's work for a seasoned mountaineer to be done in less than half a day and part of a night. But he insisted that he was a strong walker, could do a mountaineer's day's work in half a day, and would not hinder me in any way.

"Well, I have warned you," I said, "and will not assume responsibility for any trouble that may arise."

He proved to be a stout walker, and we made rapid progress across a brushy timbered flat and up the mountain slopes, open in some places, and in others thatched with dwarf firs, resting a minute here and there to refresh ourselves with huckleberries, which grew in abundance in open spots. About half an hour before sunset, when we were near a cluster of crumbling pinnacles that formed the summit, I had ceased to feel anxiety about the mountaineering strength and skill of my companion, and pushed rapidly on. In passing around the shoulder of the highest pinnacle, where the rock was rapidly disintegrating and the danger of slipping was great, I shouted in a warning voice, "Be very careful here, this is dangerous."

Mr. Young was perhaps a dozen or two yards behind me, but out of sight. I afterwards reproached myself for not stopping and lending him a steadying hand, and showing him the slight footsteps I had made by kicking out little blocks of the crumbling surface, instead of simply warning him to be careful. Only a few seconds after giving this warning, I was startled by a scream for help, and hurrying back, found the missionary face downward, his arms outstretched, clutching little crumbling knobs on the brink of a gully that plunges down a thousand feet or more to a small residual glacier. I managed to get below him, touched one of his feet, and tried to encourage him by saying, "I am below you. You are in no danger. You can't slip past me and I will soon get you out of this."

He then told me that both of his arms were dislocated. It was almost impossible to find available footholds on the treacherous rock, and I was at my wits' end to know how to get him rolled or dragged to a place where I could get about him, find out how much he was hurt, and a way back down the mountain. After narrowly scanning the cliff and making footholds, I managed to roll and lift him a few yards to a place where the slope was less steep, and there I attempted to set his arms. I found, however, that this was impossible in such a place. I therefore tied his arms to his sides with my suspenders and necktie, to prevent as much as possible inflammation from movement. I then left him, telling him to lie still, that I would be back in a few minutes, and that he was now safe from slipping. I hastily examined the ground and saw no way of getting him down except by the steep glacier gully. After scrambling to an outstanding point that commands a view of it from top to bottom, to make sure that it was not interrupted by sheer precipices, I concluded that with great care and the digging of slight footholds he could be slid down to the glacier, where I could lay him on his back and perhaps be able to set his arms. Accordingly, I cheered him up, telling him I had found a way, but that it would require lots of time and patience. Digging a footstep in the sand or crumbling rock five or six feet beneath him, I reached up, took hold of him by one of his feet, and gently slid him down on his back, placed his heels in the step, then descended another five or six feet, dug heel notches, and slid him down to them. Thus the whole distance was made by a succession of narrow steps at very short intervals, and the glacier was reached perhaps about midnight. Here I took off one of my boots, tied a handkerchief around his wrist for a good hold, placed my heel in his arm pit, and succeeded in getting one of his arms into place, but my utmost strength was insufficient to reduce the dislocation of the other. I therefore bound it closely to his side, and asked him if in his exhausted and trembling condition he was still able to walk.

"Yes," he bravely replied.

So, with a steadying arm around him and many stops for rest, I marched him slowly down in the star-light on the comparatively smooth, unfissured surface of the little glacier to the terminal moraine, a distance of perhaps a mile, crossed the moraine, bathed his head at one of the outlet streams, and after many rests reached a dry place and made a brush fire. I then went ahead looking for an open way through the bushes to where larger wood could be had, made a good lasting fire of resiny silver-fir roots, and a leafy bed beside it. I now told him I would run down the mountain, hasten back with help from the boat, and carry him down in comfort. But he would not hear of my leaving him.

"No, no," he said, "I can walk down. Don't leave me."

I reminded him of the roughness of the way, his nerve-shaken condition, and assured him I would not be gone long. But he insisted on trying, saying on no account whatever must I leave him. I therefore concluded to try to get him to the ship by short walks from one fire and resting-place to another. While he was resting I went ahead, looking for the best way through the brush and rocks, then returning, got him on his feet and made him lean on my shoulder while I steadied him to prevent his falling. This slow, staggering struggle from fire to fire lasted until long after sunrise. When at last we reached the ship and stood at the foot of the narrow single plank without side rails that reached from the bank to the deck at a considerable angle, I briefly explained to Mr. Young's companions, who stood looking down at us, that he had been hurt in an accident, and requested one of them to assist me in getting him aboard. But strange to say, instead of coming down to help, they made haste to reproach him for having gone on a "wild-goose chase" with Muir.

"These foolish adventures are well enough for Mr. Muir," they said, "but you, Mr. Young, have work to do; you have a family; you have a church, and you have no right to risk your life on treacherous peaks and precipices."

The captain, Nat Lane, son of Senator Joseph Lane, had been swearing in angry impatience for being compelled to make so late a start and thus encounter a dangerous wind in a narrow gorge, and was threatening to put the missionaries ashore to seek their lost companion, while he went on down the river about his business.

But when he heard my call for help, he hastened forward, and elbowed the divines away from the end of the gangplank, shouting in angry irreverence, "Oh, blank! This is no time for preaching! Don't you see the man is hurt?"

He ran down to our help, and while I steadied my trembling companion from behind, the captain kindly led him up the plank into the saloon, and made him drink a large glass of brandy. Then, with a man holding down his shoulders, we succeeded in getting the bone into its socket, notwithstanding the inflammation and contraction of the muscles and ligaments. Mr. Young was then put to bed, and he slept all the way back to Wrangell.

In his mission lectures in the East, Mr. Young oftentimes told this story. I made no record of it in my notebook and never intended to write a word about it; but after a miserable, sensational caricature of the story had appeared in a respectable magazine, I thought it but fair to my brave companion that it should be told just as it happened.

CHAPTER V

A Cruise in the Cassiar

Shortly after our return to Wrangell the missionaries planned a grand mission excursion up the coast of the mainland to the Chilcat country, which I gladly joined, together with Mr. Vanderbilt, his wife, and a friend from Oregon. The river steamer Cassiar was chartered, and we had her all to ourselves, ship and officers at our command to sail and stop where and when we would, and of course everybody felt important and hopeful. The main object of the missionaries was to ascertain the spiritual wants of the war-like Chilcat tribe, with a view to the establishment of a church and school in their principal village; the merchant and his party were bent on business and scenery; while my mind was on the mountains, glaciers, and forests.

This was toward the end of July, in the very brightest and best of Alaska summer weather, when the icy mountains towering in the pearly sky were displayed in all their glory, and the islands at their feet seemed to float and drowse on the shining mirror-waters.

After we had passed through the Wrangell Narrows, the mountains of the mainland came in full view, gloriously arrayed in snow and ice, some of the largest and most river-like of the glaciers flowing through wide, high-walled valleys like Yosemite, their sources far back and concealed, others in plain sight, from their highest fountains to the level of the sea.

Cares of every kind were quickly forgotten, and though the Cassiar engines soon began to wheeze and sigh with doleful solemnity, suggesting coming trouble, we were too happy to mind them. Every face glowed with natural love of wild beauty. The islands were seen in long perspective, their forests dark green in the foreground, with varying tones of blue growing more and more tender in the distance; bays full of hazy shadows, graduating into open, silvery fields of light, and lofty headlands with fine arching insteps dipping their feet in the shining water. But every eye was turned to the mountains. Forgotten now were the Chilcats and missions while the word of God was being read in these majestic hieroglyphics blazoned along the sky. The earnest, childish wonderment with which this glorious page of Nature's Bible was contemplated was delightful to see. All evinced eager desire to learn.

"Is that a glacier," they asked, "down in that cañon? And is it all solid ice?"

"Yes."

"How deep is it?"

"Perhaps five hundred or a thousand feet."

"You say it flows. How can hard ice flow?"

"It flows like water, though invisibly slow."

"And where does it come from?"

"From snow that is heaped up every winter on the mountains."

"And how, then, is the snow changed into ice?"

"It is welded by the pressure of its own weight."

"Are these white masses we see in the hollows glaciers also?"

"Yes."

"Are those bluish draggled masses hanging down from beneath the snow-fields what you call the snouts of the glaciers?"

"Yes."

"What made the hollows they are in?"

"The glaciers themselves, just as traveling animals make their own tracks."

"How long have they been there?"

"Numberless centuries," etc. I answered as best I could, keeping up a running commentary on the subject in general, while busily engaged in sketching and noting my own observations, preaching glacial gospel in a rambling way, while the Cassiar, slowly wheezing and creeping along the shore, shifted our position so that the icy cañons were opened to view and closed again in regular succession, like the leaves of a book.

About the middle of the afternoon we were directly opposite a noble group of glaciers some ten in number, flowing from a chain of crater-like snow fountains, guarded around their summits and well down their sides by jagged peaks and cols and curving mural ridges. From each of the larger clusters of fountains, a wide, sheer-walled cañon opens down to the sea. Three of the trunk glaciers descend to within a few feet of the sea-level. The largest of the three, probably about fifteen miles long, terminates in a magnificent valley like Yosemite, in an imposing wall of ice about two miles long, and from three to five hundred feet high, forming a barrier across the valley from wall to wall. It was to this glacier that the ships of the Alaska Ice Company resorted for the ice they carried to San Francisco and the Sandwich Islands, and, I believe, also to China and Japan. To load, they had only to sail up the fiord within a short distance of the front and drop anchor in the terminal moraine.

Another glacier, a few miles to the south of this one, receives two large tributaries about equal in size, and then flows down a forested valley to within a hundred feet or so of sea-level. The third of this low-descending group is four or five miles farther south, and, though less imposing than either of the two sketched above, is still a truly noble object, even as imperfectly seen from the channel, and would of itself be well worth a visit to Alaska to any lowlander so unfortunate as never to have seen a glacier.

The boilers of our little steamer were not made for sea water, but it was hoped that fresh water would be found at available points along our course where streams leap down the cliffs. In this particular we failed, however, and were compelled to use salt water an hour or two before reaching Cape Fanshawe, the supply of fifty tons of fresh water brought from Wrangell having then given out. To make matters worse, the captain and engineer were not in accord concerning the working of the engines. The captain repeatedly called for more steam, which the engineer refused to furnish, cautiously keeping the pressure low because the salt water foamed in the boilers and some of it passed over into the cylinders, causing heavy thumping at the end of each piston stroke, and threatening to knock out the cylinder-heads. At seven o'clock in the evening we had made only about seventy miles, which caused dissatisfaction, especially among the divines, who thereupon called a meeting in the cabin to consider what had better be done. In the discussions that followed much indignation and economy were brought to light. We had chartered the boat for sixty dollars per day, and the round trip was to have been made in four or five days. But at the present rate of speed it was found that the cost of the trip for each passenger would be five or ten dollars above the first estimate. Therefore, the majority ruled that we must return next day to Wrangell, the extra dollars outweighing the mountains and missions as if they had suddenly become dust in the balance.

Soon after the close of this economical meeting, we came to anchor in a beautiful bay, and as the long northern day had still hours of good light to offer, I gladly embraced the opportunity to go ashore to see the rocks and plants. One of the Indians, employed as a deck hand on the steamer, landed me at the mouth of a stream. The tide was low, exposing a luxuriant growth of algæ, which sent up a fine, fresh sea smell. The shingle was composed of slate, quartz, and granite, named in the order of abundance. The first land plant met was a tall grass, nine feet high, forming a meadow-like margin in front of the forest. Pushing my way well back into the forest, I found it composed almost entirely of spruce and two hemlocks (*Picea sitchensis, Tsuga heterophylla,* and *T. mertensiana*) with a few specimens of yellow cypress. The ferns were developed in remarkable beauty and size—aspidiums, one of which is about six feet high, a woodsia, lomaria, and several species of polypodium. The underbrush is chiefly alder, rubus, ledum, three species of vaccinium, and *Echinopanax horrida,* the whole about from six to eight

feet high, and in some places closely intertangled and hard to pene-
trate. On the opener spots beneath the trees the ground is covered to
a depth of two or three feet with mosses of indescribable freshness
and beauty, a few dwarf cornels often planted on their rich furred
bosses, together with pyrola, coptis, and Solomon's-seal. The tallest
of the trees are about a hundred and fifty feet high, with a diameter
of about four or five feet, their branches mingling together and making a perfect shade. As the twilight began to fall, I sat down on the
mossy instep of a spruce. Not a bush or tree was moving; every leaf
seemed hushed in brooding repose. One bird, a thrush, embroidered the silence with cheery notes, making the solitude familiar
and sweet, while the solemn monotone of the stream sifting through
the woods seemed like the very voice of God, humanized, terrestri-
alized, and entering one's heart as to a home prepared for it. Go
where we will, all the world over, we seem to have been there before.

The stream was bridged at short intervals with picturesque,
moss-embossed logs, and the trees on its banks, leaning over from
side to side, made high embowering arches. The log bridge I
crossed was, I think, the most beautiful of the kind I ever saw.
The massive log is plushed to a depth of six inches or more with
mosses of three or four species, their different tones of yellow
shading finely into each other, while their delicate fronded
branches and foliage lie in exquisite order, inclining outward and
down the sides in rich, furred, clasping sheets overlapping and
felted together until the required thickness is attained. The
pedicels and spore-cases give a purplish tinge, and the whole
bridge is enriched with ferns and a row of small seedling trees
and currant bushes with colored leaves, every one of which
seems to have been culled from the woods for this special use, so
perfectly do they harmonize in size, shape, and color with the
mossy cover, the width of the span, and the luxuriant, brushy
abutments.

Sauntering back to the beach, I found four or five Indian deck
hands getting water, with whom I returned aboard the steamer,
thanking the Lord for so noble an addition to my life as was this one
big mountain, forest, and glacial day.

Alaskan Hemlocks and Spruces, Sitka

Next morning most of the company seemed uncomfortably conscience-stricken, and ready to do anything in the way of compensation for our broken excursion that would not cost too much. It was not found difficult, therefore, to convince the captain and disappointed passengers that instead of creeping back to Wrangell direct we should make an expiatory branch-excursion to the largest of the three low-descending glaciers we had passed. The Indian pilot, well acquainted with this part of the coast, declared himself willing to guide us. The water in these fiord channels is generally deep and safe, and though at wide intervals rocks rise abruptly here and there, lacking only a few feet in height to enable them to take rank as islands, the flat-bottomed Cassiar drew but little more water than a duck, so that even the most timid raised no objection on this score. The cylinder-heads of our engines were the main source of anxiety; provided they could be kept on all might yet be well. But in this matter there was evidently some distrust, the engineer having imprudently informed some of the passengers that in consequence of using salt water in his frothing boilers the cylinder-heads might fly off at any moment. To the glacier, however, it was at length decided we should venture.

Arriving opposite the mouth of its fiord, we steered straight inland between beautiful wooded shores, and the grand glacier came in sight in its granite valley, glowing in the early sunshine and extending a noble invitation to come and see. After we passed between the two mountain rocks that guard the gate of the fiord, the view that was unfolded fixed every eye in wondering admiration. No words can convey anything like an adequate conception of its sublime grandeur—the noble simplicity and fineness of the sculpture of the walls; their magnificent proportions; their cascades, gardens, and forest adornments; the placid fiord between them; the great white and blue ice wall, and the snow-laden mountains beyond. Still more impotent are words in telling the peculiar awe one experiences in entering these mansions of the icy North, notwithstanding it is only the natural effect of appreciable manifestations of the presence of God.

Standing in the gateway of this glorious temple, and regarding it only as a picture, its outlines may be easily traced, the water foreground of a pale-green color, a smooth mirror sheet sweeping back five or six miles like one of the lower reaches of a great river, bounded at the head by a beveled barrier wall of blueish-white ice four or five hundred feet high. A few snowy mountain-tops appear beyond it, and on either hand rise a series of majestic, pale-gray granite rocks from three to four thousand feet high, some of them thinly forested and striped with bushes and flowery grass on narrow shelves, especially about half way up, others severely sheer and bare and built together into walls like those of Yosemite, extending far beyond the ice barrier, one immense brow appearing beyond another with their bases buried in the glacier. This is a Yosemite Valley in process of formation, the modeling and sculpture of the walls nearly completed and well planted, but no groves as yet or gardens or meadows on the raw and unfinished bottom. It is as if the explorer, in entering the Merced Yosemite, should find the walls nearly in their present condition, trees and flowers in the warm nooks and along the sunny portions of the moraine-covered brows, but the bottom of the valley still covered with water and beds of gravel and mud, and the grand glacier that formed it slowly receding but still filling the upper half of the valley.

Sailing directly up to the edge of the low, outspread, water-washed terminal moraine, scarce noticeable in a general view, we seemed to be separated from the glacier only by a bed of gravel a hundred yards or so in width; but on so grand a scale are all the main features of the valley, we afterwards found the distance to be a mile or more.

The captain ordered the Indian deck hands to get out the canoe, take as many of us ashore as wished to go, and accompany us to the glacier in case we should need their help. Only three of the company, in the first place, availed themselves of this rare opportunity of meeting a glacier in the flesh,—Mr. Young, one of the doctors, and myself. Paddling to the nearest and driest-looking part of the moraine flat, we stepped ashore, but gladly wallowed back into the canoe; for the gray mineral mud, a paste made of fine-ground mountain meal kept unstable by the tides, at once began to take us in, swallowing us feet foremost with becoming glacial deliberation. Our next attempt, made nearer the middle of the valley, was successful, and we soon found ourselves on firm gravelly ground, and made haste to the huge ice-wall, which seemed to recede as we advanced. The only difficulty we met was a network of icy streams, at the largest of which we halted, not willing to get wet in fording. The Indian attendant promptly carried us over on his back. When my turn came I told him I would ford, but he bowed his shoulders in so ludicrously persuasive a manner I thought I would try the queer mount, the only one of the kind I had enjoyed since boyhood days in playing leapfrog. Away staggered my perpendicular mule over the boulders into the brawling torrent, and in spite of top-heavy predictions to the contrary, crossed without a fall. After being ferried in this way over several more of these glacial streams, we at length reached the foot of the glacier wall. The doctor simply played tag on it, touched it gently as if it were a dangerous wild beast, and hurried back to the boat, taking the portage Indian with him for safety, little knowing what he was missing. Mr. Young and I traced the glorious crystal wall, admiring its wonderful architecture, the play of light in the rifts and caverns, and the structure of the ice as displayed in the less fractured sections, finding fresh beauty everywhere and facts for study. We then tried to climb it, and by dint of patient zigzagging and doubling among the crevasses, and cutting steps here and there, we made our way up over the brow and back a mile or two to a height of about seven hundred feet. The whole front of the glacier is gashed and sculptured into a maze of shallow caves and crevasses, and a bewildering variety of novel architectural forms, clusters of glittering lance-tipped spires, gables, and obelisks, bold outstanding bastions and plain mural cliffs, adorned along the top with fretted cornice and battlement, while every gorge and crevasse, groove and hollow, was filled with light, shimmering and throbbing in pale-blue tones of ineffable tenderness and beauty. The day was warm, and back on the broad melting bosom of the glacier beyond the crevassed front, many streams were rejoicing, gurgling, ringing, singing, in friction-less channels worn down through the white disintegrated ice of the surface into the quick and living blue, in which they flowed with a grace of motion and flashing of light to be found only on the crystal hillocks and ravines of a glacier.

Along the sides of the glacier we saw the mighty flood grinding against the granite walls with tremendous pressure, rounding outswelling bosses, and deepening the retreating hollows into the forms they are destined to have when, in the fullness of appointed time, the huge ice tool shall be withdrawn by the sun. Every feature glowed with intention, reflecting the plans of God. Back a few miles from the front, the glacier is now probably but little more than a thousand feet deep; but when we examine the records on the walls, the rounded, grooved, striated, and polished features so surely glacial, we learn that in the earlier days of the ice age they were all over-swept, and that this glacier has flowed at a height of from three to four thousand feet above its present level, when it was at least a mile deep.

Standing here, with facts so fresh and telling and held up so vividly before us, every seeing observer, not to say geologist, must readily apprehend the earth-sculpturing, landscape-making action of flowing ice. And here, too, one learns that the world, though made, is yet being made; that this is still the morning of creation; that mountains long conceived are now being born, channels traced for coming rivers, basins hollowed for lakes; that moraine soil is being ground and outspread for coming plants,—coarse boulders and gravel for forests, finer soil for grasses and flowers,—while the finest part of the grist, seen hastening out to sea in the draining streams, is being stored away in darkness and builded particle on particle, cementing and crystallizing, to make the mountains and valleys and plains of other predestined landscapes, to be followed by still others in endless rhythm and beauty.

Gladly would we have camped out on this grand old landscape mill to study its ways and works; but we had no bread and the captain was keeping the Cassiar whistle screaming for our return. Therefore, in mean haste, we threaded our way back through the crevasses and down the blue cliffs, snatched a few flowers from a warm spot on the edge of the ice, plashed across the moraine streams, and were paddled aboard, rejoicing in the possession of so blessed a day, and feeling that in very foundational truth we had been in one of God's own temples and had seen Him and heard Him working and preaching like a man.

Steaming solemnly out of the fiord and down the coast, the islands and mountains were again passed in review; the clouds that so often hide the mountain-tops even in good weather were now floating high above them, and the transparent shadows they cast were scarce perceptible on the white glacier fountains. So abundant and novel are the objects of interest in a pure wilderness that unless you are pursuing special studies it matters little where you go, or how often to the same place. Wherever you chance to be always seems at the moment of all places the best; and you feel that there can be no happiness in this world or in any other for those who may not be happy here. The bright hours were spent in making notes and sketches and getting more of the wonderful region into memory. In particular a second view of the mountains made me raise my first estimate of their height. Some of them must be seven or eight thousand feet at the least. Also the glaciers seemed larger and more numerous. I counted nearly a hundred, large and small, between a point ten or fifteen miles to the north of Cape Fanshawe and the mouth of the Stickeen River. We made no more landings, however, until we had passed through the Wrangell Narrows and dropped anchor for the night in a small sequestered bay. This was about sunset, and I eagerly seized the opportunity to go ashore in the canoe and see what I could learn. It is here only a step from the marine algæ to terrestrial vegetation of almost tropical luxuriance. Parting the alders and huckleberry bushes and the crooked stems of the prickly panax, I made my way into the woods, and lingered in the twilight doing nothing in particular, only measuring a few of the trees, listening to learn what birds and animals might be about, and gazing along the dusky aisles.

In the mean time another excursion was being invented, one of small size and price. We might have reached Fort Wrangell this evening instead of anchoring here; but the owners of the Cassiar would then receive only ten dollars fare from each person, while they had incurred considerable expense in fitting up the boat for this special trip, and had treated us well. No, under the circumstances, it would never do to return to Wrangell so meanly soon.

It was decided, therefore, that the Cassiar Company should have the benefit of another day's hire, in visiting the old deserted Stickeen village fourteen miles to the south of Wrangell.

"We shall have a good time," one of the most influential of the party said to me in a semi-apologetic tone, as if dimly recognizing my disappointment in not going on to Chilcat. "We shall probably find stone axes and other curiosities. Chief Kadachan is going to guide us, and the other Indians aboard will dig for us, and there are interesting old buildings and totem poles to be seen."

It seemed strange, however, that so important a mission to the most influential of the Alaskan tribes should end in a deserted village. But divinity abounded nevertheless; the day was divine and there was plenty of natural religion in the new-born landscapes that were being baptized in sunshine, and sermons in the glacial boulders on the beach where we landed.

The site of the old village is on an outswelling strip of ground about two hundred yards long and fifty wide, sloping gently to the water with a strip of gravel and tall grass in front, dark woods back of it, and charming views over the water among the islands—a delightful place. The tide was low when we arrived, and I noticed that the exposed boulders on the beach—granite erratics that had been dropped by the melting ice toward the close of the glacial period— were piled in parallel rows at right angles to the shore-line, out of the way of the canoes that had belonged to the village.

Most of the party sauntered along the shore; for the ruins were overgrown with tall nettles, elder bushes, and prickly rubus vines through which it was difficult to force a way. In company with the most eager of the relic-seekers and two Indians, I pushed back among the dilapidated dwellings. They were deserted some sixty or seventy years before, and some of them were at least a hundred years old. So said our guide, Kadachan, and his word was corroborated by the venerable aspect of the ruins. Though the damp climate is destructive, many of the house timbers were still in a good state of preservation, particularly those hewn from the yellow cypress, or cedar as it is called here. The magnitude of the ruins and the excellence of the workmanship manifest in them was astonishing as belonging to Indians. For example, the first dwelling we visited was about forty feet square, with walls built of planks two feet wide and six inches thick. The ridgepole of yellow cypress was two feet in diameter, forty feet long, and as round and true as if it had been turned in a lathe; and, though lying in the damp weeds, it was still perfectly sound. The nibble marks of the stone adze were still visible, though crusted over with scale lichens in most places. The pillars that had supported the ridgepole were still standing in some of the ruins. They were all, as far as I observed, carved into life-size figures of men, women, and children, fishes, birds, and various other animals, such as the beaver, wolf, or bear. Each of the wall planks had evidently been hewn out of a whole log, and must have required sturdy deliberation as well as skill. Their geometrical truthfulness was admirable. With the same tools not one in a thousand of our skilled mechanics could do as good work. Compared with it the bravest work of civilized backwoodsmen is feeble and bungling. The completeness of form, finish, and proportion of these timbers suggested skill of a wild and positive kind, like that which guides the woodpecker in drilling round holes, and the bee in making its cells.

The carved totem-pole monuments are the most striking of the objects displayed here. The simplest of them consisted of a smooth, round post fifteen or twenty feet high and about eighteen inches in diameter, with the figure of some animal on top—a bear, porpoise, eagle, or raven, about life-size or larger. These were the totems of the families that occupied the houses in front of which they stood. Others supported the figure of a man or woman, life-size or larger, usually in a sitting posture, said to resemble the dead whose ashes were contained in a closed cavity in the pole. The largest were thirty or forty feet high, carved from top to bottom into human and animal totem figures, one above another, with their limbs grotesquely doubled and folded. Some of the most imposing were said to commemorate some event of an historical character. But a

Old Chief and Totem Pole, Wrangell

telling display of family pride seemed to have been the prevailing motive. All the figures were more or less rude, and some were broadly grotesque, but there was never any feebleness or obscurity in the expression. On the contrary, every feature showed grave force and decision; while the childish audacity displayed in the designs, combined with manly strength in their execution, was truly wonderful.

The colored lichens and mosses gave them a venerable air, while the larger vegetation often found on such as were most decayed produced a picturesque effect. Here, for example, is a bear five or six feet long, reposing on top of his lichen-clad pillar, with paws comfortably folded, a tuft of grass growing in each ear and rubus bushes along his back. And yonder is an old chief poised on a taller pillar, apparently gazing out over the landscape in contemplative mood, a tuft of bushes leaning back with a jaunty air from the top of his weatherbeaten hat, and downy mosses about his massive lips. But no rudeness or grotesqueness that may appear, however combined with the decorations that nature has added, may possibly provoke mirth. The whole work is serious in aspect and brave and true in execution.

Similar monuments are made by other Thlinkit tribes. The erection of a totem pole is made a grand affair, and is often talked of for a year or two beforehand. A feast, to which many are invited, is held, and the joyous occasion is spent in eating, dancing, and the distribution of gifts. Some of the larger specimens cost a thousand dollars or more. From one to two hundred blankets, worth three dollars apiece, are paid to the genius who carves them, while the presents and feast usually cost twice as much, so that only the wealthy families can afford them. I talked with an old Indian who pointed out one of the carvings he had made in the Wrangell village, for which he told me he had received forty blankets, a gun, a canoe, and other articles, all together worth about $170. Mr. Swan, who has contributed much information concerning the British Columbian and Alaskan tribes, describes a totem pole that cost $2500. They are always planted firmly in the ground and stand fast, showing the sturdy erectness of their builders.

While I was busy with my pencil, I heard chopping going on at the north end of the village, followed by a heavy thud, as if a tree had fallen. It appeared that after digging about the old hearth in the first dwelling visited without finding anything of consequence, the archæological doctor called the steamer deck hands to one of the most interesting of the totems and directed them to cut it down, saw off the principal figure,—a woman measuring three feet three inches across the shoulders,—and convey it aboard the steamer, with a view to taking it on East to enrich some museum or other. This sacrilege came near causing trouble and would have cost us dear had the totem not chanced to belong to the Kadachan family, the representative of which is a member of the newly organized Wrangell Presbyterian Church. Kadachan looked very seriously into the face of the reverend doctor and pushed home the pertinent question: "How would you like to have an Indian go to a graveyard and break down and carry away a monument belonging to your family?"

However, the religious relations of the parties and a few trifling presents embedded in apologies served to hush and mend the matter.

Some time in the afternoon the steam whistle called us together to finish our memorable trip. There was no trace of decay in the sky; a glorious sunset gilded the water and cleared away the shadows of our meditations among the ruins. We landed at the Wrangell wharf at dusk, pushed our way through a group of inquisitive Indians, across the two crooked streets, and up to our homes in the fort. We had been away only three days, but they were so full of novel scenes and impressions the time seemed indefinitely long, and our broken Chilcat excursion, far from being a failure as it seemed to some, was one of the most memorable of my life.

CHAPTER VI

The Cassiar Trail

I made a second trip up the Stickeen in August and from the head of navigation pushed inland for general views over dry grassy hills and plains on the Cassiar trail.

Soon after leaving Telegraph Creek I met a merry trader who encouragingly assured me that I was going into the most wonderful region in the world, that "the scenery up the river was full of the very wildest freaks of nature, surpassing all other sceneries either natural or artificial, on paper or in nature. And give yourself no bothering care about provisions, for wild food grows in prodigious abundance everywhere. A man was lost four days up there, but he feasted on vegetables and berries and got back to camp in good condition. A mess of wild parsnips and pepper, for example, will actually do you good. And here's my advice—go slow and take the pleasures and sceneries as you go."

At the confluence of the first North Fork of the Stickeen I found a band of Toltan or Stick Indians catching their winter supply of salmon in willow traps, set where the fish are struggling in swift rapids on their way to the spawning-grounds. A large supply had already been secured, and of course the Indians were well fed and merry. They were camping in large booths made of poles set on end in the ground, with many binding cross-pieces on which tons of salmon were being dried. The heads were strung on separate poles and the roes packed in willow baskets, all being well smoked from fires in the middle of the floor. The largest of the booths near the bank of the river was about forty feet square. Beds made of spruce and pine boughs were spread all around the walls, on which some of the Indians lay asleep; some were braiding ropes, others sitting and lounging, gossiping and courting, while a little baby was swinging in a hammock. All seemed to be light-hearted and jolly, with work enough and wit enough to maintain health and comfort. In the winter they are said to dwell in substantial huts in the woods, where game, especially caribou, is abundant. They are pale copper-colored, have small feet and hands, are not at all negroish in lips or cheeks like some of the coast tribes, nor so thickset, short-necked, or heavy-featured in general.

One of the most striking of the geological features of this region are immense gravel deposits displayed in sections on the walls of the river gorges. About two miles above the North Fork confluence there is a bluff of basalt three hundred and fifty feet high, and above this a bed of gravel four hundred feet thick, while beneath the basalt there is another bed at least fifty feet thick.

From "Ward's," seventeen miles beyond Telegraph, and about fourteen hundred feet above sea-level, the trail ascends a gravel ridge to a pine-and-fir-covered plateau twenty-one hundred feet above the sea. Thence for three miles the trail leads through a forest of short, closely planted trees to the second North Fork of the Stickeen, where a still greater deposit of stratified gravel is displayed, a section at least six hundred feet thick resting on a red jaspery formation.

Nine hundred feet above the river there is a slightly dimpled plateau diversified with aspen and willow groves and mossy meadows. At "Wilson's," one and a half miles from the river, the ground is carpeted with dwarf manzanita and the blessed *Linnæa borealis,* and forested with small pines, spruces, and aspens, the tallest fifty to sixty feet high.

From Wilson's to "Caribou," fourteen miles, no water was visible, though the nearly level, mossy ground is swampy-looking. At

"Caribou Camp," two miles from the river, I saw two fine dogs, a Newfoundland and a spaniel. Their owner told me that he paid only twenty dollars for the team and was offered one hundred dollars for one of them a short time afterwards. The Newfoundland, he said, caught salmon on the ripples, and could be sent back for miles to fetch horses. The fine jet-black curly spaniel helped to carry the dishes from the table to the kitchen, went for water when ordered, took the pail and set it down at the stream-side, but could not be taught to dip it full. But their principal work was hauling camp-supplies on sleds up the river in winter. These two were said to be able to haul a load of a thousand pounds when the ice was in fairly good condition. They were fed on dried fish and oatmeal boiled together.

The timber hereabouts is mostly willow or poplar on the low ground, with here and there pine, birch, and spruce about fifty feet high. None seen much exceeded a foot in diameter. Thousand-acre patches have been destroyed by fire. Some of the green trees had been burned off at the root, the raised roots, packed in dry moss, being readily attacked from beneath. A range of mountains about five thousand to six thousand feet high trending nearly north and south for sixty miles is forested to the summit. Only a few cliff-faces and one of the highest points patched with snow are treeless. No part of this range as far as I could see is deeply sculptured, though the general denudation of the country must have been enormous as the gravel-beds show.

At the top of a smooth, flowery pass about four thousand feet above the sea, beautiful Dease Lake comes suddenly in sight, shining like a broad tranquil river between densely forested hills and mountains. It is about twenty-seven miles long, one to two miles wide, and its waters, tributary to the Mackenzie, flow into the Arctic Ocean by a very long, roundabout, romantic way, the exploration of which in 1789 from Great Slave Lake to the Arctic Ocean must have been a glorious task for the heroic Scotchman, Alexander Mackenzie, whose name it bears.

Dease Creek, a fine rushing stream about forty miles long and forty or fifty feet wide, enters the lake from the west, drawing its sources from grassy mountain-ridges. Thibert Creek, about the same size, and McDames and Defot Creeks, with their many branches, head together in the same general range of mountains or on moor-like tablelands on the divide between the Mackenzie and Yukon and Stickeen. All these Mackenzie streams had proved rich in gold. The wing-dams, flumes, and sluice-boxes on the lower five or ten miles of their courses showed wonderful industry, and the quantity of glacial and perhaps pre-glacial gravel displayed was enormous. Some of the beds were not unlike those of the so-called Dead Rivers of California. Several ancient drift-filled channels on Thibert Creek, blue at bed rock, were exposed and had been worked. A considerable portion of the gold, though mostly coarse, had no doubt come from considerable distances, as boulders included in some of the deposits show. The deepest beds, though known to be rich, had not yet been worked to any great depth on account of expense. Diggings that yield less than five dollars a day to the man were considered worthless. Only three of the claims on Defot Creek, eighteen miles from the mouth of Thibert Creek, were then said to pay. One of the nuggets from this creek weighed forty pounds.

While wandering about the banks of these gold-besprinkled streams, looking at the plants and mines and miners, I was so fortunate as to meet an interesting French Canadian, an old *coureur de bois,* who after a few minutes' conversation invited me to accompany him to his gold-mine on the head of Defot Creek, near the summit of a smooth, grassy mountain-ridge which he assured me commanded extensive views of the region at the heads of Stickeen, Taku, Yukon, and Mackenzie tributaries. Though heavy-laden with flour and bacon, he strode lightly along the rough trails as if his load was only a natural balanced part of his body. Our way at first lay along Thibert Creek, now on gravel benches, now on bed rock, now close down on the bouldery edge of the stream. Above the mines the stream is clear and flows with a rapid current. Its banks are embossed with moss and grass and sedge well mixed with flowers—daisies, larkspurs, solidagos, parnassia, potentilla, strawberry, etc. Small strips of meadow occur here and there, and belts of slender arrowy fir and spruce with moss-clad roots grow close to the water's edge. The creek is about forty-five miles long, and the richest of its gold-bearing beds so far discovered were on the lower four miles of the creek; the higher four-or-five-dollars-a-day diggings were considered very poor on account of the high price of provisions and shortness of the season. After crossing many smaller streams with their strips of trees and meadows, bogs and bright wild gardens, we arrived at the Le Claire cabin about the middle of the afternoon. Before entering it he threw down his burden and made haste to show me his favorite flower, a blue forget-me-not, a specimen of which he found within a few rods of the cabin, and proudly handed it to me with the finest respect, and telling its many charms and lifelong associations, showed in every endearing look and touch and gesture that the tender little plant of the mountain wilderness was truly his best-loved darling.

After luncheon we set out for the highest point on the dividing ridge about a mile above the cabin, and sauntered and gazed until sundown, admiring the vast expanse of open rolling prairie-like highlands dotted with groves and lakes, the fountain-heads of countless cool, glad streams.

Le Claire's simple, child-like love of nature, preserved undimmed through a hard wilderness life, was delightful to see. The grand landscapes with their lakes and streams, plants and animals, all were dear to him. In particular he was fond of the birds that nested near his cabin, watched the young, and in stormy weather helped their parents to feed and shelter them. Some species were so confiding they learned to perch on his shoulders and take crumbs from his hand.

A little before sunset snow began to fly, driven by a cold wind, and by the time we reached the cabin, though we had not far to go, everything looked wintry. At half-past nine we ate supper, while a good fire crackled cheerily in the ingle and a wintry wind blew hard. The little log cabin was only ten feet long, eight wide, and just high enough under the roof peak to allow one to stand upright. The bedstead was not wide enough for two, so Le Claire spread the blankets on the floor, and we gladly lay down after our long, happy walk, our heads under the bedstead, our feet against the opposite wall, and though comfortably tired, it was long ere we fell asleep, for Le Claire, finding me a good listener, told many stories of his adventurous life with Indians, bears and wolves, snow and hunger, and of his many camps in the Canadian woods, hidden like the nests and dens of wild animals; stories that have a singular interest to everybody, for they awaken inherited memories of the lang, lang syne when we were all wild. He had nine children, he told me, the youngest eight years of age, and several of his daughters were married. His home was in Victoria.

Next morning was cloudy and windy, snowy and cold, dreary December weather in August, and I gladly ran out to see what I might learn. A gray ragged-edged cloud capped the top of the divide, its snowy fringes drawn out by the wind. The flowers, though most of them were buried or partly so, were to some extent recognizable, the bluebells bent over, shining like eyes through the snow, and the gentians, too, with their corollas twisted shut; cassiope I could recognize under any disguise; and two species of dwarf willow with their seeds already ripe, one with comparatively small leaves, were growing in mere cracks and crevices of rock-ledges where the dry snow could not lie. Snowbirds and ptarmigan were flying briskly in the cold wind, and on the edge of a grove I saw a spruce from which a bear had stripped large sections of bark for food.

About nine o'clock the clouds lifted and I enjoyed another wide view from the summit of the ridge of the vast grassy fountain region with smooth rolling features. A few patches of forest broke the monotony of color, and the many lakes, one of them about five miles long, were glowing like windows. Only the highest ridges were whitened with snow, while rifts in the clouds showed beautiful bits of yellow-green sky. The limit of tree growth is about five thousand feet.

Throughout all this region from Glenora to Cassiar the grasses grow luxuriantly in openings in the woods and on dry hillsides where the trees seem to have been destroyed by fire, and over all the broad prairies above the timber-line. A kind of bunch-grass in particular is often four or five feet high, and close enough to be mowed for hay. I never anywhere saw finer or more bountiful wild pasture. Here the caribou feed and grow fat, braving the intense winter cold, often forty to sixty degrees below zero. Winter and summer seem to be the only seasons here. What may fairly be called summer lasts only two or three months, winter nine or ten, for of pure well-defined spring or autumn there is scarcely a trace. Were it not for the long severe winters, this would be a capital stock country, equaling Texas and the prairies of the old West. From my outlook on the Defot ridge I saw thousands of square miles of this prairie-like region drained by tributaries of the Stickeen, Taku, Yukon, and Mackenzie Rivers.

Le Claire told me that the caribou, or reindeer, were very abundant on this high ground. A flock of fifty or more was seen a short time before at the head of Defot Creek,—fine, hardy, able animals like their near relatives the reindeer of the Arctic tundras. The Indians hereabouts, he said, hunted them with dogs, mostly in the fall and winter. On my return trip I met several bands of these Indians on the march, going north to hunt. Some of the men and women were carrying puppies on top of their heavy loads of dried salmon, while the grown dogs had saddle-bags filled with odds and ends strapped on their backs. Small puppies, unable to carry more than five or six pounds, were thus made useful. I overtook another band going south, heavy laden with furs and skins to trade. An old woman, with short dress and leggings, was carrying a big load of furs and skins, on top of which was perched a little girl about three years old.

A brown, speckled marmot, one of Le Claire's friends, was getting ready for winter. The entrance to his burrow was a little to one side of the cabin door. A well-worn trail led to it through the grass and another to that of his companion, fifty feet away. He was a most amusing pet, always on hand at meal times for bread-crumbs and bits of bacon-rind, came when called, answering in a shrill whistle, moving like a squirrel with quick, nervous impulses, jerking his short flat tail. His fur clothing was neat and clean, fairly shining in the wintry light. The snowy weather that morning must have called winter to mind; for as soon as he got his breakfast, he ran to a tuft of dry grass, chewed it into fuzzy mouthfuls, and carried it to his nest, coming and going with admirable industry, forecast, and confidence. None watching him as we did could fail to sympathize with him; and I fancy that in practical weather wisdom no government forecaster with all his advantages surpasses this little Alaska rodent, every hair and nerve a weather instrument.

I greatly enjoyed this little inland side trip—the wide views; the miners along the branches of the great river, busy as moles and beavers; young men dreaming and hoping to strike it rich and rush home to marry their girls faithfully waiting; others hoping to clear off weary farm mortgages, and brighten the lives of the anxious home folk; but most, I suppose, just struggling blindly for gold enough to make them indefinitely rich to spend their lives in aimless affluence, honor, and ease. I enjoyed getting acquainted with the trees, especially the beautiful spruce and silver fir; the flower gardens and great grassy caribou pastures; the cheery, able marmot mountaineer; and above all the friendship and kindness of Mr. Le Claire, whom I shall never forget. Bidding good-bye, I sauntered back to the head of navigation on the Stickeen, happy and rich without a particle of obscuring gold-dust care.

CHAPTER VII

GLENORA PEAK

On the trail to the steamboat-landing at the foot of Dease Lake, I met a Douglas squirrel, nearly as red and rusty in color as his Eastern relative the chickaree. Except in color he differs but little from the California Douglas squirrel. In voice, language, gestures, temperament, he is the same fiery, indomitable little king of the woods. Another darker and probably younger specimen met near the Caribou House, barked, chirruped, and showed off in fine style on a tree within a few feet of us.

"What does the little rascal mean?" said my companion, a man I had fallen in with on the trail. "What is he making such a fuss about? I cannot frighten him."

"Never mind," I replied; "just wait until I whistle 'Old Hundred' and you will see him fly in disgust." And so he did, just as his California brethren do. Strange that no squirrel or spermophile I yet have found ever seemed to have anything like enough of Scotch religion to enjoy this grand old tune.

The taverns along the Cassiar gold trail were the worst I had ever seen, rough shacks with dirt floors, dirt roofs, and rough meals. The meals are all alike—a potato, a slice of something like bacon, some gray stuff called bread, and a cup of muddy, semi-liquid coffee like that which the California miners call "slickens" or "slumgullion." The bread was terrible and sinful. How the Lord's good wheat could be made into stuff so mysteriously bad is past finding out. The very de'il, it would seem, in wicked anger and ingenuity, had been the baker.

On our walk from Dease Lake to Telegraph Creek we had one of these rough luncheons at three o'clock in the afternoon of the first day, then walked on five miles to Ward's, where we were solemnly assured that we could not have a single bite of either supper or breakfast, but as a great favor we might sleep on his best gray bunk. We replied that, as we had lunched at the lake, supper would not be greatly missed, and as for breakfast we would start early and walk eight miles to the next road-house. We set out at half-past four, glad to escape into the fresh air, and reached the breakfast place at eight o'clock. The landlord was still abed, and when at length he came to the door, he scowled savagely at us as if our request for breakfast was preposterous and criminal beyond anything ever heard of in all goldful Alaska. A good many in those days were returning from the mines dead broke, and he probably regarded us as belonging to that disreputable class. Anyhow, we got nothing and had to tramp on.

As we approached the next house, three miles ahead, we saw the tavern-keeper keenly surveying us, and, as we afterwards learned, taking me for a certain judge whom for some cause he wished to avoid, he hurriedly locked his door and fled. Half a mile farther on we discovered him in a thicket a little way off the trail, explained our wants, marched him back to his house, and at length obtained a little sour bread, sour milk, and old salmon, our only lonely meal between the Lake and Telegraph Creek.

We arrived at Telegraph Creek, the end of my two-hundred-mile walk, about noon. After luncheon I went on down the river to Glenora in a fine canoe owned and manned by Kitty, a stout, intelligent-looking Indian woman, who charged her passengers a dollar for the fifteen-mile trip. Her crew was four Indian paddlers. In the rapids she also plied the paddle, with stout, telling strokes, and a keen-eyed old man, probably her husband, sat high in the stern and steered. All seemed exhilarated as we shot down through the narrow gorge on the rushing, roaring, throttled river, paddling all the more vigorously the faster the speed of the stream, to hold good steering way. The canoe danced lightly amid gray surges and spray as if alive and enthusiastically enjoying the adventure. Some of the passengers were pretty thoroughly drenched. In unskillful hands the frail dugout would surely have been wrecked or upset. Most of the trip season goods for the Cassiar gold camps were carried from Glenora to Telegraph Creek in canoes, the steamers not being able to overcome the rapids except during high water. Even then they had usually to line two of the rapids—that is, take a line ashore, make it fast to a tree on the bank, and pull up on the cap-stan. The freight canoes carried about three or four tons, for which fifteen dollars per ton was charged. Slow progress was made by pol-ing along the bank out of the swiftest part of the current. In the rapids a tow line was taken ashore, only one of the crew remaining aboard to steer. The trip took a day unless a favoring wind was blowing, which often happened.

Next morning I set out from Glenora to climb Glenora Peak for the general view of the great Coast Range that I failed to obtain on my first ascent on account of the accident that befell Mr. Young when we were within a minute or two of the top. It is hard to fail in reaching a mountain-top that one starts for, let the cause be what it may. This time I had no companion to care for, but the sky was threatening. I was assured by the local weather-prophets that the day would be rainy or snowy because the peaks in sight were muf-fled in clouds that seemed to be getting ready for work. I deter-mined to go ahead, however, for storms of any kind are well worth while, and if driven back I could wait and try again.

With crackers in my pocket and a light rubber coat that a kind Hebrew passenger on the steamer Gertrude loaned me, I was ready for anything that might offer, my hopes for the grand view rising and falling as the clouds rose and fell. Anxiously I watched them as they trailed their draggled skirts across the glaciers and fountain peaks as if thoughtfully looking for the places where they could do the most good. From Glenora there is first a terrace two hundred feet above the river covered mostly with bushes, yellow apocynum on the open spaces, together with carpets of dwarf manzanita, bunch-grass, and a few of the compositæ, galiums, etc. Then comes a flat stretch a mile wide, extending to the foothills, covered with birch, spruce, fir, and poplar, now mostly killed by fire and the ground strewn with charred trunks. From this black forest the mountain rises in rather steep slopes covered with a luxuriant growth of bushes, grass, flowers, and a few trees, chiefly spruce and fir, the firs gradually dwarfing into a beautiful chaparral, the most beautiful, I think, I have ever seen, the flat fan-shaped plumes thickly foliaged and imbricated by snow pressure, forming a smooth, handsome thatch which bears cones and thrives as if this repressed condition were its very best. It extends up to an elevation of about fifty-five hundred feet. Only a few trees more than a foot in diameter and more than fifty feet high are found higher than four thousand feet above the sea. A few poplars and willows occur on moist places, gradually dwarfing like the conifers. Alder is the most generally distributed of the chaparral bushes, growing nearly everywhere; its crinkled stems an inch or two thick form a trouble-some tangle to the mountaineer. The blue geranium, with leaves red and showy at this time of the year, is perhaps the most telling of the flowering plants. It grows up to five thousand feet or more. Larkspurs are common, with epilobium, senecio, erigeron, and a few solidagos. The harebell appears at about four thousand feet and extends to the summit, dwarfing in stature but maintaining the size of its handsome bells until they seem to be lying loose and de-tached on the ground as if like snow flowers they had fallen from the sky; and, though frail and delicate-looking, none of its compan-ions is more enduring or rings out the praises of beauty-loving Nature in tones more appreciable to mortals, not forgetting even Cassiope, who also is here and her companion, Bryanthus, the loveliest and most widely distributed of the alpine shrubs. Then come crowberry, and two species of huckleberry, one of them from about six inches to a foot high with delicious berries, the other a most lavishly prolific and contented-looking dwarf, few of the bushes being more than two inches high, counting to the topmost leaf, yet each bearing from ten to twenty or more large berries. Perhaps more than half the bulk of the whole plant is fruit, the largest and finest-flavored of all the huckleberries or blueberries I ever tasted, spreading fine feasts for the grouse and ptarmigan and many others of Nature's mountain people. I noticed three species of dwarf willows, one with narrow leaves, growing at the very summit of the mountain in cracks of the rocks, as well as on patches of soil, another with large, smooth leaves now turning yellow. The third species grows between the others as to elevation; its leaves, then orange-colored, are strikingly pitted and reticulated. Another alpine shrub, a species of sericocarpus, covered with handsome heads of feathery achenia, beautiful dwarf echiverias with flocks of purple flowers pricked into their bright grass-green, cushion-like bosses of moss-like foliage, and a fine forget-me-not reach to the summit. I may also mention a large mertensia, a fine anemone, a veratrum, six feet high, a large blue daisy, growing up to three to four thousand feet, and at the summit a dwarf species, with dusky, hairy involucres, and a few ferns, aspidium, gymnogramma, and small rock cheilanthes, leaving scarce a foot of ground bare, though the mountain looks bald and brown in the distance like those of the desert ranges of the Great Basin in Utah and Nevada.

Charmed with these plant people, I had almost forgotten to watch the sky until I reached the top of the highest peak, when one of the greatest and most impressively sublime of all the mountain views I have ever enjoyed came full in sight—more than three hundred miles of closely packed peaks of the great Coast Range, sculptured in the boldest manner imaginable, their naked tops and dividing ridges dark in color, their sides and the cañons, gorges, and valleys between them loaded with glaciers and snow. From this standpoint I counted upwards of two hundred glaciers, while dark-centred luminous clouds with fringed edges hovered and crawled over them, now slowly descending, casting transparent shadows on the ice and snow, now rising high above them, lingering like loving angels guarding the crystal gifts they had bestowed. Although the range as seen from this Glenora mountain-top seems regular in its trend, as if the main axis were simple and continuous, it is, on the contrary, far from simple. In front of the highest ranks of peaks are others of the same form with their own glaciers, and lower peaks before these, and yet lower ones with their ridges and cañons, valleys and foothills. Alps rise beyond alps as far as the eye can reach, and clusters of higher peaks here and there closely crowded together; clusters, too, of needles and pinnacles innumerable like trees in groves. Everywhere the peaks seem comparatively slender and closely packed, as if Nature had here been trying to see how many noble well-dressed mountains could be crowded into one grand range.

The black rocks, too steep for snow to lie upon, were brought into sharp relief by white clouds and snow and glaciers, and these again were outlined and made tellingly plain by the rocks. The glaciers so grandly displayed are of every form, some crawling through gorge and valley like monster glittering serpents; others like broad cataracts pouring over cliffs into shadowy gulfs; others, with their main trunks winding through narrow cañons, display long, white finger-like tributaries descending from the summits of pinnacled ridges. Others lie back in fountain cirques walled in all around save at the lower edge, over which they pour in blue cascades. Snow, too, lay in folds and patches of every form on blunt, rounded ridges in curves, arrowy lines, dashes, and narrow ornamental flutings among the summit peaks and in broad radiating wings on smooth slopes. And on many a bulging headland and lower ridge there lay heavy, over-curling copings and smooth, white domes where wind-driven snow was pressed and wreathed and packed into every form and in every possible place and condition. I never before had seen so richly sculptured a range or so many awe-inspiring inaccessible mountains crowded together. If a line were drawn east and west from the peak on which I stood, and extended both ways to the horizon, cutting the whole round landscape in two equal parts, then all of the south half would be bounded by these icy peaks, which would seem to curve around half the horizon and about twenty degrees more, though extending in a general straight, or but moderately curved, line. The deepest and thickest and highest of all this wilderness of peaks lie to the southwest. They are probably from about nine to twelve thousand feet high, springing to this elevation from near the sea-level. The peak on which these observations were made is somewhere about seven thousand feet high, and from here I estimated the height of the range. The highest peak of all, or that seemed so to me, lies to the westward at an estimated distance of about one hundred and fifty or two hundred miles. Only its solid white summit was visible. Possibly it may be the topmost peak of St. Elias. Now look northward around the other half of the horizon, and instead of countless peaks crowding into the sky, you see a low brown region, heaving and swelling in gentle curves, apparently scarcely more waved than a rolling prairie. The so-called cañons of several forks of the upper Stickeen are visible, but even where best seen in the foreground and middle ground of the picture, they are like mere sunken gorges, making scarce perceptible marks on the landscape, while the tops of the highest mountain-swells show only small patches of snow and no glaciers.

Glenora Peak, on which I stood, is the highest point of a spur that puts out from the main range in a northerly direction. It seems to have been a rounded, broad-backed ridge which has been sculptured into its present irregular form by short residual glaciers, some of which, a mile or two long, are still at work.

As I lingered, gazing on the vast show, luminous shadowy clouds seemed to increase in glory of color and motion, now fondling the highest peaks with infinite tenderness of touch, now hovering above them like eagles over their nests.

When night was drawing near, I ran down the flowery slopes exhilarated, thanking God for the gift of this great day. The setting sun fired the clouds. All the world seemed new-born. Every thing, even the commonest, was seen in new light and was looked at with new interest as if never seen before. The plant people seemed glad, as if rejoicing with me, the little ones as well as the trees, while every feature of the peak and its traveled boulders seemed to know what I had been about and the depth of my joy, as if they could read faces.

CHAPTER VIII

EXPLORATION OF THE STICKEEN GLACIERS

Next day I planned an excursion to the so-called Dirt Glacier, the most interesting to Indians and steamer men of all the Stickeen glaciers from its mysterious floods. I left the steamer Gertrude for the glacier delta an hour or two before sunset. The captain kindly loaned me his canoe and two of his Indian deck hands, who seemed much puzzled to know what the rare service required of them might mean, and on leaving bade a merry adieu to their companions. We camped on the west side of the river opposite the front of the glacier, in a spacious valley surrounded by snowy mountains. Thirteen small glaciers were in sight and four waterfalls. It was a fine, serene evening, and the highest peaks were wearing turbans of flossy, gossamer cloud-stuff. I had my supper before leaving the steamer, so I had only to make a camp-fire, spread my blanket, and lie down. The Indians had their own bedding and lay beside their own fire.

The Dirt Glacier is noted among the river men as being subject to violent flood outbursts once or twice a year, usually in the late summer. The delta of this glacier stream is three or four miles wide where it fronts the river, and the many rough channels with which it is guttered and the uprooted trees and huge boulders that roughen its surface manifest the power of the floods that swept them to their places; but under ordinary conditions the glacier discharges its drainage water into the river through only four or five of the delta-channels.

Our camp was made on the south or lower side of the delta, below all the draining streams, so that I would not have to ford any of them on my way to the glacier. The Indians chose a sand-pit to sleep in; I chose a level spot back of a drift log. I had but little to say to my companions as they could speak no English, nor I much Thlinkit or Chinook. In a few minutes after landing they retired to their pit and were soon asleep and asnore. I lingered by the fire until after ten o'clock, for the night sky was clear, and the great white mountains in the starlight seemed nearer than by day and to be looking down like guardians of the valley, while the waterfalls, and the torrents escaping from beneath the big glacier, roared in a broad, low monotone, sounding as if close at hand, though, as it proved next day, the nearest was three miles away. After wrapping myself in my blankets, I still gazed into the marvelous sky and made out to sleep only about two hours. Then, without waking the noisy sleepers, I arose, ate a piece of bread, and set out in my shirt-sleeves, determined to make the most of the time at my disposal. The captain was to pick us up about noon at a woodpile about a mile from here; but if in the mean time the steamer should run aground and he should need his canoe, a three-whistle signal would be given.

Following a dry channel for about a mile, I came suddenly upon the main outlet of the glacier, which in the imperfect light seemed as large as the river, about one hundred and fifty feet wide, and perhaps three or four feet deep. A little farther up it was only about fifty feet wide and rushing on with impetuous roaring force in its rocky channel, sweeping forward sand, gravel, cobblestones, and boulders, the bump and rumble sounds of the largest of these rolling stones being readily heard in the midst of the roaring. It was too swift and rough to ford, and no bridge tree could be found, for the great floods had cleared everything out of their way. I was therefore compelled to keep on up the right bank, however difficult the way. Where a strip of bare boulders lined the margin, the walking was easy, but where the current swept close along the ragged edge of the forest, progress was difficult and slow on account of snow-crinkled and interlaced thickets of alder and willow, reinforced with fallen trees and thorny devil's-club (*Echinopanax horridum*), making a jungle all but impenetrable. The mile of this extravagantly difficult growth through which I struggled, inch by inch, will not soon be forgotten. At length arriving within a few hundred yards of the glacier, full of panax barbs, I found that both the glacier and its unfordable stream were pressing hard against a shelving cliff, dangerously steep, leaving no margin, and compelling me to scramble along its face before I could get on to the glacier. But by sunrise all these cliff, jungle, and torrent troubles were overcome and I gladly found myself free on the magnificent ice-river.

The curving, out-bulging front of the glacier is about two miles wide, two hundred feet high, and its surface for a mile or so above the front is strewn with moraine detritus, giving it a strangely dirty, dusky look, hence its name, the "Dirt Glacier," this detritus-laden portion being all that is seen in passing up the river. A mile or two beyond the moraine-covered part I was surprised to find alpine plants growing on the ice, fresh and green, some of them in full flower. These curious glacier gardens, the first I had seen, were evidently planted by snow avalanches from the high walls. They were well watered, of course, by the melting surface of the ice and fairly well nourished by humus still attached to the roots, and in some places formed beds of considerable thickness. Seedling trees and bushes also were growing among the flowers. Admiring these novel floating gardens, I struck out for the middle of the pure white glacier, where the ice seemed smoother, and then held straight on for about eight miles, where I reluctantly turned back to meet the steamer, greatly regretting that I had not brought a week's supply of hardtack to allow me to explore the glacier to its head, and then trust to some passing canoe to take me down to Buck Station, from which I could explore the Big Stickeen Glacier.

Altogether, I saw about fifteen or sixteen miles of the main trunk. The grade is almost regular, and the walls on either hand are about from two to three thousand feet high, sculptured like those of Yosemite Valley. I found no difficulty of an extraordinary kind. Many a crevasse had to be crossed, but most of them were narrow and easily jumped, while the few wide ones that lay in my way were crossed on sliver bridges or avoided by passing around them. The structure of the glacier was strikingly revealed on its melting surface. It is made up of thin vertical or inclined sheets or slabs set on edge and welded together. They represent, I think, the successive snowfalls from heavy storms on the tributaries. One of the tributaries on the right side, about three miles above the front, has been entirely melted off from the trunk and has receded two or three miles, forming an independent glacier. Across the mouth of this abandoned part of its channel the main glacier flows, forming a dam which gives rise to a lake. On the head of the detached tributary there are some five or six small residual glaciers, the drainage of which, with that of the snowy mountain slopes above them, discharges into the lake, whose outlet is through a channel or channels beneath the damming glacier. Now these sub-channels are occasionally blocked and the water rises until it flows alongside of the glacier, but as the dam is a moving one, a grand outburst is sometimes made, which, draining the large lake, produces a flood of amazing power, sweeping down immense quantities of moraine material and raising the river all the way down to its mouth, so that several trips may occasionally be made by the steamers after the season of low water has laid them up for the year. The occurrence of these floods are, of course, well known to the Indians and steamboat men, though they know nothing of their cause. They simply remark, "The Dirt Glacier has broken out again."

I greatly enjoyed my walk up this majestic ice-river, charmed by the pale-blue, ineffably fine light in the crevasses, moulins, and wells, and the innumerable azure pools in basins of azure ice, and the network of surface streams, large and small, gliding, swirling with wonderful grace of motion in their frictionless channels, calling forth devout admiration at almost every step and filling the mind with a sense of Nature's endless beauty and power. Looking ahead from the middle of the glacier, you see the broad white flood, though apparently rigid as iron, sweeping in graceful curves between its high mountain-like walls, small glaciers hanging in the hollows on either side, and snow in every form above them, and the great down-plunging granite buttresses and headlands of the walls marvelous in bold massive sculpture; forests in side cañons to within fifty feet of the glacier; avalanche pathways overgrown with alder and willow; innumerable cascades keeping up a solemn harmony of water sounds blending with those of the glacier moulins and rills; and as far as the eye can reach, tributary glaciers at short intervals silently descending from their high, white fountains to swell the grand central ice-river.

In the angle formed by the main glacier and the lake that gives rise to the river floods, there is a massive granite dome sparsely feathered with trees, and just beyond this yosemitic rock is a mountain, perhaps ten thousand feet high, laden with ice and snow which seemed pure pearly white in the morning light. Last evening as seen from camp it was adorned with a cloud streamer, and both the streamer and the peak were flushed in the alpenglow. A mile or two above this mountain, on the opposite side of the glacier, there is a rock like the Yosemite Sentinel; and in general all the wall rocks as far as I saw them are more or less yosemitic in form and color and streaked with cascades.

But wonderful as this noble ice-river is in size and depth and in power displayed, far more wonderful was the vastly greater glacier three or four thousand feet, or perhaps a mile, in depth, whose size and general history is inscribed on the sides of the walls and over the tops of the rocks in characters which have not yet been greatly dimmed by the weather. Comparing its present size with that when it was in its prime, is like comparing a small rivulet to the same stream when it is a roaring torrent.

The return trip to the camp past the shelving cliff and through the weary devil's-club jungle was made in a few hours. The Indians had gone off picking berries, but were on the watch for me and hailed me as I approached. The captain had called for me, and, after waiting three hours, departed for Wrangell without leaving any food, to make sure, I suppose, of a quick return of his Indians and canoe. This was no serious matter, however, for the swift current swept us down to Buck Station, some thirty-five miles distant, by eight o'clock. Here I remained to study the "Big Stickeen Glacier," but the Indians set out for Wrangell soon after supper, though I invited them to stay till morning.

The weather that morning, August 27, was dark and rainy, and I tried to persuade myself that I ought to rest a day before setting out on new ice work. But just across the river the "Big Glacier" was staring me in the face, pouring its majestic flood through a broad mountain gateway and expanding in the spacious river valley to a width of four or five miles, while dim in the gray distance loomed its high mountain fountains. So grand an invitation displayed in characters so telling was of course irresistible, and body-care and weather-care vanished.

Mr. Choquette, the keeper of the station, ferried me across the river, and I spent the day in getting general views and planning the work that had been long in mind. I first traced the broad, complicated terminal moraine to its southern extremity, climbed up the west side along the lateral moraine three or four miles, making my way now on the glacier, now on the moraine-covered bank, and now compelled to climb up through the timber and brush in order to pass some rocky headland, until I reached a point commanding a good general view of the lower end of the glacier. Heavy, blotting rain then began to fall, and I retraced my steps, oftentimes stopping to admire the blue ice-caves into which glad, rejoicing streams from the mountain-side were hurrying as if going home, while the glacier seemed to open wide its crystal gateways to welcome them.

The following morning blotting rain was still falling, but time and work was too precious to mind it. Kind Mr. Choquette put me across the river in a canoe, with a lot of biscuits his Indian wife had baked for me and some dried salmon, a little sugar and tea, a blanket, and a piece of light sheeting for shelter from rain during the night, all rolled into one bundle.

"When shall I expect you back?" inquired Choquette, when I bade him good-bye.

"Oh, any time," I replied. "I shall see as much as possible of the glacier, and I know not how long it will hold me."

"Well, but when will I come to look for you, if anything happens? Where are you going to try to go? Years ago Russian officers from Sitka went up the glacier from here and none ever returned. It's a mighty dangerous glacier, all full of damn deep holes and cracks. You've no idea what ticklish deceiving traps are scattered over it."

"Yes, I have," I said. "I have seen glaciers before, though none so big as this one. Do not look for me until I make my appearance on the river-bank. Never mind me. I am used to caring for myself." And so, shouldering my bundle, I trudged off through the moraine boulders and thickets.

My general plan was to trace the terminal moraine to its extreme north end, pitch my little tent, leave the blanket and most of the hardtack, and from this main camp go and come as hunger required or allowed.

After examining a cross-section of the broad moraine, roughened by concentric masses, marking interruptions in the recession of the glacier of perhaps several centuries, in which the successive moraines were formed and shoved together in closer or wider order, I traced the moraine to its northeastern extremity and ascended the glacier for several miles along the left margin, then crossed it at the grand cataract and down the right side to the river, and along the moraine to the point of beginning.

On the older portions of this moraine I discovered several kettles in process of formation and was pleased to find that they conformed in the most striking way with the theory I had already been led to make from observations on the old kettles which form so curious a feature of the drift covering Wisconsin and Minnesota and some of the larger moraines of the residual glaciers in the California Sierra. I found a pit eight or ten feet deep with raw shifting sides countersunk abruptly in the rough moraine material, and at the bottom, on sliding down by the aid of a lithe spruce tree that was being undermined, I discovered, after digging down a foot or two, that the bottom was resting on a block of solid blue ice which had been buried in the moraine perhaps a century or more, judging by the age of the tree that had grown above it. Probably more than another century will be required to complete the formation of this kettle by the slow melting of the buried ice-block. The moraine material of course was falling in as the ice melted, and the sides maintained an angle as steep as the material would lie. All sorts of theories have been advanced for the formation of these kettles, so abundant in the drift over a great part of the United States, and I was glad to be able to set the question at rest, at least as far as I was concerned.

The glacier and the mountains about it are on so grand a scale and so generally inaccessible in the ordinary sense, it seemed to matter but little what course I pursued. Everything was full of interest, even the weather, though about as unfavorable as possible for wide views, and scrambling through the moraine jungle brush kept one as wet as if all the way was beneath a cascade.

I pushed on, with many a rest and halt to admire the bold and marvelously sculptured ice-front, looking all the grander and more striking in the gray mist with all the rest of the glacier shut out, until I came to a lake about two hundred yards wide and two miles long with scores of small bergs floating in it, some aground, close inshore against the moraine, the light playing on their angles and shimmering in their blue caves in ravishing tones. This proved to be the largest of the series of narrow lakelets that lie in shallow troughs between the moraine and the glacier, a miniature Arctic Ocean, its ice-cliffs played upon by whispering, rippling wavelets and its small berg floes drifting in its currents or with the wind, or stranded here and there along its rocky moraine shore.

Hundreds of small rills and good-sized streams were falling into the lake from the glacier, singing in low tones, some of them pouring in sheer falls over blue cliffs from narrow ice-valleys, some spouting from pipe-like channels in the solid front of the glacier, others gurgling out of arched openings at the base. All these water-streams were riding on the parent ice-stream, their voices joined in one grand anthem telling the wonders of their near and far-off fountains. The lake itself is resting in a basin of ice, and the forested moraine, though seemingly cut off from the glacier and probably more than a century old, is in great part resting on buried ice left behind as the glacier receded, and melting slowly on account of the protection afforded by the moraine detritus, which keeps shifting and falling on the inner face long after it is overgrown with lichens, mosses, grasses, bushes, and even good-sized trees; these changes going on with marvelous deliberation until in fullness of time the whole moraine settles down upon its bedrock foundation.

The outlet of the lake is a large stream, almost a river in size, one of the main draining streams of the glacier. I attempted to ford it where it begins to break in rapids in passing over the moraine, but found it too deep and rough on the bottom. I then tried to ford at its head, where it is wider and glides smoothly out of the lake, bracing myself against the current with a pole, but found it too deep, and when the icy water reached my shoulders I cautiously struggled back to the moraine. I next followed it down through the rocky jungle to a place where in breaking across the moraine dam it was only about thirty-five feet wide. Here I found a spruce tree, which I felled for a bridge; it reached across, about ten feet of the top holding in the bank brush. But the force of the torrent, acting on the submerged branches and the slender end of the trunk, bent it like a bow and made it very unsteady, and after testing it by going out about a third of the way over, it seemed likely to be carried away when bent deeper into the current by my weight. Fortunately, I discovered another larger tree well situated a little farther down, which I felled, and though a few feet in the middle was submerged, it seemed perfectly safe.

As it was now getting late, I started back to the lakeside where I had left my bundle, and in trying to hold a direct course found the interlaced jungle still more difficult than it was along the bank of the torrent. For over an hour I had to creep and struggle close to the rocky ground like a fly in a spider-web without being able to obtain a single glimpse of any guiding feature of the landscape. Finding a little willow taller than the surrounding alders, I climbed it, caught sight of the glacier-front, took a compass bearing, and sunk again into the dripping, blinding maze of brush, and at length emerged on the lakeshore seven hours after leaving it, all this time as wet as though I had been swimming, thus completing a trying day's work. But everything was deliciously fresh, and I found new and old plant friends, and lessons on Nature's Alaska moraine landscape-gardening that made everything bright and light.

It was now near dark, and I made haste to make up my flimsy little tent. The ground was desperately rocky. I made out, however, to level down a strip large enough to lie on, and by means of slim alder stems bent over it and tied together soon had a home. While thus busily engaged I was startled by a thundering roar across the lake. Running to the top of the moraine, I discovered that the tremendous noise was only the outcry of a new-born berg about fifty or sixty feet in diameter, rocking and wallowing in the waves it had raised as if enjoying its freedom after its long grinding work as part of the glacier. After this fine last lesson I managed to make a small fire out of wet twigs, got a cup of tea, stripped off my dripping clothing, wrapped myself in a blanket and lay brooding on the gains of the day and plans for the morrow, glad, rich, and almost comfortable.

It was raining hard when I awoke, but I made up my mind to disregard the weather, put on my dripping clothing, glad to know it was fresh and clean; ate biscuits and a piece of dried salmon without attempting to make a tea fire; filled a bag with hardtack, slung it over my shoulder, and with my indispensable ice-axe plunged once more into the dripping jungle. I found my bridge holding bravely in place against the swollen torrent, crossed it and beat my way around pools and logs and through two hours of tangle back to the moraine on the north side of the outlet,—a wet, weary battle but not without enjoyment. The smell of the washed ground and vegetation made every breath a pleasure, and I found *Calypso borealis,* the first I had seen on this side of the continent, one of my darlings, worth any amount of hardship; and I saw one of my Douglas squirrels on the margin of a grassy pool. The drip of the rain on the various leaves was pleasant to hear. More especially marked were the flat low-toned bumps and splashes of large drops from the trees on the broad horizontal leaves of *Echinopanax horridum,* like the drumming of thunder-shower drops on veratrum and palm leaves, while the mosses were indescribably beautiful, so fresh, so bright, so cheerily green, and all so low and calm and silent, however heavy and wild the wind and the rain blowing and pouring above them. Surely never a particle of dust has touched leaf or crown of all these blessed mosses; and how bright were the red rims of the cladonia cups beside them, and the fruit of the dwarf cornel! And the wet berries, Nature's precious jewelry, how beautiful they were!—huckleberries with pale bloom and a crystal drop on each; red and yellow salmon-berries, with clusters of smaller drops; and the glittering, berry-like raindrops adorning the interlacing arches of bent grasses and sedges around the edges of the pools, every drop a mirror with all the landscape in it. A' that and a' that and twice as muckle's a' that in this glorious Alaska day, recalling, however different, George Herbert's "Sweet day, so cool, so calm, so bright."

In the gardens and forests of this wonderful moraine one might spend a whole joyful life.

When I at last reached the end of the great moraine and the front of the mountain that forms the north side of the glacier basin, I tried to make my way along its side, but, finding the climbing tedious and difficult, took to the glacier and fared well, though a good deal of step-cutting was required on its ragged, crevassed margin. When night was drawing nigh, I scanned the steep mountainside in search of an accessible bench, however narrow, where a bed and a fire might be gathered for a camp. About dark great was my delight to find a little shelf with a few small mountain hemlocks growing in cleavage joints. Projecting knobs below it enabled me to build a platform for a fireplace and a bed, and by industrious creeping from one fissure to another, cutting bushes and small trees and sliding them down to within reach of my rock-shelf, I made out to collect wood enough to last through the night. In an hour or two I had a cheery fire, and spent the night in turning from side to side, steaming and drying after being wet two days and a night. Fortunately this night it did not rain, but it was very cold.

Pushing on next day, I climbed to the top of the glacier by ice-steps and along its side to the grand cataract two miles wide where the whole majestic flood of the glacier pours like a mighty surging river down a steep declivity in its channel. After gazing a long time on the glorious show, I discovered a place beneath the edge of the cataract where it flows over a hard, resisting granite rib, into which I crawled and enjoyed the novel and instructive view of a glacier pouring over my head, showing not only its grinding, polishing action, but how it breaks off large angular boulder-masses—a most telling lesson in earth-sculpture, confirming many I had already learned in the glacier basins of the High Sierra of California. I then crossed to the south side, noting the forms of the huge blocks into which the glacier was broken in passing over the brow of the cataract, and how they were welded.

The weather was now clear, opening views according to my own heart far into the high snowy fountains. I saw what seemed the farthest mountains, perhaps thirty miles from the front, everywhere winter-bound, but thick forested, however steep, for a distance of at least fifteen miles from the front, the trees, hemlock and spruce, clinging to the rock by root-holds among cleavage joints. The greatest discovery was in methods of denudation displayed beneath the glacier.

After a few more days of exhilarating study I returned to the river-bank opposite Choquette's landing. Promptly at sight of the signal I made, the kind Frenchman came across for me in his canoe. At his house I enjoyed a rest while writing out notes; then examined the smaller glacier fronting the one I had been exploring, until a passing canoe bound for Fort Wrangell took me aboard.

CHAPTER IX

A CANOE VOYAGE TO NORTHWARD

I arrived at Wrangell in a canoe with a party of Cassiar miners in October while the icy regions to the northward still burned in my mind. I had met several prospectors who had been as far as Chilcat at the head of Lynn Canal, who told wonderful stories about the great glaciers they had seen there. All the high mountains up there, they said, seemed to be made of ice, and if glaciers "are what you are after, that's the place for you," and to get there "all you have to do is to hire a good canoe and Indians who know the way."

But it now seemed too late to set out on so long a voyage. The days were growing short and winter was drawing nigh when all the land would be buried in snow. On the other hand, though this wilderness was new to me, I was familiar with storms and enjoyed them. The main channels extending along the coast remain open all winter, and, their shores being well forested, I knew that it would be easy to keep warm in camp, while abundance of food could be carried. I determined, therefore, to go ahead as far north as possible, to see and learn what I could, especially with reference to future work. When I made known my plans to Mr. Young, he offered to go with me, and, being acquainted with the Indians, procured a good canoe and crew, and with a large stock of provisions and blankets, we left Wrangell October 14, eager to welcome weather of every sort, as long as food lasted.

I was anxious to make an early start, but it was half-past two in the afternoon before I could get my Indians together—Toyatte, a grand old Stickeen nobleman, who was made captain, not only because he owned the canoe, but for his skill in woodcraft and seamanship; Kadachan, the son of a Chilcat chief; John, a Stickeen, who acted as interpreter; and Sitka Charley. Mr. Young, my companion, was an adventurous evangelist, and it was the opportunities the trip might afford to meet the Indians of the different tribes on our route with reference to future missionary work, that induced him to join us.

When at last all were aboard and we were about to cast loose from the wharf, Kadachan's mother, a woman of great natural dignity and force of character, came down the steps alongside the canoe oppressed with anxious fears for the safety of her son. Standing silent for a few moments, she held the missionary with her dark, bodeful eyes, and with great solemnity of speech and gesture accused him of using undue influence in gaining her son's consent to go on a dangerous voyage among unfriendly tribes; and like an ancient sibyl foretold a long train of bad luck from storms and enemies, and finished by saying, "If my son comes not back, on you will be his blood, and you shall pay. I say it."

Mr. Young tried in vain to calm her fears, promising Heaven's care as well as his own for her precious son, assuring her that he would faithfully share every danger that he encountered, and if need be die in his defense.

"We shall see whether or not you die," she said, and turned away.

Toyatte also encountered domestic difficulties. When he stepped into the canoe I noticed a cloud of anxiety on his grand old face, as if his doom now drawing near was already beginning to overshadow him. When he took leave of his wife, she refused to shake hands with him, wept bitterly, and said that his enemies, the Chilcat chiefs, would be sure to kill him in case he reached their village. But it was not on this trip that the old hero was to meet his fate, and when we were fairly free in the wilderness and a gentle breeze pressed us joyfully over the shining waters these gloomy forebodings vanished.

We first pursued a westerly course, through Sumner Strait, between Kupreanof and Prince of Wales Islands, then, turning northward, sailed up the Kiku Strait through the midst of innumerable picturesque islets, across Prince Frederick's Sound, up Chatham Strait, thence northwestward through Icy Strait and around the then uncharted Glacier Bay. Thence returning through Icy Strait, we sailed up the beautiful Lynn Canal to the Davidson Glacier and the lower village of the Chilcat tribe and returned to Wrangell along the coast of the mainland, visiting the icy Sum Dum Bay and the Wrangell Glacier on our route. Thus we made a journey more than eight hundred miles long, and though hardships and perhaps dangers were encountered, the great wonderland made compensation beyond our most extravagant hopes. Neither rain nor snow stopped us, but when the wind was too wild, Kadachan and the old captain stayed on guard in the camp and John and Charley went into the woods deer-hunting, while I examined the adjacent rocks and woods. Most of our camp-grounds were in sheltered nooks where good firewood was abundant, and where the precious canoe could be safely drawn up beyond reach of the waves. After supper we sat long around the fire, listening to the Indians' stories about the wild animals, their hunting-adventures, wars, traditions, religion, and customs. Every Indian party we met we interviewed, and visited every village we came to.

Our first camp was made at a place called the Island of the Standing Stone, on the shore of a shallow bay. The weather was fine. The mountains of the mainland were unclouded, excepting one, which had a horizontal ruff of dull slate color, but its icy summit covered with fresh snow towered above the cloud, flushed like its neighbors in the alpenglow. All the large islands in sight were densely forested, while many small rock islets in front of our camp were treeless or nearly so. Some of them were distinctly glaciated even below the tide-line, the effects of wave washing and general weathering being scarce appreciable as yet. Some of the larger islets had a few trees, others only grass. One looked in the distance like a two-masted ship flying before the wind under press of sail.

Next morning the mountains were arrayed in fresh snow that had fallen during the night down to within a hundred feet of the sea-level. We made a grand fire, and after an early breakfast pushed merrily on all day along beautiful forested shores embroidered with autumn-colored bushes. I noticed some pitchy trees that had been deeply hacked for kindling-wood and torches, precious conveniences to belated voyagers on stormy nights. Before sundown we camped in a beautiful nook of Deer Bay, shut in from every wind by gray-bearded trees and fringed with rose bushes, rubus, potentilla, asters, etc. Some of the lichen tresses depending from the branches were six feet in length.

A dozen rods or so from our camp we discovered a family of Kake Indians snugly sheltered in a portable bark hut, a stout middle-aged man with his wife, son, and daughter, and his son's wife. After our tent was set and fire made, the head of the family paid us a visit and presented us with a fine salmon, a pair of mallard ducks, and a mess of potatoes. We paid a return visit with gifts of rice and tobacco, etc. Mr. Young spoke briefly on mission affairs and inquired whether their tribe would be likely to welcome a teacher or missionary. But they seemed unwilling to offer an opinion on so important a subject. The following words from the head of the family was the only reply:—

"We have not much to say to you fellows. We always do to Boston men as we have done to you, give a little of whatever we have, treat everybody well and never quarrel. This is all we have to say."

Our Kake neighbors set out for Fort Wrangell next morning, and we pushed gladly on toward Chilcat. We passed an island that had lost all its trees in a storm, but a hopeful crop of young ones was springing up to take their places. I found no trace of fire in these woods. The ground was covered with leaves, branches, and fallen trunks perhaps a dozen generations deep, slowly decaying, forming a grand mossy mass of ruins, kept fresh and beautiful. All that is repulsive about death was here hidden beneath abounding life. Some rocks along the shore were completely covered with crimson-leafed huckleberry bushes; one species still in fruit might well be called the winter huckleberry. In a short walk I found vetches eight feet high leaning on raspberry bushes, and tall ferns and *Smilacina unifolia* with leaves six inches wide growing on yellow-green moss, producing a beautiful effect.

Our Indians seemed to be enjoying a quick and merry reaction from the doleful domestic dumps in which the voyage was begun. Old and young behaved this afternoon like a lot of truant boys on a lark. When we came to a pond fenced off from the main channel by a moraine dam, John went ashore to seek a shot at ducks. Creeping up behind the dam, he killed a mallard fifty or sixty feet from the shore and attempted to wave it within reach by throwing stones back of it. Charley and Kadachan went to his help, enjoying the sport, especially enjoying their own blunders in throwing in front of it and thus driving the duck farther out. To expedite the business John then tried to throw a rope across it, but failed after repeated trials, and so did each in turn, all laughing merrily at their awkward bungling. Next they tied a stone to the end of the rope to carry it further and with better aim, but the result was no better. Then majestic old Toyatte tried his hand at the game. He tied the rope to one of the canoe-poles, and taking aim threw it, harpoon fashion, beyond the duck, and the general merriment was redoubled when the pole got loose and floated out to the middle of the pond. At length John stripped, swam to the duck, threw it ashore, and brought in the pole in his teeth, his companions meanwhile making merry at his expense by splashing the water in front of him and making the dead duck go through the motions of fighting and biting him in the face as he landed.

The morning after this delightful day was dark and threatening. A high wind was rushing down the strait dead against us, and just as we were about ready to start, determined to fight our way by creeping close inshore, pelting rain began to fly. We concluded therefore to wait for better weather. The hunters went out for deer and I to see the forests. The rain brought out the fragrance of the drenched trees, and the wind made wild melody in their tops, while every brown bole was embroidered by a network of rain rills. Perhaps the most delightful part of my ramble was along a stream that flowed through a leafy arch beneath overleaning trees which met at the top. The water was almost black in the deep pools and fine clear amber in the shallows. It was the pure, rich wine of the woods with a pleasant taste, bringing spicy spruce groves and widespread bog and beaver meadows to mind. On this amber stream I discovered an interesting fall. It is only a few feet high, but remarkably fine in the curve of its brow and blending shades of color, while the mossy, bushy pool into which it plunges is inky black, but wonderfully brightened by foam bells larger than common that drift in clusters on the smooth water around the rim, each of them carrying a picture of the overlooking trees leaning together at the tips like the teeth of moss capsules before they rise.

I found most of the trees here fairly loaded with mosses. Some broadly palmated branches had beds of yellow moss so wide and deep that when wet they must weigh a hundred pounds or even more. Upon these moss-beds ferns and grasses and even good-sized seedling trees grow, making beautiful hanging gardens in which the curious spectacle is presented of old trees holding hundreds of their own children in their arms, nourished by rain and dew and the decaying leaves showered down to them by their parents. The branches upon which these beds of mossy soil rest become flat and irregular like weathered roots or the antlers of deer, and at length die; and when the whole tree has thus been killed it seems to be standing on its head with roots in the air. A striking example of this sort stood near the camp and I called the missionary's attention to it.

"Come, Mr. Young," I shouted. "Here's something wonderful, the most wonderful tree you ever saw; it is standing on its head."

"How in the world," said he in astonishment, "could that tree have been plucked up by the roots, carried high in the air, and dropped down head foremost into the ground. It must have been the work of a tornado."

Toward evening the hunters brought in a deer. They had seen four others, and at the camp-fire talk said that deer abounded on all the islands of considerable size and along the shores of the mainland. But few were to be found in the interior on account of wolves that ran them down where they could not readily take refuge in the water. The Indians, they said, hunted them on the islands with trained dogs which went into the woods and drove them out, while the hunters lay in wait in canoes at the points where they were likely to take to the water. Beaver and black bear also abounded on this large island. I saw but few birds there, only ravens, jays, and wrens. Ducks, gulls, bald eagles, and jays are the commonest birds hereabouts. A flock of swans flew past, sounding their startling human-like cry which seemed yet more striking in this lonely wilderness. The Indians said that geese, swans, cranes, etc., making their long journeys in regular order thus called aloud to encourage each other and enable them to keep stroke and time like men in rowing or marching (a sort of "Row, brothers, row," or "Hip, hip" of marching soldiers).

October 18 was about half sunshine, half rain and wet snow, but we paddled on through the midst of the innumerable islands in more than half comfort, enjoying the changing effects of the weather on the dripping wilderness. Strolling a little way back into the woods when we went ashore for luncheon, I found fine specimens of cedar, and here and there a birch, and small thickets of wild apple. A hemlock, felled by Indians for bread-bark, was only twenty inches thick at the butt, a hundred and twenty feet long, and about five hundred and forty years old at the time it was felled. The first hundred of its rings measured only four inches, showing that for a century it had grown in the shade of taller trees and at the age of one hundred years was yet only a sapling in size. On the mossy trunk of an old prostrate spruce about a hundred feet in length thousands of seedlings were growing. I counted seven hundred on a length of eight feet, so favorable is this climate for the development of tree seeds and so fully do these trees obey the command to multiply and replenish the earth. No wonder these islands are densely clothed with trees. They grow on solid rocks and logs as well as on fertile soil. The surface is first covered with a plush of mosses in which the seeds germinate; then the interlacing roots form a sod, fallen leaves soon cover their feet, and the young trees, closely crowded together, support each other, and the soil becomes deeper and richer from year to year.

I greatly enjoyed the Indians' camp-fire talk this evening on their ancient customs, how they were taught by their parents ere the whites came among them, their religion, ideas connected with the next world, the stars, plants, the behavior and language of animals under different circumstances, manner of getting a living, etc. When our talk was interrupted by the howling of a wolf on the opposite side of the strait, Kadachan puzzled the minister with the question, "Have wolves souls?" The Indians believe that they have, giving as foundation for their belief that they are wise creatures who know how to catch seals and salmon by swimming slyly upon them with their heads hidden in a mouthful of grass, hunt deer in company, and always bring forth their young at the same and most favorable time of the year. I inquired how it was that with enemies so wise and powerful the deer were not all killed. Kadachan replied that wolves knew better than to kill them all and thus cut off their most important food-supply. He said they were numerous on all the large islands, more so than on the mainland, that Indian hunters were afraid of them and never ventured far into the woods alone, for these large gray and black wolves attacked man whether they were hungry or not. When attacked, the Indian hunter, he said, climbed a tree or stood with his back against a tree or rock as a wolf never attacks face to face. Wolves, and not bears, Indians regard as masters of the woods, for they sometimes attack and kill bears, but the wolverine they never attack, "for," said John, "wolves and wolverines are companions in sin and equally wicked and cunning."

On one of the small islands we found a stockade, sixty by thirty-five feet, built, our Indians said, by the Kake tribe during one of their many war-like quarrels. Toyatte and Kadachan said these forts were common throughout the canoe waters, showing that in this foodful, kindly wilderness, as in all the world beside, man may be man's worst enemy.

We discovered small bits of cultivation here and there, patches of potatoes and turnips, planted mostly on the cleared sites of deserted villages. In spring the most industrious families sailed to their little farms of perhaps a quarter of an acre or less, and ten or fifteen miles from their villages. After preparing the ground, and planting it, they visited it again in summer to pull the weeds and speculate on the size of the crop they were likely to have to eat with their fat salmon. The Kakes were then busy digging their potatoes, which they complained were this year injured by early frosts.

We arrived at Klugh-Quan, one of the Kupreanof Kake villages, just as a funeral party was breaking up. The body had been burned and gifts were being distributed—bits of calico, handkerchiefs, blankets, etc., according to the rank and wealth of the deceased. The death ceremonies of chiefs and head men, Mr. Young told me, are very weird and imposing, with wild feasting, dancing, and singing. At this little place there are some eight totem poles of bold and intricate design, well executed, but smaller than those of the Stickeens. As elsewhere throughout the archipelago, the bear, raven, eagle, salmon, and porpoise are the chief figures. Some of the poles have square cavities, mortised into the back, which are said to contain the ashes of members of the family. These recesses are closed by a plug. I noticed one that was caulked with a rag where the joint was imperfect.

Strolling about the village, looking at the tangled vegetation, sketching the totems, etc., I found a lot of human bones scattered on the surface of the ground or partly covered. In answer to my inquiries, one of our crew said they probably belonged to Sitka Indians slain in war. These Kakes are shrewd, industrious, and rather good-looking people. It was at their largest village that an American schooner was seized and all the crew except one man murdered. A gunboat sent to punish them burned the village. I saw the anchor of the ill-fated vessel lying near the shore.

Though all the Thlinkit tribes believe in witchcraft, they are less superstitious in some respects than many of the lower classes of whites. Chief Yana Taowk seemed to take pleasure in kicking the Sitka bones that lay in his way, and neither old nor young showed the slightest trace of superstitious fear of the dead at any time.

It was at the northmost of the Kupreanof Kake villages that Mr. Young held his first missionary meeting, singing hymns, praying, and preaching, and trying to learn the number of the inhabitants and their readiness to receive instruction. Neither here nor in any of the other villages of the different tribes that we visited was there anything like a distinct refusal to receive school-teachers or ministers. On the contrary, with but one or two exceptions, all with apparent good faith declared their willingness to receive them, and many seemed heartily delighted at the prospect of gaining light on subjects so important and so dark to them. All had heard ere this of the wonderful work of the Reverend Mr. Duncan at Metlakatla, and even those chiefs who were not at all inclined to anything like piety were yet anxious to procure schools and churches that their people should not miss the temporal advantages of knowledge, which with their natural shrewdness they were not slow to recognize. "We are all children," they said, "groping in the dark. Give us this light and we will do as you bid us."

The chief of the first Kupreanof Kake village we came to was a venerable-looking man, perhaps seventy years old, with massive head and strongly marked features, a bold Roman nose, deep, tranquil eyes, shaggy eyebrows, a strong face set in a halo of long gray hair. He seemed delighted at the prospect of receiving a teacher for his people. "This is just what I want," he said. "I am ready to bid him welcome."

"This," said Yana Taowk, chief of the larger north village, "is a good word you bring us. We will be glad to come out of our darkness into your light. You Boston men must be favorites of the Great Father. You know all about God, and ships and guns and the growing of things to eat. We will sit quiet and listen to the words of any teacher you send us."

While Mr. Young was preaching, some of the congregation smoked, talked to each other, and answered the shouts of their companions outside, greatly to the disgust of Toyatte and Kadachan, who regarded the Kakes as mannerless barbarians. A little girl, frightened at the strange exercises, began to cry and was turned out of doors. She cried in a strange, low, wild tone, quite unlike the screech crying of the children of civilization.

The following morning we crossed Prince Frederick's Sound to the west coast of Admiralty Island. Our frail shell of a canoe was tossed like a bubble on the swells coming in from the ocean. Still, I suppose, the danger was not so great as it seemed. In a good canoe, skillfully handled, you may safely sail from Victoria to Chilcat, a thousand-mile voyage frequently made by Indians in their trading operations before the coming of the whites. Our Indians, however, dreaded this crossing so late in the season. They spoke of it repeatedly before we reached it as the one great danger of our voyage.

John said to me just as we left the shore, "You and Mr. Young will be scared to death on this broad water."

"Never mind us, John," we merrily replied, "perhaps some of you brave Indian sailors may be the first to show fear."

Toyatte said he had not slept well a single night thinking of it, and after we rounded Cape Gardner and entered the comparatively smooth Chatham Strait, they all rejoiced, laughing and chatting like frolicsome children.

We arrived at the first of the Hootsenoo villages on Admiralty Island shortly after noon and were welcomed by everybody. Men, women, and children made haste to the beach to meet us, the children staring as if they had never before seen a Boston man. The chief, a remarkably good-looking and intelligent fellow, stepped forward, shook hands with us Boston fashion, and invited us to his house. Some of the curious children crowded in after us and stood around the fire staring like half-frightened wild animals. Two old women drove them out of the house, making hideous gestures, but taking good care not to hurt them. The merry throng poured through the round door, laughing and enjoying the harsh gestures and threats of the women as all a joke, indicating mild parental government in general. Indeed, in all my travels I never saw a child, old or young, receive a blow or even a harsh word. When our cook began to prepare luncheon our host said through his interpreter that he was sorry we could not eat Indian food, as he was anxious to entertain us. We thanked him, of course, and expressed our sense of his kindness. His brother, in the mean time, brought a dozen turnips, which he peeled and sliced and served in a clean dish. These we ate raw as dessert, reminding me of turnip-field feasts when I was a boy in Scotland. Then a box was brought from some corner and opened. It seemed to be full of tallow or butter. A sharp

Admiralty Island

stick was thrust into it, and a lump of something five or six inches long, three or four wide, and an inch thick was dug up, which proved to be a section of the back fat of a deer, preserved in fish oil and seasoned with boiled spruce and other spicy roots. After stripping off the lard-like oil, it was cut into small pieces and passed round. It seemed white and wholesome, but I was unable to taste it even for manner's sake. This disgust, however, was not noticed, as the rest of the company did full justice to the precious tallow and smacked their lips over it as a great delicacy. A lot of potatoes about the size of walnuts, boiled and peeled and added to a potful of salmon, made a savory stew that all seemed to relish. An old, cross-looking, wrinkled crone presided at the steaming chowder-pot, and as she peeled the potatoes with her fingers she, at short intervals, quickly thrust one of the best into the mouth of a little wild-eyed girl that crouched beside her, a spark of natural love which charmed her withered face and made all the big gloomy house shine. In honor of our visit, our host put on a genuine white shirt. His wife also dressed in her best and put a pair of dainty trousers on her two-year-old boy, who seemed to be the pet and favorite of the large family and indeed of the whole village. Toward evening messengers were sent through the village to call everybody to a meeting. Mr. Young delivered the usual missionary sermon and I also was called on to say something. Then the chief arose and made an eloquent reply, thanking us for our good words and for the hopes we had inspired of obtaining a teacher for their children. In particular, he said, he wanted to hear all we could tell him about God.

This village was an offshoot of a larger one, ten miles to the north, called Killisnoo. Under the prevailing patriarchal form of government each tribe is divided into comparatively few families; and because of quarrels, the chief of this branch moved his people to this little bay, where the beach offered a good landing for canoes. A stream which enters it yields abundance of salmon, while in the adjacent woods and mountains berries, deer, and wild goats abound.

"Here," he said, "we enjoy peace and plenty; all we lack is a church and a school, particularly a school for the children." His dwelling so much with benevolent aspect on the children of the tribe showed, I think, that he truly loved them and had a right intelligent insight concerning their welfare. We spent the night under his roof, the first we had ever spent with Indians, and I never felt more at home. The loving kindness bestowed on the little ones made the house glow.

Next morning, with the hearty good wishes of our Hootsenoo friends, and encouraged by the gentle weather, we sailed gladly up the coast, hoping soon to see the Chilcat glaciers in their glory. The rock hereabouts is mostly a beautiful blue marble, waveworn into a multitude of small coves and ledges. Fine sections were thus revealed along the shore, which with their colors, brightened with showers and late-blooming leaves and flowers, beguiled the weariness of the way. The shingle in front of these marble cliffs is also mostly marble, well polished and rounded and mixed with a small percentage of glacier-borne slate and granite erratics.

We arrived at the upper village about half-past one o'clock. Here we saw Hootsenoo Indians in a very different light from that which illumined the lower village. While we were yet half a mile or more away, we heard sounds I had never before heard—a storm of strange howls, yells, and screams rising from a base of gasping, bellowing grunts and groans. Had I been alone, I should have fled as from a pack of fiends, but our Indians quietly recognized this awful sound, if such stuff could be called sound, simply as the "whiskey howl" and pushed quietly on. As we approached the landing, the demoniac howling so greatly increased I tried to dissuade Mr. Young from attempting to say a single word in the village, and as for preaching one might as well try to preach in Tophet. The whole village was afire with bad whiskey. This was the first time in my life that I learned the meaning of the phrase "a howling drunk." Even our Indians hesitated to venture ashore, notwithstanding whiskey storms were far from novel to them. Mr. Young, however, hoped that in this Indian Sodom at least one man might be found so righteous as to be in his right mind and able to give trustworthy information. Therefore I was at length prevailed on to yield consent to land. Our canoe was drawn up on the beach and one of the crew left to guard it. Cautiously we strolled up the hill to the main row of houses, now a chain of alcoholic volcanoes. The largest house, just opposite the landing, was about forty feet square, built of immense planks, each hewn from a whole log, and, as usual, the only opening was a mere hole about two and a half feet in diameter, closed by a massive hinged plug like the breach of a cannon. At the dark door-hole a few black faces appeared and were suddenly withdrawn. Not a single person was to be seen on the street. At length a couple of old, crouching men, hideously blackened, ventured out and stared at us, then, calling to their companions, other black and burning heads appeared, and we began to fear that like the Alloway Kirk witches the whole legion was about to sally forth. But, instead, those outside suddenly crawled and tumbled in again. We were thus allowed to take a general view of the place and return to our canoe unmolested. But ere we could get away, three old women came swaggering and grinning down to the beach, and Toyatte was discovered by a man with whom he had once had a business misunderstanding, who, burning for revenge, was now jumping and howling and threatening as only a drunken Indian may, while our heroic old captain, in severe icy majesty, stood erect and motionless, uttering never a word. Kadachan, on the contrary, was well nigh smothered with the drunken caresses of one of his father's *tillicums* (friends), who insisted on his going back with him into the house. But reversing the words of St. Paul in his account of his shipwreck, it came to pass that we all at length got safe to sea and by hard rowing managed to reach a fine harbor before dark, fifteen sweet, serene miles from the howlers.

Our camp this evening was made at the head of a narrow bay bordered by spruce and hemlock woods. We made our beds beneath a grand old Sitka spruce five feet in diameter, whose broad, wing-like branches were outspread immediately above our heads. The night picture as I stood back to see it in the firelight was this one great tree, relieved against the gloom of the woods back of it, the light on the low branches revealing the shining needles, the brown, sturdy trunk grasping an outswelling mossy bank, and a fringe of illuminated bushes within a few feet of the tree with the firelight on the tips of the sprays.

Next morning, soon after we left our harbor, we were caught in a violent gust of wind and dragged over the seething water in a passionate hurry, though our sail was close-reefed, flying past the gray headlands in most exhilarating style, until fear of being capsized made us drop our sail and run into the first little nook we came to for shelter. Captain Toyatte remarked that in this kind of wind no Indian would dream of traveling, but since Mr. Young and I were with him he was willing to go on, because he was sure that the Lord loved us and would not allow us to perish.

We were now within a day or two of Chilcat. We had only to hold a direct course up the beautiful Lynn Canal to reach the large Davidson and other glaciers at its head in the cañons of the Chilcat and Chilcoot Rivers. But rumors of trouble among the Indians there now reached us. We found a party taking shelter from the stormy wind in a little cove, who confirmed the bad news that the Chilcats were drinking and fighting, that Kadachan's father had been shot, and that it would be far from safe to venture among them until blood-money had been paid and the quarrels settled. I decided, therefore, in the mean time, to turn westward and go in search of the wonderful "ice-mountains" that Sitka Charley had been telling us about. Charley, the youngest of my crew, noticing my interest in glaciers, said that when he was a boy he had gone with his father to hunt seals in a large bay full of ice, and that though it was long since he had been there, he thought he could find his way to it. Accordingly, we pushed eagerly on across Chatham Strait to the north end of Icy Strait, toward the new and promising ice-field.

On the south side of Icy Strait we ran into a picturesque bay to visit the main village of the Hoona tribe. Rounding a point on the north shore of the bay, the charmingly located village came in sight, with a group of the inhabitants gazing at us as we approached. They evidently recognized us as strangers or visitors from the shape and style of our canoe, and perhaps even determining that white men were aboard, for these Indians have wonderful eyes. While we were yet half a mile off, we saw a flag unfurled on a tall mast in front of the chief's house. Toyatte hoisted his United

States flag in reply, and thus arrayed we made for the landing. Here we were met and received by the chief, Kashoto, who stood close to the water's edge, barefooted and bareheaded, but wearing so fine a robe and standing so grave, erect, and serene, his dignity was complete. No white man could have maintained sound dignity under circumstances so disadvantageous. After the usual formal salutations, the chief, still standing as erect and motionless as a tree, said that he was not much acquainted with our people and feared that his house was too mean for visitors so distinguished as we were. We hastened of course to assure him that we were not proud of heart, and would be glad to have the honor of his hospitality and friendship. With a smile of relief he then led us into his large fort house to the seat of honor prepared for us. After we had been allowed to rest unnoticed and unquestioned for fifteen minutes or so, in accordance with good Indian manners in case we should be weary or embarrassed, our cook began to prepare luncheon; and the chief expressed great concern at his not being able to entertain us in Boston fashion.

Luncheon over, Mr. Young as usual requested him to call his people to a meeting. Most of them were away at outlying camps gathering winter stores. Some ten or twelve men, however, about the same number of women, and a crowd of wondering boys and girls were gathered in, to whom Mr. Young preached the usual gospel sermon. Toyatte prayed in Thlinkit, and the other members of the crew joined in the hymn-singing. At the close of the mission exercises the chief arose and said that he would now like to hear what the other white chief had to say. I directed John to reply that I was not a missionary, that I came only to pay a friendly visit and see the forests and mountains of their beautiful country. To this he replied, as others had done in the same circumstances, that he would like to hear me on the subject of their country and themselves; so I had to get on my feet and make some sort of a speech, dwelling principally on the brotherhood of all races of people, assuring them that God loved them and that some of their white brethren were beginning to know them and become interested in their welfare; that I seemed this evening to be among old friends with whom I had long been acquainted, though I had never been here before; that I would always remember them and the kind reception they had given us; advised them to heed the instructions of sincere self-denying mission men who wished only to do them good and desired nothing but their friendship and welfare in return. I told them that in some far-off countries, instead of receiving the missionaries with glad and thankful hearts, the Indians killed and ate them; but I hoped, and indeed felt sure, that his people would find a better use for missionaries than putting them, like salmon, in pots for food. They seemed greatly interested, looking into each other's faces with emphatic nods and a-ahs and smiles.

The chief then slowly arose and, after standing silent a minute or two, told us how glad he was to see us; that he felt as if his heart had enjoyed a good meal; that we were the first to come humbly to his little out-of-the-way village to tell his people about God; that they were all like children groping in darkness, but eager for light; that they would gladly welcome a missionary and teacher and use them well; that he could easily believe that whites and Indians were the children of one Father just as I had told them in my speech; that they differed little and resembled each other a great deal, calling attention to the similarity of hands, eyes, legs, etc., making telling gestures in the most natural style of eloquence and dignified composure. "Oftentimes," he said, "when I was on the high mountains in the fall, hunting wild sheep for meat, and for wool to make blankets, I have been caught in snowstorms and held in camp until there was nothing to eat, but when I reached my home and got warm, and had a good meal, then my body felt good. For a long time my heart has been hungry and cold, but to-night your words have warmed my heart, and given it a good meal, and now my heart feels good."

The most striking characteristic of these people is their serene dignity in circumstances that to us would be novel and embarrassing. Even the little children behave with natural dignity, come to the white men when called, and restrain their wonder at the strange prayers, hymn-singing, etc. This evening an old woman fell asleep in the meeting and began to snore; and though both old and young were shaken with suppressed mirth, they evidently took great pains to conceal it. It seems wonderful to me that these so-called savages can make one feel at home in their families. In good breeding, intelligence, and skill in accomplishing whatever they try to do with tools they seem to me to rank above most of our uneducated white laborers. I have never yet seen a child ill-used, even to the extent of an angry word. Scolding, so common a curse in civilization, is not known here at all. On the contrary the young are fondly indulged without being spoiled. Crying is very rarely heard.

In the house of this Hoona chief a pet marmot (Parry's) was a great favorite with old and young. It was therefore delightfully confiding and playful and human. Cats were petted, and the confidence with which these cautious, thoughtful animals met strangers showed that they were kindly treated.

There were some ten or a dozen houses, all told, in the village. The count made by the chief for Mr. Young showed some seven hundred and twenty-five persons in the tribe.

CHAPTER X

THE DISCOVERY OF GLACIER BAY

From here, on October 24, we set sail for Guide Charley's ice-mountains. The handle of our heaviest axe was cracked, and as Charley declared that there was no firewood to be had in the big ice-mountain bay, we would have to load the canoe with a store for cooking at an island out in the Strait a few miles from the village. We were therefore anxious to buy or trade for a good sound axe in exchange for our broken one. Good axes are rare in rocky Alaska. Soon or late an unlucky stroke on a stone concealed in moss spoils the edge. Finally one in almost perfect condition was offered by a young Hoona for our broken-handled one and a half-dollar to boot; but when the broken axe and money were given he promptly demanded an additional twenty-five cents' worth of tobacco. The tobacco was given him, then he required a half-dollar's worth more of tobacco, which was also given; but when he still demanded something more, Charley's patience gave way and we sailed in the same condition as to axes as when we arrived. This was the only contemptible commercial affair we encountered among these Alaskan Indians.

We reached the wooded island about one o'clock, made coffee, took on a store of wood, and set sail direct for the icy country, finding it very hard indeed to believe the woodless part of Charley's description of the Icy Bay, so heavily and uniformly are all the shores forested wherever we had been. In this view we were joined by John, Kadachan, and Toyatte, none of them on all their lifelong canoe travels having ever seen a woodless country.

We held a northwesterly course until long after dark, when we reached a small inlet that sets in near the mouth of Glacier Bay, on the west side. Here we made a cold camp on a desolate snow-covered beach in stormy sleet and darkness. At daybreak I looked eagerly in every direction to learn what kind of place we were in; but gloomy rain-clouds covered the mountains, and I could see nothing that would give me a clue, while Vancouver's chart, hitherto a faithful guide, here failed us altogether. Nevertheless, we made haste to be off; and fortunately, for just as we were leaving the shore, a faint smoke was seen across the inlet, toward which Charley, who now seemed lost, gladly steered. Our sudden appearance so early that gray morning had evidently alarmed our neighbors, for as soon as we were within hailing distance an Indian with his face blackened fired a shot over our heads, and in a blunt, bellowing voice roared, "Who are you?"

Our interpreter shouted, "Friends and the Fort Wrangell missionary."

Then men, women, and children swarmed out of the hut, and awaited our approach on the beach. One of the hunters having brought his gun with him, Kadachan sternly rebuked him, asking with superb indignation whether he was not ashamed to meet a missionary with a gun in his hands. Friendly relations, however, were speedily established, and as a cold rain was falling, they invited us to enter their hut. It seemed very small and was jammed full of oily boxes and bundles; nevertheless, twenty-one persons managed to find shelter in it about a smoky fire. Our hosts proved to be Hoona seal-hunters laying in their winter stores of meat and skins. The packed hut was passably well ventilated, but its heavy, meaty smells were not the same to our noses as those we were accustomed to in the sprucy nooks of the evergreen woods. The circle of black eyes peering at us through a fog of reek and smoke made a novel picture. We were glad, however, to get within reach of information, and of course asked many questions concerning the ice-mountains and the strange bay, to most of which our inquisitive Hoona friends replied with counter-questions as to our object in coming to such a place, especially so late in the year. They had heard of Mr. Young and his work at Fort Wrangell, but could not understand what a missionary could be doing in such a place as this. Was he going to preach to the seals and gulls, they asked, or to the ice-mountains? And could they take his word? Then John explained that only the friend of the missionary was seeking ice-mountains, that Mr. Young had already preached many good words in the villages we had visited, their own among the others, that our hearts were good and every Indian was our friend. Then we gave them a little rice, sugar, tea, and tobacco, after which they began to gain confidence and to speak freely. They told us that the big bay was called by them Sit-a-da-kay, or Ice Bay; that there were many large ice-mountains in it, but no gold-mines; and that the ice-mountain they knew best was at the head of the bay, where most of the seals were found.

Notwithstanding the rain, I was anxious to push on and grope our way beneath the clouds as best we could, in case worse weather should come; but Charley was ill at ease, and wanted one of the seal-hunters to go with us, for the place was much changed. I promised to pay well for a guide, and in order to lighten the canoe proposed to leave most of our heavy stores in the hut until our return. After a long consultation one of them consented to go. His wife got ready his blanket and a piece of cedar matting for his bed, and some provisions—mostly dried salmon, and seal sausage made of strips of lean meat plaited around a core of fat. She followed us to the beach, and just as we were pushing off said with a pretty smile, "It is my husband that you are taking away. See that you bring him back."

We got under way about 10 A.M. The wind was in our favor, but a cold rain pelted us, and we could see but little of the dreary, tree-less wilderness which we had now fairly entered. The bitter blast, however, gave us good speed; our bedraggled canoe rose and fell on the waves as solemnly as a big ship. Our course was northwestward, up the southwest side of the bay, near the shore of what seemed to be the mainland, smooth marble islands being on our right. About noon we discovered the first of the great glaciers, the one I afterward named for James Geikie, the noted Scotch geologist. Its lofty blue cliffs, looming through the draggled skirts of the clouds, gave a tremendous impression of savage power, while the roar of the new-born icebergs thickened and emphasized the general roar of the storm. An hour and a half beyond the Geikie Glacier we ran into a slight harbor where the shore is low, dragged the canoe beyond the reach of drifting icebergs, and, much against my desire to push ahead, encamped, the guide insisting that the big ice-mountain at the head of the bay could not be reached before dark, that the landing there was dangerous even in daylight, and that this was the only safe harbor on the way to it. While camp was being made, I strolled along the shore to examine the rocks and the fossil timber that abounds here. All the rocks are freshly glaciated, even below the sea-level, nor have the waves as yet worn off the surface polish, much less the heavy scratches and grooves and lines of glacial contour.

The next day being Sunday, the minister wished to stay in camp; and so, on account of the weather, did the Indians. I therefore set out on an excursion, and spent the day alone on the mountain-slopes above the camp, and northward, to see what I might learn. Pushing on through rain and mud and sludgy snow, crossing many brown, boulder-choked torrents, wading, jumping, and wallowing in snow up to my shoulders was mountaineering of the most trying kind. After crouching cramped and benumbed in the canoe, poulticed in wet or damp clothing night and day, my limbs had been asleep. This day they were awakened and in the hour of trial proved that they had not lost the cunning learned on many a mountain peak of the High Sierra. I reached a height of fifteen hundred feet, on the ridge that bounds the second of the great glaciers. All the landscape was smothered in clouds and I began to fear that as far as wide views were concerned I had climbed in vain. But at length the clouds lifted a little, and beneath their gray fringes I saw the berg-filled expanse of the bay, and the feet of the mountains that stand about it, and the imposing fronts of five huge glaciers, the nearest being immediately beneath me. This was my first general view of Glacier Bay, a solitude of ice and snow and new-born rocks, dim, dreary, mysterious. I held the ground I had so dearly won for an hour or two, sheltering myself from the blast as best I could, while with benumbed fingers I sketched what I could see of the landscape, and wrote a few lines in my notebook. Then, breasting the snow again, crossing the shifting avalanche slopes and torrents, I reached camp about dark, wet and weary and glad.

While I was getting some coffee and hardtack, Mr. Young told me that the Indians were discouraged, and had been talking about turning back, fearing that I would be lost, the canoe broken, or in some other mysterious way the expedition would come to grief if I persisted in going farther. They had been asking him what possible motive I could have in climbing mountains when storms were blowing; and when he replied that I was only seeking knowledge, Toyatte said, "Muir must be a witch to seek knowledge in such a place as this and in such miserable weather."

After supper, crouching about a dull fire of fossil wood, they became still more doleful, and talked in tones that accorded well with the wind and waters and growling torrents about us, telling sad old stories of crushed canoes, drowned Indians, and hunters frozen in snowstorms. Even brave old Toyatte, dreading the treeless, forlorn appearance of the region, said that his heart was not strong, and that he feared his canoe, on the safety of which our lives depended, might be entering a skookum-house (jail) of ice, from which there might be no escape; while the Hoona guide said bluntly that if I was so fond of danger, and meant to go close up to the noses of the ice-mountains, he would not consent to go any farther; for we should all be lost, as many of his tribe had been, by the sudden rising of bergs from the bottom. They seemed to be losing heart with every howl of the wind, and, fearing that they might fail me now that I was in the midst of so grand a congregation of glaciers, I made haste to reassure them, telling them that for ten years I had wandered alone among mountains and storms, and good luck always followed me; that with me, therefore, they need fear nothing. The storm would soon cease and the sun would shine to show us the way we should go, for God cares for us and guides us as long as we are trustful and brave, therefore all childish fear must be put away. This little speech did good. Kadachan, with some show of enthusiasm, said he liked to travel with good-luck people; and dignified old Toyatte declared that now his heart was strong again, and he would venture on with me as far as I liked for my "wawa" was "delait" (my talk was very good). The old warrior even became a little sentimental, and said that even if the canoe was broken he would not greatly care, because on the way to the other world he would have good companions.

Next morning it was still raining and snowing, but the south wind swept us bravely forward and swept the bergs from our course. In about an hour we reached the second of the big glaciers, which I afterwards named for Hugh Miller. We rowed up its fiord and landed to make a slight examination of its grand frontal wall. The berg-producing portion we found to be about a mile and a half wide, and broken into an imposing array of jagged spires and pyramids, and flat-topped towers and battlements, of many shades of blue, from pale, shimmering, limpid tones in the crevasses and hollows, to the most startling, chilling, almost shrieking vitriol blue on the plain mural spaces from which bergs had just been discharged. Back from the front for a few miles the glacier rises in a series of wide steps, as if this portion of the glacier had sunk in successive sections as it reached deep water, and the sea had found its way beneath it. Beyond this it extends indefinitely in a gently rising prairie-like expanse, and branches along the slopes and cañons of the Fairweather Range.

From here a run of two hours brought us to the head of the bay, and to the mouth of the northwest fiord, at the head of which lie the Hoona sealing-grounds, and the great glacier now called the Pacific, and another called the Hoona. The fiord is about five miles long, and two miles wide at the mouth. Here our Hoona guide had a store of dry wood, which we took aboard. Then, setting sail, we were driven wildly up the fiord, as if the storm-wind were saying, "Go, then, if you will, into my icy chamber; but you shall stay in until I am ready to let you out." All this time sleety rain was falling on the bay, and snow on the mountains; but soon after we landed the sky began to open. The camp was made on a rocky bench near the front of the Pacific Glacier, and the canoe was carried beyond the reach of the bergs and berg-waves. The bergs were now crowded in a dense pack against the discharging front, as if the storm-wind had determined to make the glacier take back her crystal offspring and keep them at home.

While camp affairs were being attended to, I set out to climb a mountain for comprehensive views; and before I had reached a height of a thousand feet the rain ceased, and the clouds began to rise from the lower altitudes, slowly lifting their white skirts, and lingering in majestic, wing-shaped masses about the mountains that rise out of the broad, icy sea, the highest of all the white mountains, and the greatest of all the glaciers I had yet seen. Climbing higher for a still broader outlook, I made notes and sketched, improving the precious time while sunshine streamed through the luminous fringes of the clouds and fell on the green waters of the fiord, the glittering bergs, the crystal bluffs of the vast glacier, the intensely white, far-spreading fields of ice, and the ineffably chaste and spiritual heights of the Fairweather Range, which were now hidden, now partly revealed, the whole making a picture of icy wildness unspeakably pure and sublime.

Looking southward, a broad ice-sheet was seen extending in a gently undulating plain from the Pacific Fiord in the foreground to the horizon, dotted and ridged here and there with mountains which were as white as the snow-covered ice in which they were half, or more than half, submerged. Several of the great glaciers of the bay flow from this one grand fountain. It is an instructive example of a general glacier covering the hills and dales of a country that is not yet ready to be brought to the light of day—not only covering but creating a landscape with the features it is destined to have when, in the fullness of time, the fashioning ice-sheet shall be lifted by the sun, and the land become warm and fruitful. The view to the westward is bounded and almost filled by the glorious Fairweather Mountains, the highest among them springing aloft in sublime beauty to a height of nearly sixteen thousand feet, while from base to summit every peak and spire and dividing ridge of all the mighty host was spotless white, as if painted. It would seem that snow could never be made to lie on the steepest slopes and precipices unless plastered on when wet, and then frozen. But this snow could not have been wet. It must have been fixed by being driven and set in small particles like the storm-dust of drifts, which, when in this condition, is fixed not only on sheer cliffs, but in massive, overcurling cornices. Along the base of this majestic range sweeps the Pacific Glacier, fed by innumerable cascading tributaries, and discharging into the head of its fiord by two mouths only partly separated by the brow of an island rock about one thousand feet high, each nearly a mile wide.

Dancing down the mountain to camp, my mind glowing like the sunbeaten glaciers, I found the Indians seated around a good fire, entirely happy now that the farthest point of the journey was safely reached and the long, dark storm was cleared away. How hopefully, peacefully bright that night were the stars in the frosty sky, and how impressive was the thunder of the icebergs, rolling, swelling, reverberating through the solemn stillness! I was too happy to sleep.

About daylight next morning we crossed the fiord and landed on the south side of the rock that divides the wall of the great glacier. The whiskered faces of seals dotted the open spaces between the bergs, and I could not prevent John and Charley and Kadachan from shooting at them. Fortunately, few, if any, were hurt. Leaving the Indians in charge of the canoe, I managed to climb to the top of the wall by a good deal of step-cutting between the ice and dividing rock, and gained a good general view of the glacier. At one favorable place I descended about fifty feet below the side of the glacier, where its denuding, fashioning action was clearly shown. Pushing back from here, I found the surface crevassed and sunken in steps, like the Hugh Miller Glacier, as if it were being undermined by the action of tide-waters. For a distance of fifteen or twenty miles the river-like ice-flood is nearly level, and when it recedes, the ocean water will follow it, and thus form a long extension of the fiord, with features essentially the same as those now extending into the continent farther south, where many great glaciers once poured into the sea, though scarce a vestige of them now exists. Thus the domain of the sea has been, and is being, extended in these ice-sculptured lands, and the scenery of their shores enriched. The brow of the dividing rock is about a thousand feet high, and is hard beset by the glacier. A short time ago it was at least two thousand feet below the surface of the over-sweeping ice; and under present climatic conditions it will soon take its place as a glacier-polished island in the middle of the fiord, like a thousand others in the magnificent archipelago. Emerging from its icy sepulchre, it gives a most telling illustration of the birth of a marked feature of a landscape. In this instance it is not the mountain, but the glacier, that is in labor, and the mountain itself is being brought forth.

The Hoona Glacier enters the fiord on the south side, a short distance below the Pacific, displaying a broad and far-reaching expanse, over which many lofty peaks are seen; but the front wall, thrust into the fiord, is not nearly so interesting as that of the Pacific, and I did not observe any bergs discharged from it.

In the evening, after witnessing the unveiling of the majestic peaks and glaciers and their baptism in the down-pouring sunbeams, it seemed inconceivable that nature could have anything finer to show us. Nevertheless, compared with what was to come the next morning, all that was as nothing. The calm dawn gave no promise of anything uncommon. Its most impressive features were the frosty clearness of the sky and a deep, brooding stillness made all the more striking by the thunder of the new-born bergs. The sunrise we did not see at all, for we were beneath the shadows of the fiord cliffs; but in the midst of our studies, while the Indians were getting ready to sail, we were startled by the sudden appearance of a red light burning with a strange unearthly splendor on the topmost peak of the Fairweather Mountains. Instead of vanishing as suddenly as it had appeared, it spread and spread until the whole range down to the level of the glaciers was filled with the celestial fire. In color it was at first a vivid crimson, with a thick, furred appearance, as fine as the alpenglow, yet indescribably rich and deep—not in the least like a garment or mere external flush or bloom through which one might expect to see the rocks or snow, but every mountain apparently was glowing from the heart like molten metal fresh from a furnace. Beneath the frosty shadows of the fiord we stood hushed and awe-stricken, gazing at the holy vision; and had we seen the heavens opened and God made manifest, our attention could not have been more tremendously strained. When the highest peak began to burn, it did not seem to be steeped in sunshine, however glorious, but rather as if it had been thrust into the body of the sun itself. Then the supernal fire slowly descended, with a sharp line of demarkation separating it from the cold, shaded region beneath; peak after peak, with their spires and ridges and cascading glaciers, caught the heavenly glow, until all the mighty host stood transfigured, hushed, and thoughtful, as if awaiting the coming of the Lord. The white, rayless light of morning, seen when I was alone amid the peaks of the California Sierra, had always seemed to me the most telling of all the terrestrial manifestations of God. But here the mountains themselves were made divine, and declared His glory in terms still more impressive. How long we gazed I never knew. The glorious vision passed away in a gradual, fading change through a thousand tones of color to pale yellow and white, and then the work of the ice-world went on again in everyday beauty. The green waters of the fiord were filled with sun-spangles; the fleet of icebergs set forth on their voyages with the upspringing breeze; and on the innumerable mirrors and prisms of these bergs, and on those of the shattered crystal walls of the glaciers, common white light and rainbow light began to burn, while the mountains shone in their frosty jewelry, and loomed again in the thin azure in serene terrestrial majesty. We turned and sailed away, joining the outgoing bergs, while "Gloria in excelsis" still seemed to be sounding over all the white landscape, and our burning hearts were ready for any fate, feeling that, whatever the future might have in store, the treasures we had gained this glorious morning would enrich our lives forever.

When we arrived at the mouth of the fiord, and rounded the massive granite headland that stands guard at the entrance on the north side, another large glacier, now named the Reid, was discovered at the head of one of the northern branches of the bay. Pushing ahead into this new fiord, we found that it was not only packed with bergs, but that the spaces between the bergs were crusted with new ice, compelling us to turn back while we were yet several miles from the discharging frontal wall. But though we were not then allowed to set foot on this magnificent glacier, we obtained a fine view of it, and I made the Indians cease rowing while I sketched its principal features. Thence, after steering northeastward a few miles, we discovered still another large glacier, now named the Carroll. But the fiord into which this glacier flows was, like the last, utterly inaccessible on account of ice, and we had to be content with a general view and sketch of it, gained as we rowed slowly past at a distance of three or four miles. The mountains back of it and on each side of its inlet are sculptured in a singularly rich and striking style of architecture, in which subordinate peaks and gables appear in wonderful profusion, and an imposing conical mountain with a wide, smooth base stands out in the main current of the glacier, a mile or two back from the discharging ice-wall.

We now turned southward down the eastern shore of the bay, and in an hour or two discovered a glacier of the second class, at the head of a comparatively short fiord that winter had not yet closed. Here we landed, and climbed across a mile or so of rough boulder-beds, and back upon the wildly broken, receding front of the glacier, which, though it descends to the level of the sea, no longer sends off bergs. Many large masses, detached from the wasting front by irregular melting, were partly buried beneath mud, sand, gravel, and boulders of the terminal moraine. Thus protected, these fossil icebergs remain unmelted for many years, some of them for a century or more, as shown by the age of trees growing above them, though there are no trees here as yet. At length melting, a pit with sloping sides is formed by the falling in of the overlying moraine material into the space at first occupied by the buried ice. In this way are formed the curious depressions in drift-covered regions called kettles or sinks. On these decaying glaciers we may also find many interesting lessons on the formation of boulders and boulder-beds, which in all glaciated countries exert a marked influence on scenery, health, and fruitfulness.

Three or four miles farther down the bay, we came to another fiord, up which we sailed in quest of more glaciers, discovering one in each of the two branches into which the fiord divides. Neither of these glaciers quite reaches tide-water. Notwithstanding the apparent fruitfulness of their fountains, they are in the first stage of decadence, the waste from melting and evaporation being greater now than the supply of new ice from their snowy fountains. We reached the one in the north branch, climbed over its wrinkled brow, and gained a good view of the trunk and some of the tributaries, and also of the sublime gray cliffs of its channel.

Then we sailed up the south branch of the inlet, but failed to reach the glacier there, on account of a thin sheet of new ice. With the tent-poles we broke a lane for the canoe for a little distance; but it was slow work, and we soon saw that we could not reach the glacier before dark. Nevertheless, we gained a fair view of it as it came sweeping down through its gigantic gateway of massive Yosemite rocks three or four thousand feet high. Here we lingered until sundown, gazing and sketching; then turned back, and encamped on a bed of cobblestones between the forks of the fiord.

We gathered a lot of fossil wood and after supper made a big fire, and as we sat around it the brightness of the sky brought on a long talk with the Indians about the stars; and their eager, child-like attention was refreshing to see as compared with the death-like apathy of weary town-dwellers, in whom natural curiosity has been quenched in toil and care and poor shallow comfort.

After sleeping a few hours, I stole quietly out of the camp, and climbed the mountain that stands between the two glaciers. The ground was frozen, making the climbing difficult in the steepest places; but the views over the icy bay, sparkling beneath the stars, were enchanting. It seemed then a sad thing that any part of so precious a night had been lost in sleep. The star-light was so full that I distinctly saw not only the berg-filled bay, but most of the lower portions of the glaciers, lying pale and spirit-like amid the mountains. The nearest glacier in particular was so distinct that it seemed to be glowing with light that came from within itself. Not even in dark nights have I ever found any difficulty in seeing large glaciers; but on this mountain-top, amid so much ice, in the heart of so clear and frosty a night, everything was more or less luminous, and I seemed to be poised in a vast hollow between two skies of almost equal brightness. This exhilarating scramble made me glad and strong and I rejoiced that my studies called me before the glorious night succeeding so glorious a morning had been spent!

I got back to camp in time for an early breakfast, and by daylight we had everything packed and were again under way. The fiord was frozen nearly to its mouth, and though the ice was so thin it gave us but little trouble in breaking a way for the canoe, yet it showed us that the season for exploration in these waters was well-nigh over. We were in danger of being imprisoned in a jam of icebergs, for the water-spaces between them freeze rapidly, binding the floes into one mass. Across such floes it would be almost impossible to drag a canoe, however industriously we might ply the axe, as our Hoona guide took great pains to warn us. I would have kept straight down the bay from here, but the guide had to be taken home, and the provisions we left at the bark hut had to be got on board. We therefore crossed over to our Sunday storm-camp, cautiously boring a way through the bergs. We found the shore lavishly adorned with a fresh arrival of assorted bergs that had been left stranded at high tide. They were arranged in a curving row, looking intensely clear and pure on the gray sand, and, with the sunbeams pouring through them, suggested the jewel-paved streets of the New Jerusalem.

On our way down the coast, after examining the front of the beautiful Geikie Glacier, we obtained our first broad view of the great glacier afterwards named the Muir, the last of all the grand company to be seen, the stormy weather having hidden it when we first entered the bay. It was now perfectly clear, and the spacious, prairie-like glacier, with its many tributaries extending far back into the snowy recesses of its fountains, made a magnificent display of its wealth, and I was strongly tempted to go and explore it at all hazards. But winter had come, and the freezing of its fiords was an insurmountable obstacle. I had, therefore, to be content for the present with sketching and studying its main features at a distance.

When we arrived at the Hoona hunting-camp, men, women, and children came swarming out to welcome us. In the neighborhood of this camp I carefully noted the lines of demarkation between the forested and deforested regions. Several mountains here are only in part deforested, and the lines separating the bare and the forested portions are well defined. The soil, as well as the trees, had slid off the steep slopes, leaving the edge of the woods raw-looking and rugged.

At the mouth of the bay a series of moraine islands show that the trunk glacier that occupied the bay halted here for some time and deposited this island material as a terminal moraine; that more of the bay was not filled in shows that, after lingering here, it receded comparatively fast. All the level portions of trunks of glaciers occupying ocean fiords, instead of melting back gradually in times of general shrinking and recession, as inland glaciers with sloping channels do, melt almost uniformly over all the surface until they become thin enough to float. Then, of course, with each rise and fall of the tide, the sea water, with a temperature usually considerably above the freezing-point, rushes in and out beneath them, causing rapid waste of the nether surface, while the upper is being wasted by the weather, until at length the fiord portions of these great glaciers become comparatively thin and weak and are broken up and vanish almost simultaneously.

Glacier Bay is undoubtedly young as yet. Vancouver's chart, made only a century ago, shows no trace of it, though found admirably faithful in general. It seems probable, therefore, that even then the entire bay was occupied by a glacier of which all those described above, great though they are, were only tributaries. Nearly as great a change has taken place in Sum Dum Bay since Vancouver's visit, the main trunk glacier there having receded from eighteen to twenty-five miles from the line marked on his chart. Charley, who was here when a boy, said that the place had so changed that he hardly recognized it, so many new islands had been born in the mean time and so much ice had vanished. As we

The Muir Glacier in the Seventies, Showing Ice Cliffs and Stranded Ice

have seen, this Icy Bay is being still farther extended by the recession of the glaciers. That this whole system of fiords and channels was added to the domain of the sea by glacial action is to my mind certain.

We reached the island from which we had obtained our store of fuel about half-past six and camped here for the night, having spent only five days in Sitadaka, sailing round it, visiting and sketching all the six glaciers excepting the largest, though I landed only on three of them,—the Geikie, Hugh Miller, and Grand Pacific,—the freezing of the fiords in front of the others rendering them inaccessible at this late season.

CHAPTER XI

The Country of the Chilcats

On October 30 we visited a camp of Hoonas at the mouth of a salmon-chuck. We had seen some of them before, and they received us kindly. Here we learned that peace reigned in Chilcat. The reports that we had previously heard were, as usual in such cases, wildly exaggerated. The little camp hut of these Indians was crowded with the food-supplies they had gathered—chiefly salmon, dried and tied in bunches of convenient size for handling and transporting to their villages, bags of salmon-roe, boxes of fish-oil, a lot of mountain-goat mutton, and a few porcupines. They presented us with some dried salmon and potatoes, for which we gave them tobacco and rice. About 3 P.M. we reached their village, and in the best house, that of a chief, we found the family busily engaged in making whiskey. The still and mash were speedily removed and hidden away with apparent shame as soon as we came in sight. When we entered and passed the regular greetings, the usual apologies as to being unable to furnish Boston food for us and inquiries whether we could eat Indian food were gravely made. Toward six or seven o'clock Mr. Young explained the object of his visit and held a short service. The chief replied with grave deliberation, saying that he would be heartily glad to have a teacher sent to his poor ignorant people, upon whom he now hoped the light of a better day was beginning to break. Hereafter he would gladly do whatever the white teachers told him to do and would have no will of his own. This under the whiskey circumstances seemed too good to be quite true. He thanked us over and over again for coming so far to see him, and complained that Port Simpson Indians, sent out on a missionary tour by Mr. Crosby, after making a good-luck board for him and nailing it over his door, now wanted to take it away. Mr. Young promised to make him a new one, should this threat be executed, and remarked that since he had offered to do his bidding he hoped he would make no more whiskey. To this the chief replied with fresh complaints concerning the threatened loss of his precious board, saying that he thought the Port Simpson Indians were very mean in seeking to take it away, but that now he would tell them to take it as soon as they liked for he was going to get a better one at Wrangell. But no effort of the missionary could bring him to notice or discuss the whiskey business. The luck board nailed over the door was about two feet long and had the following inscription: "The Lord will bless those who do his will. When you rise in the morning, and when you retire at night, give him thanks. Heccla Hockla Popla."

This chief promised to pray like a white man every morning, and to bury the dead as the whites do. "I often wondered," he said, "where the dead went to. Now I am glad to know"; and at last acknowledged the whiskey, saying he was sorry to have been caught making the bad stuff. The behavior of all, even the little ones circled around the fire, was very good. There was no laughter when the strange singing commenced. They only gazed like curious, intelligent animals. A little daughter of the chief with the glow of the fire-light on her eyes made an interesting picture, head held aslant. Another in the group, with upturned eyes, seeming to half understand the strange words about God, might have passed for one of Raphael's angels.

The chief's house was about forty feet square, of the ordinary fort kind, but better built and cleaner than usual. The side-room doors were neatly paneled, though all the lumber had been nibbled into shape with a small narrow Indian adze. We had our tent pitched on a grassy spot near the beach, being afraid of wee beasties; which greatly offended Kadachan and old Toyatte, who said, "If this is the way you are to do up at Chilcat, we will be ashamed of you." We promised them to eat Indian food and in every way behave like good Chilcats.

We set out direct for Chilcat in the morning against a brisk head wind. By keeping close inshore and working hard, we made about ten miles by two or three o'clock, when, the tide having turned against us, we could make scarce any headway, and therefore landed in a sheltered cove a few miles up the west side of Lynn Canal. Here I discovered a fine growth of yellow cedar, but none of the trees were very large, the tallest only seventy-five to one hundred feet high. The flat, drooping, plume-like branchlets hang edgewise, giving the trees a thin, open, airy look. Nearly every tree that I saw in a long walk was more or less marked by the knives and axes of the Indians, who use the bark for matting, for covering house-roofs, and making temporary portable huts. For this last purpose sections five or six feet long and two or three wide are pressed flat and secured from warping or splitting by binding them with thin strips of wood at the end. These they carry about with them in their canoes, and in a few minutes they can be put together against slim poles and made into a rainproof hut. Every paddle that I have seen along the coast is made of the light, tough, handsome yellow wood of this tree. It is a tree of moderately rapid growth and usually chooses ground that is rather boggy and mossy. Whether its network of roots makes the bog or not, I am unable as yet to say.

Three glaciers on the opposite side of the canal were in sight, descending nearly to sea-level, and many smaller ones that melt a little below timber-line. While I was sketching these, a canoe hove in sight, coming on at a flying rate of speed before the wind. The owners, eager for news, paid us a visit. They proved to be Hoonas, a man, his wife, and four children, on their way home from Chilcat. The man was sitting in the stern steering and holding a sleeping child in his arms. Another lay asleep at his feet. He told us that

Sitka Jack had gone up to the main Chilcat village the day before he left, intending to hold a grand feast and potlatch, and that whiskey up there was flowing like water. The news was rather depressing to Mr. Young and myself, for we feared the effect of the poison on Toyatte's old enemies. At 8.30 P.M. we set out again on the turn of the tide, though the crew did not relish this night work. Naturally enough, they liked to stay in camp when wind and tide were against us, but didn't care to make up lost time after dark however wooingly wind and tide might flow and blow. Kadachan, John, and Charley rowed, and Toyatte steered and paddled, assisted now and then by me. The wind moderated and almost died away, so that we made about fifteen miles in six hours, when the tide turned and snow began to fall. We ran into a bay nearly opposite Berner's Bay, where three or four families of Chilcats were camped, who shouted when they heard us landing and demanded our names. Our men ran to the huts for news before making camp. The Indians proved to be hunters, who said there were plenty of wild sheep on the mountains back a few miles from the head of the bay. This interview was held at three o'clock in the morning, a rather early hour. But Indians never resent any such disturbance provided there is anything worth while to be said or done. By four o'clock we had our tents set, a fire made and some coffee, while the snow was falling fast. Toyatte was out of humor with this night business. He wanted to land an hour or two before we did, and then, when the snow began to fall and we all wanted to find a camping-ground as soon as possible, he steered out into the middle of the canal, saying grimly that the tide was good. He turned, however, at our orders, but read us a lecture at the first opportunity, telling us to start early if we were in a hurry, but not to travel in the night like thieves.

After a few hours' sleep, we set off again, with the wind still against us and the sea rough. We were all tired after making only about twelve miles, and camped in a rocky nook where we found a family of Hoonas in their bark hut beside their canoe. They presented us with potatoes and salmon and a big bucketful of berries, salmon-roe, and grease of some sort, probably fish-oil, which the crew consumed with wonderful relish.

A fine breeze was blowing next morning from the south, which would take us to Chilcat in a few hours, but unluckily the day was Sunday and the good wind was refused. Sunday, it seemed to me, could be kept as well by sitting in the canoe and letting the Lord's wind waft us quietly on our way. The day was rainy and the clouds hung low. The trees here are remarkably well developed, tall and straight. I observed three or four hemlocks which had been struck by lightning,—the first I noticed in Alaska. Some of the species on windy outjutting rocks become very picturesque, almost as much so as old oaks, the foliage becoming dense and the branchlets tufted in heavy plume-shaped horizontal masses.

Monday was a fine clear day, but the wind was dead ahead, making hard, dull work with paddles and oars. We passed a long stretch of beautiful marble cliffs enlivened with small merry waterfalls, and toward noon came in sight of the front of the famous Chilcat or Davidson Glacier, a broad white flood reaching out two or three miles into the canal with wonderful effect. I wanted to camp beside it but the head wind tired us out before we got within six or eight miles of it. We camped on the west side of a small rocky island in a narrow cove. When I was looking among the rocks and bushes for a smooth spot for a bed, I found a human skeleton. My Indians seemed not in the least shocked or surprised, explaining that it was only the remains of a Chilcat slave. Indians never bury or burn the bodies of slaves, but just cast them away anywhere. Kind Nature was covering the poor bones with moss and leaves, and I helped in the pitiful work.

The wind was fair and joyful in the morning, and away we glided to the famous glacier. In an hour or so we were directly in front of it and beheld it in all its crystal glory descending from its white mountain fountains and spreading out in an immense fan three or four miles wide against its tree-fringed terminal moraine. But, large as it is, it long ago ceased to discharge bergs.

The Chilcats are the most influential of all the Thlinkit tribes. Whenever on our journey I spoke of the interesting characteristics of other tribes we had visited, my crew would invariably say, "Oh, yes, these are pretty good Indians, but wait till you have seen the

Chilcats." We were now only five or six miles distant from their lower village, and my crew requested time to prepare themselves to meet their great rivals. Going ashore on the moraine with their boxes that had not been opened since we left Fort Wrangell, they sat on boulders and cut each other's hair, carefully washed and perfumed themselves and made a complete change in their clothing, even to white shirts, new boots, new hats, and bright neckties. Meanwhile, I scrambled across the broad, brushy, forested moraine, and on my return scarcely recognized my crew in their dress suits. Mr. Young also made some changes in his clothing, while I, having nothing dressy in my bag, adorned my cap with an eagle's feather I found on the moraine, and thus arrayed we set forth to meet the noble Thlinkits.

We were discovered while we were several miles from the village, and as we entered the mouth of the river we were hailed by a messenger from the chief, sent to find out who we were and the objects of our extraordinary visit.

"Who are you?" he shouted in a heavy, far-reaching voice. "What are your names? What do you want? What have you come for?"

On receiving replies, he shouted the information to another messenger, who was posted on the river-bank at a distance of a quarter of a mile or so, and he to another and another in succession, and by this living telephone the news was delivered to the chief as he sat by his fireside. A salute was then fired to welcome us, and a swarm of musket-bullets, flying scarce high enough for comfort, pinged over our heads. As soon as we reached the landing at the village, a dignified young man stepped forward and thus addressed us:—

"My chief sent me to meet you, and to ask if you would do him the honor to lodge in his house during your stay in our village?"

We replied, of course, that we would consider it a great honor to be entertained by so distinguished a chief.

The messenger then ordered a number of slaves, who stood behind him, to draw our canoe out of the water, carry our provisions and bedding into the chief's house, and then carry the canoe back from the river where it would be beyond the reach of floating ice. While we waited, a lot of boys and girls were playing on a meadow near the landing—running races, shooting arrows, and wading in the icy river without showing any knowledge of our presence beyond quick stolen glances. After all was made secure, he conducted us to the house, where we found seats of honor prepared for us.

The old chief sat barefooted by the fireside, clad in a calico shirt and blanket, looking down, and though we shook hands as we passed him he did not look up. After we were seated, he still gazed into the fire without taking the slightest notice of us for about ten or fifteen minutes. The various members of the chief's family, also,—men, women, and children,—went about their usual employment and play as if entirely unconscious that strangers were in the house, it being considered impolite to look at visitors or speak to them before time had been allowed them to collect their thoughts and prepare any message they might have to deliver.

At length, after the politeness period had passed, the chief slowly raised his head and glanced at his visitors, looked down again, and at last said, through our interpreter:—

"I am troubled. It is customary when strangers visit us to offer them food in case they might be hungry, and I was about to do so, when I remembered that the food of you honorable white chiefs is so much better than mine that I am ashamed to offer it."

We, of course, replied that we would consider it a great honor to enjoy the hospitality of so distinguished a chief as he was.

Hearing this, he looked up, saying, "I feel relieved"; or, in John the interpreter's words, "He feels good now, he says he feels good."

He then ordered one of his family to see that the visitors were fed. The young man who was to act as steward took up his position in a corner of the house commanding a view of all that was going on, and ordered the slaves to make haste to prepare a good meal; one to bring a lot of the best potatoes from the cellar and wash them well; another to go out and pick a basketful of fresh berries; another to broil a salmon; while others made a suitable fire, pouring oil on the wet wood to make it blaze. Speedily the feast was prepared and passed around. The first course was potatoes, the second fish-oil and salmon, next berries and rose-hips; then the steward

shouted the important news, in a loud voice like a herald address-
ing an army, "That's all!" and left his post.

Then followed all sorts of questions from the old chief. He
wanted to know what Professor Davidson had been trying to do a
year or two ago on a mountain-top back of the village, with many
strange things looking at the sun when it grew dark in the daytime;
and we had to try to explain eclipses. He asked us if we could tell
him what made the water rise and fall twice a day, and we tried to
explain that the sun and moon attracted the sea by showing how a
magnet attracted iron.

Mr. Young, as usual, explained the object of his visit and requested that the people might be called together in the evening to
hear his message. Accordingly all were told to wash, put on their
best clothing, and come at a certain hour. There was an audience of
about two hundred and fifty, to whom Mr. Young preached. Toyatte
led in prayer, while Kadachan and John joined in the singing of several hymns. At the conclusion of the religious exercises the chief
made a short address of thanks, and finished with a request for the
message of the other chief. I again tried in vain to avoid a speech by
telling the interpreter to explain that I was only traveling to see the
country, the glaciers, and mountains and forests, etc., but these subjects, strange to say, seemed to be about as interesting as the gospel,
and I had to deliver a sort of lecture on the fine foodful country
God had given them and the brotherhood of man, along the same
general lines I had followed at other villages. Some five similar
meetings were held here, two of them in the daytime, and we began
to feel quite at home in the big block-house with our hospitable
and war-like friends.

At the last meeting an old white-haired shaman of grave and
venerable aspect, with a high wrinkled forehead, big, strong Roman
nose and light-colored skin, slowly and with great dignity arose
and spoke for the first time.

"I am an old man," he said, "but I am glad to listen to those
strange things you tell, and they may well be true, for what is more
wonderful than the flight of birds in the air? I remember the first
white man I ever saw. Since that long, long-ago time I have seen

many, but never until now have I ever truly known and felt a white man's heart. All the white men I have heretofore met wanted to get something from us. They wanted furs and they wished to pay for them as small a price as possible. They all seemed to be seeking their own good—not our good. I might say that through all my long life I have never until now heard a white man speak. It has always seemed to me while trying to speak to traders and those seeking gold-mines that it was like speaking to a person across a broad stream that was running fast over stones and making so loud a noise that scarce a single word could be heard. But now, for the first time, the Indian and the white man are on the same side of the river, eye to eye, heart to heart. I have always loved my people. I have taught them and ministered to them as well as I could. Hereafter, I will keep silent and listen to the good words of the missionaries, who know God and the places we go to when we die so much better than I do."

At the close of the exercises, after the last sermon had been preached and the last speech of the Indian chief and head men had been made, a number of the sub-chiefs were talking informally together. Mr. Young, anxious to know what impression he had made on the tribe with reference to mission work, requested John to listen and tell him what was being said.

"They are talking about Mr. Muir's speech," he reported. "They say he knows how to talk and beats the preacher far." Toyatte also, with a teasing smile, said: "Mr. Young, mika tillicum hi yu tola wawa" (your friend leads you far in speaking).

Later, when the sending of a missionary and teacher was being considered, the chief said they wanted me, and, as an inducement, promised that if I would come to them they would always do as I directed, follow my councils, give me as many wives as I liked, build a church and school, and pick all the stones out of the paths and make them smooth for my feet.

They were about to set out on an expedition to the Hootsenoos to collect blankets as indemnity or blood-money for the death of a Chilcat woman from drinking whiskey furnished by one of the Hootsenoo tribe. In case of their refusal to pay, there would be fighting, and one of the chiefs begged that we would pray them good luck, so that no one would be killed. This he asked as a favor, after begging that we would grant permission to go on this expedition, promising that they would avoid bloodshed if possible. He spoke in a very natural and easy tone and manner, always serene and so much of a polished diplomat that all polish was hidden. The younger chief stood while speaking, the elder sat on the floor. None of the congregation had a word to say, though they gave approving nods and shrugs.

The house was packed at every meeting, two a day. Some climbed on the roof to listen around the smoke opening. I tried in vain to avoid speechmaking, but, as usual, I had to say something at every meeting. I made five speeches here, all of which seemed to be gladly heard, particularly what I said on the different kinds of white men and their motives, and their own kindness and good manners in making strangers feel at home in their houses.

The chief had a slave, a young and good-looking girl, who waited on him, cooked his food, lighted his pipe for him, etc. Her servitude seemed by no means galling. In the morning, just before we left on the return trip, interpreter John overheard him telling her that after the teacher came from Wrangell, he was going to dress her well and send her to school and use her in every way as if she were his own daughter. Slaves are still owned by the richest of the Thlinkits. Formerly, many of them were sacrificed on great occasions, such as the opening of a new house or the erection of a totem pole. Kadachan ordered John to take a pair of white blankets out of his trunk and wrap them about the chief's shoulders, as he sat by the fire. This gift was presented without ceremony or saying a single word. The chief scarcely noticed the blankets, only taking a corner in his hand, as if testing the quality of the wool. Toyatte had been an inveterate enemy and fighter of the Chilcats, but now, having joined the church, he wished to forget the past and bury all the hard feuds and be universally friendly and peaceful. It was evident, however, that he mistrusted the proud and warlike Chilcats and doubted the acceptance of his friendly advances, and as we approached their village became more and more thoughtful.

"My wife said that my old enemies would be sure to kill me. Well, never mind. I am an old man and may as well die as not." He was troubled with palpitation, and oftentimes, while he suffered, he put his hand over his heart and said, "I hope the Chilcats will shoot me here."

Before venturing up the river to the principal village, located some ten miles up the river, we sent Sitka Charley and one of the young Chilcats as messengers to announce our arrival and inquire whether we would be welcome to visit them, informing the chief that both Kadachan and Toyatte were Mr. Young's friends and mine, that we were "all one meat" and any harm done them would also be done to us.

While our messengers were away, I climbed a pure-white, dome-crowned mountain about fifty-five hundred feet high and gained noble telling views to the northward of the main Chilcat glaciers and the multitude of mighty peaks from which they draw their sources. At a height of three thousand feet I found a mountain hemlock, considerably dwarfed, in company with Sitka spruce and the common hemlock, the tallest about twenty feet high, sixteen inches in diameter. A few stragglers grew considerably higher, say at about four thousand feet. Birch and two-leaf pine were common.

The messengers returned next day, bringing back word that we would all be heartily welcomed excepting Toyatte; that the guns were loaded and ready to be fired to welcome us, but that Toyatte, having insulted a Chilcat chief not long ago in Wrangell, must not come. They also informed us in their message that they were very busy merrymaking with other visitors, Sitka Jack and his friends, but that if we could get up to the village through the running ice on the river, they would all be glad to see us; they had been drinking and Kadachan's father, one of the principal chiefs, said plainly that he had just waked up out of a ten days' sleep. We were anxious to make this visit, but, taking the difficulties and untoward circumstances into account, the danger of being frozen in at so late a time, while Kadachan would not be able to walk back on account of a shot in his foot, the danger also from whiskey, the awakening of old feuds on account of Toyatte's presence, etc., we reluctantly concluded to start back on the home journey at once. This was on Friday and a fair wind was blowing, but our crew, who loved dearly to rest and eat in these big hospitable houses, all said that Monday would be *hyas klosh* for the starting-day. I insisted, however, on starting Saturday morning, and succeeded in getting away from our friends at ten o'clock. Just as we were leaving, the chief who had entertained us so handsomely requested a written document to show that he had not killed us, so in case we were lost on the way home he could not be held accountable in any way for our death.

CHAPTER XII

THE RETURN TO FORT WRANGELL

The day of our start for Wrangell was bright and the Hoon, the north wind, strong. We passed around the east side of the larger island which lies near the south extremity of the point of land between the Chilcat and the Chilcoot channels and thence held a direct course down the east shore of the canal. At sunset we encamped in a small bay at the head of a beautiful harbor three or four miles south of Berner's Bay, and the next day, being Sunday, we remained in camp as usual, though the wind was fair and it is not a sin to go home. The Indians spent most of the day in washing, mending, eating, and singing hymns with Mr. Young, who also gave them a Bible lesson, while I wrote notes and sketched. Charley made a sweathouse and all the crew got good baths. This is one of the most delightful little bays we have thus far enjoyed, girdled with tall trees whose branches almost meet, and with views of pure-white mountains across the broad, river-like canal.

Seeing smoke back in the dense woods, we went ashore to seek it and discovered a Hootsenoo whiskey-factory in full blast. The Indians said that an old man, a friend of theirs, was about to die and they were making whiskey for his funeral.

Our Indians were already out of oily flesh, which they regard as a necessity and consume in enormous quantities. The bacon was nearly gone and they eagerly inquired for flesh at every camp we passed. Here we found skinned carcasses of porcupines and a heap of wild mutton lying on the confused hut floor. Our cook boiled the porcupines in a big pot with a lot of potatoes we obtained at the same hut, and although the potatoes were protected by their skins, the awfully wild penetrating porcupine flavor found a way through the skins and flavored them to the very heart. Bread and beans and dried fruit we had in abundance, and none of these rank aboriginal dainties ever came nigh any meal of mine. The Indians eat the hips of wild roses entire like berries, and I was laughed at for eating only the outside of this fruit and rejecting the seeds.

When we were approaching the village of the Auk tribe, venerable Toyatte seemed to be unusually pensive, as if weighed down by some melancholy thought. This was so unusual that I waited attentively to find out the cause of his trouble.

When at last he broke silence it was to say, "Mr. Young, Mr. Young,"—he usually repeated the name,—"I hope you will not stop at the Auk village."

"Why, Toyatte?" asked Mr. Young.

"Because they are a bad lot, and preaching to them can do no good."

"Toyatte," said Mr. Young, "have you forgotten what Christ said to his disciples when he charged them to go forth and preach the gospel to everybody; and that we should love our enemies and do good to those who use us badly?"

"Well," replied Toyatte, "if you preach to them, you must not call on me to pray, because I cannot pray for Auks."

"But the Bible says we should pray for all men, however bad they may be."

"Oh, yes, I know that, Mr. Young; I know it very well. But Auks are not men, good or bad,—they are dogs."

It was now nearly dark and quite so ere we found a harbor, not far from the fine Auk Glacier which descends into the narrow channel that separates Douglas Island from the mainland. Two of the Auks followed us to our camp after eight o'clock and inquired into our object in visiting them, that they might carry the news to their chief. One of the chief's houses is opposite our camp a mile or two distant, and we concluded to call on him next morning.

I wanted to examine the Auk Glacier in the morning, but tried to be satisfied with a general view and sketch as we sailed around its wide fan-shaped front. It is one of the most beautiful of all the coast glaciers that are in the first stage of decadence. We called on the Auk chief at daylight, when he was yet in bed, but he arose good-naturedly, put on a calico shirt, drew a blanket around his legs, and comfortably seated himself beside a small fire that gave light enough to show his features and those of his children and the three women that one by one came out of the shadows. All listened attentively to Mr. Young's message of good-will. The chief was a serious, sharp-featured, dark-complexioned man, sensible-looking and with good manners. He was very sorry, he said, that his people had been drinking in his absence and had used us so ill; he would like to hear us talk and would call his people together if we would return to the village. This offer we had to decline. We gave him good words and tobacco and bade him good-bye.

The scenery all through the channel is magnificent, something like Yosemite Valley in its lofty avalanche-swept wall cliffs, especially on the mainland side, which are so steep few trees can find footing. The lower island side walls are mostly forested. The trees are heavily draped with lichens, giving the woods a remarkably gray, ancient look. I noticed a good many two-leafed pines in boggy spots. The water was smooth, and the reflections of the lofty walls striped with cascades were charmingly distinct.

It was not easy to keep my crew full of wild flesh. We called at an Indian summer camp on the mainland about noon, where there were three very squalid huts crowded and jammed full of flesh of many colors and smells, among which we discovered a lot of bright fresh trout, lovely creatures about fifteen inches long, their sides adorned with vivid red spots. We purchased five of them and a couple of salmon for a box of gun-caps and a little tobacco. About the middle of the afternoon we passed through a fleet of icebergs, their number increasing as we neared the mouth of the Taku Fiord, where we camped, hoping to explore the fiord and see the glaciers where the bergs, the first we had seen since leaving Icy Bay, are derived.

We left camp at six o'clock, nearly an hour before daybreak. My Indians were glad to find the fiord barred by a violent wind, against which we failed to make any headway; and as it was too late in the season to wait for better weather, I reluctantly gave up this promising work for another year, and directed the crew to go straight ahead down the coast. We sailed across the mouth of the happy inlet at fine speed, keeping a man at the bow to look out for the smallest of the bergs, not easily seen in the dim light, and another bailing the canoe as the tops of some of the white caps broke over us. About two o'clock we passed a large bay or fiord, out of which a violent wind was blowing, though the main Stephens Passage was calm. About dusk, when we were all tired and anxious to get into camp, we reached the mouth of Sum Dum Bay, but nothing like a safe landing could we find. Our experienced captain was indignant, as well he might be, because we did not see fit to stop early in the afternoon at a good camp-ground he had chosen. He seemed determined to give us enough of night sailing as a punishment to last us for the rest of the voyage. Accordingly, though the night was dark and rainy and the bay full of icebergs, he pushed grimly on, saying that we must try to reach an Indian village on the other side of the bay or an old Indian fort on an island in the middle of it. We made slow, weary, anxious progress while Toyatte, who was well acquainted with every feature of this part of the coast and could find his way in the dark, only laughed at our misery. After a mile or two of this dismal night work we struck across toward the island, now invisible, and came near being wrecked on a rock which showed a smooth round back over which the waves were breaking. In the hurried Indian shouts that followed and while we were close against the rock, Mr. Young shouted, as he leaned over against me, "It's a whale, a whale!" evidently fearing its tail, several specimens of these animals, which were probably still on his mind, having been seen in the forenoon. While we were passing along the east shore of the island we saw a light on the opposite shore, a joyful sight, which Toyatte

Stranded Icebergs, Taku Glacier

took for a fire in the Indian village, and steered for it. John stood in the bow, as guide through the bergs. Suddenly, we ran aground on a sand bar. Clearing this, and running back half a mile or so, we again stood for the light, which now shone brightly. I thought it strange that Indians should have so large a fire. A broad white mass dimly visible back of the fire Mr. Young took for the glow of the fire on the clouds. This proved to be the front of a glacier. After we had effected a landing and stumbled up toward the fire over a ledge of slippery, algæ-covered rocks, and through the ordinary tangle of shore grass, we were astonished to find white men instead of Indians, the first we had seen for a month. They proved to be a party of seven gold-seekers from Fort Wrangell. It was now about eight o'clock and they were in bed, but a jolly Irishman got up to make coffee for us and find out who we were, where we had come from, where going, and the objects of our travels. We unrolled our chart and asked for information as to the extent and features of the bay. But our benevolent friend took great pains to pull wool over our eyes, and made haste to say that if "ice and sceneries" were what we were looking for, this was a very poor, dull place. There were "big rocks, gulches, and sceneries" of a far better quality down the coast on the way to Wrangell. He and his party were prospecting, he said, but thus far they had found only a few colors and they proposed going over to Admiralty Island in the morning to try their luck.

In the morning, however, when the prospectors were to have gone over to the island, we noticed a smoke half a mile back on a large stream, the outlet of the glacier we had seen the night before, and an Indian told us that the white men were building a big log house up there. It appeared that they had found a promising placer mine in the moraine and feared we might find it and spread the news. Daylight revealed a magnificent fiord that brought Glacier Bay to mind. Miles of bergs lay stranded on the shores, and the waters of the branch fiords, not on Vancouver's chart, were crowded with them as far as the eye could reach. After breakfast we set out to explore an arm of the bay that trends southeastward, and managed to force a way through the bergs about ten miles. Farther we could not go. The pack was so close no open water was in sight, and, convinced at last that this part of my work would have to be left for another year, we struggled across to the west side of the fiord and camped.

I climbed a mountain next morning, hoping to gain a view of the great fruitful glaciers at the head of the fiord or, at least, of their snowy fountains. But in this also I failed; for at a distance of about sixteen miles from the mouth of the fiord a change to the north-ward in its general trend cut off all its upper course from sight.

Returning to camp baffled and weary, I ordered all hands to pack up and get out of the ice as soon as possible. And how gladly was that order obeyed! Toyatte's grand countenance glowed like a sun-filled glacier, as he joyfully and teasingly remarked that "the big Sum Dum ice-mountain had hidden his face from me and refused to let me pay him a visit." All the crew worked hard boring a way down the west side of the fiord, and early in the afternoon we reached comparatively open water near the mouth of the bay. Resting a few minutes among the drifting bergs, taking last linger-ing looks at the wonderful place I might never see again, and feel-ing sad over my weary failure to explore it, I was cheered by a friend I little expected to meet here. Suddenly, I heard the familiar whir of an ousel's wings, and, looking up, saw my little comforter coming straight from the shore. In a second or two he was with me, and flew three times around my head with a happy salute, as if say-ing, "Cheer up, old friend, you see I am here and all's well." He then flew back to the shore, alighted on the topmost jag of a stranded iceberg, and began to nod and bow as though he were on one of his favorite rocks in the middle of a sunny California mountain cataract.

Mr. Young regretted not meeting the Indians here, but mission work also had to be left until next season. Our happy crew hoisted sail to a fair wind, shouted "Good-bye, Sum Dum!" and soon after dark reached a harbor a few miles north of Hobart Point.

We made an early start the next day, a fine, calm morning, glided smoothly down the coast, admiring the magnificent mountains ar-rayed in their winter robes, and early in the afternoon reached a lovely harbor on an island five or six miles north of Cape Fanshawe. Toyatte predicted a heavy winter storm, though only a mild rain was falling as yet. Everybody was tired and hungry, and as the voyage was nearing the end, I consented to stop here. While the shelter tents were being set up and our blankets stowed under cover, John went out to hunt and killed a deer within two hundred yards of the camp. When we were at the camp-fire in Sum Dum Bay, one of the prospectors, replying to Mr. Young's complaint that they were oftentimes out of meat, asked Toyatte why he and his men did not shoot plenty of ducks for the minister. "Because the duck's friend would not let us," said Toyatte; "when we want to shoot, Mr. Muir always shakes the canoe."

Just as we were passing the south headland of Port Houghton Bay, we heard a shout, and a few minutes later saw four Indians in a canoe paddling rapidly after us. In about an hour they overtook us. They were an Indian, his son, and two women with a load of fish-oil and dried salmon to sell and trade at Fort Wrangell. They camped within a dozen yards of us; with their sheets of cedar bark and poles they speedily made a hut, spread spruce boughs in it for a carpet, unloaded the canoe, and stored their goods under cover. Toward evening the old man came smiling with a gift for Toyatte, —a large fresh salmon, which was promptly boiled and eaten by our captain and crew as if it were only a light refreshment like a biscuit between meals. A few minutes after the big salmon had vanished, our generous neighbor came to Toyatte with a second gift of dried salmon, which after being toasted a few minutes tranquilly followed the fresh one as though it were a mere mouthful. Then, from the same generous hands, came a third gift,—a large milk-panful of huckleberries and grease boiled together,—and, strange to say, this wonderful mess went smoothly down to rest on the broad and deep salmon foundation. Thus refreshed, and appetite sharpened, my sturdy crew made haste to begin on the buck, beans, bread, etc., and, boiling and roasting, managed to get comfortably full on but little more than half of it by sundown, making a good deal of sport of my pity for the deer and refusing to eat any of it and nicknaming me the ice *ancou* and the deer and duck's *tillicum*.

Sunday was a wild, driving, windy day with but little rain but big promise of more. I took a walk back in the woods. The timber here is very fine, about as large as any I have seen in Alaska, much better than farther north. The Sitka spruce and the common hemlock, one hundred and fifty and two hundred feet high, are slender and handsome. The Sitka spruce makes good firewood even when green, the hemlock very poor. Back a little way from the sea, there was a good deal of yellow cedar, the best I had yet seen. The largest specimen that I saw and measured on the trip was five feet three inches in diameter and about one hundred and forty feet high. In the evening Mr. Young gave the Indians a lesson, calling in our Indian neighbors. He told them the story of Christ coming to save the world. The Indians wanted to know why the Jews had killed him. The lesson was listened to with very marked attention. Toyatte's generous friend caught a devil-fish about three feet in diameter to add to his stores of food. It would be very good, he said, when boiled in berry and colicon-oil soup. Each arm of this savage animal with its double row of button-like suction discs closed upon any object brought within reach with a grip nothing could escape. The Indians tell me that devil-fish live mostly on crabs, mussels, and clams, the shells of which they easily crunch with their strong, parrot-like beaks. That was a wild, stormy, rainy night. How the rain soaked us in our tents!

"Just feel that," said the minister in the night, as he took my hand and plunged it into a pool about three inches deep in which he was lying.

"Never mind," I said, "it is only water. Everything is wet now. It will soon be morning and we will dry at the fire."

Our Indian neighbors were, if possible, still wetter. Their hut had been blown down several times during the night. Our tent leaked badly, and we were lying in a mossy bog, but around the big camp-fire we were soon warm and half dry. We had expected to reach Wrangell by this time. Toyatte said the storm might last several days longer. We were out of tea and coffee, much to Mr. Young's distress. On my return from a walk I brought in a good big bunch of glandular ledum and boiled it in the teapot. The result of this experiment was a bright, clear amber-colored, rank-smelling liquor which I did not taste, but my suffering companion drank the whole potful and praised it. The rain was so heavy we decided not to attempt to leave camp until the storm somewhat abated, as we were assured by Toyatte that we would not be able to round Cape Fanshawe, a sheer, outjutting headland, the nose as he called it, past which the wind sweeps with great violence in these southeastern storms. With what grateful enthusiasm the trees welcomed the life-giving rain! Strong, towering spruces, hemlocks, and cedars tossed their arms, bowing, waving, in every leap, quivering and rejoicing together in the gray, roaring storm. John and Charley put on their gun-coats and went hunting for another deer, but returned later in the afternoon with clean hands, having fortunately failed to shed any more blood. The wind still held in the south, and Toyatte, grimly trying to comfort us, told us that we might be held here a week or more, which we should not have minded much, for we had abundance of provisions. Mr. Young and I shifted our tent and tried to dry blankets. The wind moderated considerably, and at 7 A.M. we started but met a rough sea and so stiff a wind we barely succeeded in rounding the cape by all hands pulling their best. Thence we struggled down the coast, creeping close to the shore and taking advantage of the shelter of protecting rocks, making slow, hard-won progress until about the middle of the afternoon, when the sky opened and the blessed sun shone out over the beautiful waters and forests with rich amber light; and the high, glacier-laden mountains, adorned with fresh snow, slowly came to view in all their grandeur, the bluish-gray clouds crawling and lingering and dissolving until every vestige of them vanished. The sunlight made the upper snow-fields pale creamy yellow, like that seen on the Chilcat mountains the first day of our return trip. Shortly after the sky cleared, the wind abated and changed around to the north, so that we ventured to hoist our sail, and then the weary Indians had rest. It was interesting to note how speedily the heavy swell that had been rolling for the last two or three days was subdued by the comparatively light breeze from the opposite direction. In a few minutes the sound was smooth and no trace of the storm was left, save the fresh snow and the discoloration of the water. All the water of the sound as far as I noticed was pale coffee-color like that of the streams in boggy woods. How much of this color was due to the inflow of the flooded streams many times increased in size and number by the rain, and how much to the beating of the waves along the shore stirring up vegetable matter in shallow bays, I cannot determine. The effect, however, was very marked.

About four o'clock we saw smoke on the shore and ran in for news. We found a company of Taku Indians, who were on their way to Fort Wrangell, some six men and about the same number of women. The men were sitting in a bark hut, handsomely reinforced and embowered with fresh spruce boughs. The women were out at the side of a stream, washing their many bits of calico. A little girl, six or seven years old, was sitting on the gravelly beach, building a playhouse of white quartz pebbles, scarcely caring to stop her work to gaze at us. Toyatte found a friend among the men, and wished to encamp beside them for the night, assuring us that this was the only safe harbor to be found within a good many miles. But we resolved to push on a little farther and make use of the smooth weather after being stormbound so long, much to Toyatte and his companion's disgust. We rowed about a couple of miles and ran into a cozy cove where wood and water were close at hand. How beautiful and home-like it was! plushy moss for mattresses decked with red cornel berries, noble spruce standing guard about us and spreading kindly protecting arms. A few ferns, aspidiums, polypodiums, with dewberry vines, coptis, pyrola, leafless huckleberry bushes, and ledum grow beneath the trees. We retired at eight o'clock, and just then Toyatte, who had been attentively studying the sky, presaged rain and another southeaster for the morrow.

The sky was a little cloudy next morning, but the air was still and the water smooth. We all hoped that Toyatte, the old weather prophet, had misread the sky signs. But before reaching Point Vanderpeut the rain began to fall and the dreaded southeast wind to blow, which soon increased to a stiff breeze, next thing to a gale, that lashed the sound into ragged white caps. Cape Vanderpeut is part of the terminal of an ancient glacier that once extended six or

eight miles out from the base of the mountains. Three large glaciers that once were tributaries still descend nearly to the sea-level,
though their fronts are back in narrow fiords, eight or ten miles
from the sound. A similar point juts out into the sound five or six
miles to the south, while the missing portion is submerged and
forms a shoal.

All the cape is forested save a narrow strip about a mile long, composed of large boulders against which the waves beat with loud roaring. A bar of foam a mile or so farther out showed where the waves
were breaking on a submerged part of the moraine, and I supposed
that we would be compelled to pass around it in deep water, but
Toyatte, usually so cautious, determined to cross it, and after giving
particular directions, with an encouraging shout every oar and paddle
was strained to shoot through a narrow gap. Just at the most critical
point a big wave heaved us aloft and dropped us between two huge
rounded boulders, where, had the canoe been a foot or two closer to
either of them, it must have been smashed. Though I had offered no
objection to our experienced pilot's plan, it looked dangerous, and I
took the precaution to untie my shoes so they could be quickly shaken
off for swimming. But after crossing the bar we were not yet out of
danger, for we had to struggle hard to keep from being driven ashore
while the waves were beating us broadside on. At length we discovered a little inlet, into which we gladly escaped. A pure-white iceberg,
weathered to the form of a cross, stood amid drifts of kelp and the
black rocks of the wave-beaten shore in sign of safety and welcome. A
good fire soon warmed and dried us into common comfort. Our narrow escape was the burden of conversation as we sat around the fire.
Captain Toyatte told us of two similar adventures while he was a
strong young man. In both of them his canoe was smashed and he
swam ashore out of the surge with a gun in his teeth. He says that if we
had struck the rocks he and Mr. Young would have been drowned, all
the rest of us probably would have been saved. Then, turning to me,
he asked me if I could have made a fire in such a case without
matches, and found a way to Wrangell without canoe or food.

We started about daybreak from our blessed white cross harbor,
and, after rounding a bluff cape opposite the mouth of Wrangell

Narrows, a fleet of icebergs came in sight, and of course I was eager to trace them to their source. Toyatte naturally enough was greatly excited about the safety of his canoe and begged that we should not venture to force a way through the bergs, risking the loss of the canoe and our lives now that we were so near the end of our long voyage.

"Oh, never fear, Toyatte," I replied. "You know we are always lucky—the weather is good. I only want to see the Thunder Glacier for a few minutes, and should the bergs be packed dangerously close, I promise to turn back and wait until next summer."

Thus assured, he pushed rapidly on until we entered the fiord, where we had to go cautiously slow. The bergs were close packed almost throughout the whole extent of the fiord, but we managed to reach a point about two miles from the head—commanding a good view of the down-plunging lower end of the glacier and blue, jagged ice-wall. This was one of the most imposing of the first-class glaciers I had as yet seen, and with its magnificent fiord formed a fine triumphant close for our season's ice work. I made a few notes and sketches and turned back in time to escape from the thickest packs of bergs before dark. Then Kadachan was stationed in the bow to guide through the open portion of the mouth of the fiord and across Soutchoi Strait. It was not until several hours after dark that we were finally free from ice. We occasionally encountered stranded packs on the delta, which in the starlight seemed to extend indefinitely in every direction. Our danger lay in breaking the canoe on small bergs hard to see and in getting too near the larger ones that might split or roll over.

"Oh, when will we escape from this ice?" moaned much-enduring old Toyatte.

We ran aground in several places in crossing the Stickeen delta, but finally succeeded in groping our way over muddy shallows before the tide fell, and encamped on the boggy shore of a small island, where we discovered a spot dry enough to sleep on, after tumbling about in a tangle of bushes and mossy logs.

We left our last camp November 21 at daybreak. The weather was calm and bright. Wrangell Island came into view beneath a lovely rosy sky, all the forest down to the water's edge silvery gray with a dusting of snow. John and Charley seemed to be seriously distressed to find themselves at the end of their journey while a portion of the stock of provisions remained uneaten. "What is to be done about it?" they asked, more than half in earnest. The fine, strong, and specious deliberation of Indians was well illustrated on this eventful trip. It was fresh every morning. They all behaved well, however, exerted themselves under tedious hardships without flinching for days or weeks at a time; never seemed in the least non-plussed; were prompt to act in every exigency; good as servants, fellow travelers, and even friends.

We landed on an island in sight of Wrangell and built a big smoky signal fire for friends in town, then set sail, unfurled our flag, and about noon completed our long journey of seven or eight hundred miles. As we approached the town, a large canoeful of friendly Indians came flying out to meet us, cheering and handshaking in lusty Boston fashion. The friends of Mr. Young had intended to come out in a body to welcome him back, but had not had time to complete their arrangements before we landed. Mr. Young was eager for news. I told him there could be no news of importance about a town. We only had real news, drawn from the wilderness. The mail steamer had left Wrangell eight days before, and Mr. Vanderbilt and family had sailed on her to Portland. I had to wait a month for the next steamer, and though I would have liked to go again to Nature, the mountains were locked for the winter and canoe excursions no longer safe.

So I shut myself up in a good garret alone to wait and work. I was invited to live with Mr. Young but concluded to prepare my own food and enjoy quiet work. How grandly long the nights were and short the days! At noon the sun seemed to be about an hour high, the clouds colored like sunset. The weather was rather stormy. North winds prevailed for a week at a time, sending down the temperature to near zero and chilling the vapor of the bay into white reek, presenting a curious appearance as it streamed forward on the wind, like combed wool. At Sitka the minimum was eight degrees plus; at Wrangell, near the storm-throat of the Stickeen, zero. This is said to be the coldest weather ever experienced in southeastern Alaska.

CHAPTER XIII

ALASKA INDIANS

Looking back on my Alaska travels, I have always been glad that good luck gave me Mr. Young as a companion, for he brought me into confiding contact with the Thlinkit tribes, so that I learned their customs, what manner of men they were, how they lived and loved, fought and played, their morals, religion, hopes and fears, and superstitions, how they resembled and differed in their characteristics from our own and other races. It was easy to see that they differed greatly from the typical American Indian of the interior of this continent. They were doubtless derived from the Mongol stock. Their down-slanting oval eyes, wide cheek-bones, and rather thick, outstanding upper lips at once suggest their connection with the Chinese or Japanese. I have not seen a single specimen that looks in the least like the best of the Sioux, or indeed of any of the tribes to the east of the Rocky Mountains. They also differ from other North American Indians in being willing to work, when free from the contamination of bad whites. They manage to feed themselves well, build good substantial houses, bravely fight their enemies, love their wives and children and friends, and cherish a quick sense of honor. The best of them prefer death to dishonor, and sympathize with their neighbors in their misfortunes and sorrows.

Thus when a family loses a child by death, neighbors visit them to cheer and console. They gather around the fire and smoke, talk kindly and naturally, telling the sorrowing parents not to grieve too much, reminding them of the better lot of their child in another world and of the troubles and trials the little ones escape by dying young, all this in a perfectly natural, straightforward way, wholly unlike the vacant, silent, hesitating behavior of most civilized friends, who oftentimes in such cases seem nonplussed, awkward, and afraid to speak, however sympathetic.

The Thlinkits are fond and indulgent parents. In all my travels I never heard a cross, fault-finding word, or anything like scolding inflicted on an Indian child, or ever witnessed a single case of spanking, so common in civilized communities. They consider the want of a son to bear their name and keep it alive the saddest and most deplorable ill-fortune imaginable.

The Thlinkit tribes give a hearty welcome to Christian missionaries. In particular they are quick to accept the doctrine of the atonement, because they themselves practice it, although to many of the civilized whites it is a stumbling-block and rock of offense. As an example of their own doctrine of atonement they told Mr. Young and me one evening that twenty or thirty years ago there was a bitter war between their own and the Sitka tribe, great fighters, and pretty evenly matched. After fighting all summer in a desultory, squabbling way, fighting now under cover, now in the open, watching for every chance for a shot, none of the women dared venture to the salmon-streams or berry-fields to procure their winter stock of food. At this crisis one of the Stickeen chiefs came out of his block-house fort into an open space midway between their fortified camps, and shouted that he wished to speak to the leader of the Sitkas.

When the Sitka chief appeared he said:—

"My people are hungry. They dare not go to the salmon-streams or berry-fields for winter supplies, and if this war goes on much longer most of my people will die of hunger. We have fought long enough; let us make peace. You brave Sitka warriors go home, and we will go home, and we will all set out to dry salmon and berries before it is too late."

The Sitka chief replied:—

"You may well say let us stop fighting, when you have had the best of it. You have killed ten more of my tribe than we have killed of yours. Give us ten Stickeen men to balance our blood-account; then, and not till then, will we make peace and go home."

"Very well," replied the Stickeen chief, "you know my rank. You know that I am worth ten common men and more. Take me and make peace."

This noble offer was promptly accepted; the Stickeen chief stepped forward and was shot down in sight of the fighting bands. Peace was thus established, and all made haste to their homes and ordinary work. That chief literally gave himself a sacrifice for his people. He died that they might live. Therefore, when missionaries preached the doctrine of atonement, explaining that when all mankind had gone astray, had broken God's laws and deserved to die, God's son came forward, and, like the Stickeen chief, offered himself as a sacrifice to heal the cause of God's wrath and set all the people of the world free, the doctrine was readily accepted.

"Yes, your words are good," they said. "The Son of God, the Chief of chiefs, the Maker of all the world, must be worth more than all mankind put together; therefore, when His blood was shed, the salvation of the world was made sure."

A telling illustration of the ready acceptance of this doctrine was displayed by Shakes, head chief of the Stickeens at Fort Wrangell. A few years before my first visit to the Territory, when the first missionary arrived, he requested Shakes to call his people together to hear the good word he had brought them. Shakes accordingly sent out messengers throughout the village, telling his people to wash their faces, put on their best clothing, and come to his block-house to hear what their visitor had to say. When all were assembled, the missionary preached a Christian sermon on the fall of man and the atonement whereby Christ, the Son of God, the Chief of chiefs, had redeemed all mankind, provided that this redemption was voluntarily accepted with repentance of their sins and the keeping of his commandments.

When the missionary had finished his sermon, Chief Shakes slowly arose, and, after thanking the missionary for coming so far to bring them good tidings and taking so much unselfish interest in the welfare of his tribe, he advised his people to accept the new religion, for he felt satisfied that because the white man knew so much more than the Indian, the white man's religion was likely to be better than theirs.

"The white man," said he, "makes great ships. We, like children, can only make canoes. He makes his big ships go with the wind, and he also makes them go with fire. We chop down trees with stone axes; the Boston man with iron axes, which are far better. In everything the ways of the white man seem to be better than ours. Compared with the white man we are only blind children, knowing not how best to live either here or in the country we go to after we die. So I wish you to learn this new religion and teach it to your children, that you may all go when you die into that good heaven country of the white man and be happy. But I am too old to learn a new religion, and besides, many of my people who have died were bad and foolish people, and if this word the missionary has brought us is true, and I think it is, many of my people must be in that bad country the missionary calls 'Hell,' and I must go there also, for a Stickeen chief never deserts his people in time of trouble. To that bad country, therefore, I will go, and try to cheer my people and help them as best I can to endure their misery."

Toyatte was a famous orator. I was present at the meeting at Fort Wrangell at which he was examined and admitted as a member of the Presbyterian Church. When called upon to answer the questions as to his ideas of God, and the principal doctrines of Christianity, he slowly arose in the crowded audience, while the missionary said, "Toyatte, you do not need to rise. You can answer the questions seated."

To this he paid no attention, but stood several minutes without speaking a word, never for a moment thinking of sitting down like a tired woman while making the most important of all the speeches of his life. He then explained in detail what his mother had taught him as to the character of God, the great Maker of the world; also what the shamans had taught him; the thoughts that often came to his mind when he was alone on hunting expeditions, and what he first thought of the religion which the missionaries had brought them. In all his gestures, and in the language in which he expressed himself, there was a noble simplicity and earnestness and majestic bearing which made the sermons and behavior of the three distinguished divinity doctors present seem commonplace in comparison.

Soon after our return to Fort Wrangell this grand old man was killed in a quarrel in which he had taken no other part than that of peacemaker. A number of the Taku tribe came to Fort Wrangell, camped near the Stickeen village, and made merry, manufacturing and drinking *hootchenoo,* a vile liquor distilled from a mash made of flour, dried apples, sugar, and molasses, and drunk hot from the still. The manufacture of *hootchenoo* being illegal, and several of Toyatte's tribe having been appointed deputy constables to prevent it, they went to the Taku camp and destroyed as much of the liquor as they could find. The Takus resisted, and during the quarrel one of the Stickeens struck a Taku in the face—an unpardonable offense. The next day messengers from the Taku camp gave notice to the Stickeens that they must make atonement for that blow, or fight with guns. Mr. Young, of course, was eager to stop the quarrel and so was Toyatte. They advised the Stickeen who had struck the Taku to return to their camp and submit to an equal blow in the face from the Taku. He did so; went to the camp, said he was ready to make atonement, and invited the person whom he had struck to strike him. This the Taku did with so much force that the balance of justice was again disturbed. The attention of the Takus was called to the fact that this atoning blow was far harder than the one to be atoned for, and immediately a sort of general free fist-fight began, and the quarrel was thus increased in bitterness rather than diminished.

Next day the Takus sent word to the Stickeens to get their guns ready, for to-morrow they would come up and fight them, thus boldly declaring war. The Stickeens in great excitement assembled and loaded their guns for the coming strife. Mr. Young ran hither and thither amongst the men of his congregation, forbidding them to fight, reminding them that Christ told them when they were struck to offer the other cheek instead of giving a blow in return, doing everything in his power to still the storm, but all in vain.

Toyatte stood outside one of the big block-houses with his men about him, awaiting the onset of the Takus. Mr. Young tried hard to get him away to a place of safety, reminding him that he belonged to his church and no longer had any right to fight. Toyatte calmly replied:—

"Mr. Young, Mr. Young, I am not going to fight. You see I have no gun in my hand; but I cannot go inside of the fort to a place of safety like women and children while my young men are exposed to the bullets of their enemies. I must stay with them and share their dangers, but I will not fight. But you, Mr. Young, *you* must go away; you are a minister and you are an important man. It would not do for you to be exposed to bullets. Go to your home in the fort; pretty soon 'hi yu poogh' " (much shooting).

At the first fire Toyatte fell, shot through the breast. Thus died for his people the noblest old Roman of them all.

On this first Alaska excursion I saw Toyatte under all circumstances,—in rain and snow, landing at night in dark storms, making fires, building shelters, exposed to all kinds of discomfort, but never under any circumstances did I ever see him do anything, or make a single gesture, that was not dignified, or hear him say a word that might not be uttered anywhere. He often deplored the fact that he had no son to take his name at his death, and expressed himself as very grateful when I told him that his name would not be forgotten, —that I had named one of the Stickeen glaciers for him.

PART TWO

THE TRIP OF
1880

CHAPTER XIV

SUM DUM BAY

I arrived early on the morning of the eighth of August on the steamer California to continue my explorations of the fiords to the northward which were closed by winter the previous November. The noise of our cannon and whistle was barely sufficient to awaken the sleepy town. The morning shout of one good rooster was the only evidence of life and health in all the place. Everything seemed kindly and familiar—the glassy water; evergreen islands; the Indians with their canoes and baskets and blankets and berries; the jet ravens, prying and flying about the streets and spruce trees; and the bland, hushed atmosphere brooding tenderly over all.

How delightful it is, and how it makes one's pulses bound to get back into this reviving northland wilderness! How truly wild it is, and how joyously one's heart responds to the welcome it gives, its waters and mountains shining and glowing like enthusiastic human faces! Gliding along the shores of its network of channels, we may travel thousands of miles without seeing any mark of man, save at long intervals some little Indian village or the faint smoke of a camp-fire. Even these are confined to the shore. Back a few yards from the beach the forests are as trackless as the sky, while the mountains, wrapped in their snow and ice and clouds, seem never before to have been even looked at.

For those who really care to get into hearty contact with the coast region, travel by canoe is by far the better way. The larger canoes carry from one to three tons, rise lightly over any waves likely to be met on the inland channels, go well under sail, and are easily paddled alongshore in calm weather or against moderate winds, while snug harbors where they may ride at anchor or be pulled up on a smooth beach are to be found almost everywhere. With plenty of provisions packed in boxes, and blankets and warm clothing in rubber or canvas bags, you may be truly independent, and enter into partnership with Nature; to be carried with the winds and currents, accept the noble invitations offered all along your way to enter the mountain fiords, the homes of the waterfalls and glaciers, and encamp almost every night beneath hospitable trees.

I left Fort Wrangell the 16th of August, accompanied by Mr. Young, in a canoe about twenty-five feet long and five wide, carrying two small square sails and manned by two Stickeen Indians— Captain Tyeen and Hunter Joe—and a half-breed named Smart Billy. The day was calm, and bright, fleecy, clouds hung about the lowest of the mountain-brows, while far above the clouds the peaks were seen stretching grandly away to the northward with their ice and snow shining in as calm a light as that which was falling on the glassy waters. Our Indians welcomed the work that lay before them, dipping their oars in exact time with hearty good-will as we glided past island after island across the delta of the Stickeen into Soutchoi Channel.

By noon we came in sight of a fleet of icebergs from Hutli Bay. The Indian name of this icy fiord is Hutli, or Thunder Bay, from the sound made by the bergs in falling and rising from the front of the inflowing glacier.

As we floated happily on over the shining waters, the beautiful islands, in ever-changing pictures, were an unfailing source of enjoyment; but chiefly our attention was turned upon the mountains. Bold granite headlands with their feet in the channel, or some broad-shouldered peak of surpassing grandeur, would fix the eye, or some one of the larger glaciers, with far-reaching tributaries clasping entire groups of peaks and its great crystal river pouring down through the forest between gray ridges and domes. In these grand picture lessons the day was spent, and we spread our blankets beneath a Menzies spruce on moss two feet deep.

Next morning we sailed around an outcurving bank of boulders and sand ten miles long, the terminal moraine of a grand old glacier on which last November we met a perilous adventure. It is located just opposite three large converging glaciers which formerly united to form the vanished trunk of the glacier to which the submerged moraine belonged. A few centuries ago it must have been the grandest feature of this part of the coast, and, so well preserved are the monuments of its greatness, the noble old ice-river may be seen again in imagination about as vividly as if present in the flesh, with snow-clouds crawling about its fountains, sunshine sparkling on its broad flood, and its ten-mile ice-wall planted in the deep waters of the channel and sending off its bergs with loud resounding thunder.

About noon we rounded Cape Fanshawe, scudding swiftly before a fine breeze, to the delight of our Indians, who had now only to steer and chat. Here we overtook two Hoona Indians and their families on their way home from Fort Wrangell. They had exchanged five sea-otter furs, worth about a hundred dollars apiece, and a considerable number of fur-seal, land-otter, marten, beaver, and other furs and skins, some $800 worth, for a new canoe valued at eighty dollars, some flour, tobacco, blankets, and a few barrels of molasses for the manufacture of whiskey. The blankets were not to wear, but to keep as money, for the almighty dollar of these tribes is a Hudson's Bay blanket. The wind died away soon after we met, and as the two canoes glided slowly side by side, the Hoonas made minute inquiries as to who we were and what we were doing so far north. Mr. Young's object in meeting the Indians as a missionary they could in part understand, but mine in searching for rocks and glaciers seemed past comprehension, and they asked our Indians whether gold-mines might not be the main object. They remembered, however, that I had visited their Glacier Bay ice-mountains a year ago, and seemed to think there might be, after all, some mysterious interest about them of which they were ignorant. Toward the middle of the afternoon they engaged our crew in a race. We pushed a little way ahead for a time, but, though possessing a considerable advantage, as it would seem, in our long oars, they at length overtook us and kept up until after dark, when we camped together in the rain on the bank of a salmon-stream among dripping grass and bushes some twenty-five miles beyond Cape Fanshawe.

These cold northern waters are at times about as brilliantly phosphorescent as those of the warm South, and so they were this evening in the rain and darkness, with the temperature of the water at forty-nine degrees, the air fifty-one. Every stroke of the oar made a vivid surge of white light, and the canoes left shining tracks.

As we neared the mouth of the well-known salmon-stream where we intended making our camp, we noticed jets and flashes of silvery light caused by the startled movement of the salmon that were on their way to their spawning-grounds. These became more and more numerous and exciting, and our Indians shouted joyfully, "Hi yu salmon! Hi yu muck-a-muck!" while the water about the canoe and beneath the canoe was churned by thousands of fins into silver fire. After landing two of our men to commence camp-work, Mr. Young and I went up the stream with Tyeen to the foot of a rapid, to see him catch a few salmon for supper. The stream was so filled with them there seemed to be more fish than water in it, and we appeared to be sailing in boiling, seething silver light marvelously relieved in the jet darkness. In the midst of the general auroral glow and the specially vivid flashes made by the frightened fish darting ahead and to right and left of the canoe, our attention was suddenly fixed by a long, steady, comet-like blaze that seemed to be made by some frightful monster that was pursuing us. But when the portentous object reached the canoe, it proved to be only our little dog, Stickeen.

After getting the canoe into a side eddy at the foot of the rapids, Tyeen caught half a dozen salmon in a few minutes by means of a large hook fastened to the end of a pole. They were so abundant that he simply groped for them in a random way, or aimed at them by the light they themselves furnished. That food to last a month or two may thus be procured in less than an hour is a striking illustration of the fruitfulness of these Alaskan waters.

Our Hoona neighbors were asleep in the morning at sunrise, lying in a row, wet and limp like dead salmon. A little boy about six years old, with no other covering than a remnant of a shirt, was lying peacefully on his back, like Tam o' Shanter, despising wind and rain and fire. He is up now, looking happy and fresh, with no clothes to dry and no need of washing while this weather lasts. The two babies are firmly strapped on boards, leaving only their heads and hands free. Their mothers are nursing them, holding the boards on end, while they sit on the ground with their breasts level with the little prisoners' mouths.

This morning we found out how beautiful a nook we had got into. Besides the charming picturesqueness of its lines, the colors about it, brightened by the rain, made a fine study. Viewed from the shore, there was first a margin of dark-brown algæ, then a bar of yellowish-brown, next a dark bar on the rugged rocks marking the highest tides, then a bar of granite boulders with grasses in the seams, and above this a thick, bossy, overleaning fringe of bushes colored red and yellow and green. A wall of spruces and hemlocks draped and tufted with gray and yellow lichens and mosses embowered the camp-ground and overarched the little river, while the camp-fire smoke, like a stranded cloud, lay motionless in their branches. Down on the beach ducks and sandpipers in flocks of hundreds were getting their breakfasts, bald eagles were seen perched on dead spars along the edge of the woods, heavy-looking and overfed, gazing stupidly like gorged vultures, and porpoises were blowing and plunging outside.

As for the salmon, as seen this morning urging their way up the swift current,—tens of thousands of them, side by side, with their backs out of the water in shallow places now that the tide was low,—nothing that I could write might possibly give anything like a fair conception of the extravagance of their numbers. There was more salmon apparently, bulk for bulk, than water in the stream. The struggling multitudes, crowding one against another, could not get out of

Vegetation at High-Tide Line, Sitka Harbor

our way when we waded into the midst of them. One of our men amused himself by seizing them above the tail and swinging them over his head. Thousands could thus be taken by hand at low tide, while they were making their way over the shallows among the stones.

Whatever may be said of other resources of the Territory, it is hardly possible to exaggerate the importance of the fisheries. Not to mention cod, herring, halibut, etc., there are probably not less than a thousand salmon-streams in southeastern Alaska as large or larger than this one (about forty feet wide) crowded with salmon several times a year. The first run commenced that year in July, while the king salmon, one of the five species recognized by the Indians, was in the Chilcat River about the middle of the November before.

From this wonderful salmon-camp we sailed joyfully up the coast to explore icy Sum Dum Bay, beginning my studies where I left off the previous November. We started about six o'clock, and pulled merrily on through fog and rain, the beautiful wooded shore on our right, passing bergs here and there, the largest of which, though not over two hundred feet long, seemed many times larger as they loomed gray and indistinct through the fog. For the first five hours the sailing was open and easy, nor was there anything very exciting to be seen or heard, save now and then the thunder of a falling berg rolling and echoing from cliff to cliff, and the sustained roar of cataracts.

About eleven o'clock we reached a point where the fiord was packed with ice all the way across, and we ran ashore to fit a block of wood on the cutwater of our canoe to prevent its being battered or broken. While Captain Tyeen, who had had considerable experience among berg ice, was at work on the canoe, Hunter Joe and Smart Billy prepared a warm lunch.

The sheltered hollow where we landed seems to be a favorite camping-ground for the Sum Dum seal-hunters. The pole-frames of tents, tied with cedar bark, stood on level spots strewn with seal bones, bits of salmon, and spruce bark.

We found the work of pushing through the ice rather tiresome. An opening of twenty or thirty yards would be found here and there, then a close pack that had to be opened by pushing the smaller bergs aside with poles. I enjoyed the labor, however, for the fine lessons I got, and in an hour or two we found zigzag lanes of water, through which we paddled with but little interruption, and had leisure to study the wonderful variety of forms the bergs presented as we glided past them. The largest we saw did not greatly exceed two hundred feet in length, or twenty-five or thirty feet in height above the water. Such bergs would draw from one hundred and fifty to two hundred feet of water. All those that have floated long undisturbed have a projecting base at the water-line, caused by the more rapid melting of the immersed portion. When a portion of the berg breaks off, another base line is formed, and the old one, sharply cut, may be seen rising at all angles, giving it a marked character. Many of the oldest bergs are beautifully ridged by the melting out of narrow furrows strictly parallel throughout the mass, revealing the bedded structure of the ice, acquired perhaps centuries ago, on the mountain snow fountains. A berg suddenly going to pieces is a grand sight, especially when the water is calm and no motion is visible save perchance the slow drift of the tide-current. The prolonged roar of its fall comes with startling effect, and heavy swells are raised that haste away in every direction to tell what has taken place, and tens of thousands of its neighbors rock and swash in sympathy, repeating the news over and over again. We were too near several large ones that fell apart as we passed them, and our canoe had narrow escapes. The seal-hunters, Tyeen says, are frequently lost in these sudden berg accidents.

In the afternoon, while we were admiring the scenery, which, as we approached the head of the fiord, became more and more sublime, one of our Indians called attention to a flock of wild goats on a mountain overhead, and soon afterwards we saw two other flocks, at a height of about fifteen hundred feet, relieved against the mountains as white spots. They are abundant here and throughout the Alaskan Alps in general, feeding on the grassy slopes above the timber-line. Their long, yellowish hair is shed at this time of year and they were snowy white. None of nature's cattle are better fed or better protected from the cold. Tyeen told us that before the introduction of guns they used to hunt them with spears, chasing them with their wolf-dogs, and thus bringing them to bay among the rocks, where they were easily approached and killed.

The upper half of the fiord is about from a mile to a mile and a half wide, and shut in by sublime Yosemite cliffs, nobly sculptured, and adorned with waterfalls and fringes of trees, bushes, and patches of flowers; but amid so crowded a display of novel beauty it was not easy to concentrate the attention long enough on any portion of it without giving more days and years than our lives could afford. I was determined to see at least the grand fountain of all this ice. As we passed headland after headland, hoping as each was rounded we should obtain a view of it, it still remained hidden.

"Ice-mountain hi yu kumtux hide,"—glaciers know how to hide extremely well,—said Tyeen, as he rested for a moment after rounding a huge granite shoulder of the wall whence we expected to gain a view of the extreme head of the fiord. The bergs, however, were less closely packed and we made good progress, and at half-past eight o'clock, fourteen and a half hours after setting out, the great glacier came in sight at the head of a branch of the fiord that comes in from the northeast.

The discharging front of this fertile, fast-flowing glacier is about three quarters of a mile wide, and probably eight or nine hundred feet deep, about one hundred and fifty feet of its depth rising above the water as a grand blue barrier wall. It is much wider a few miles farther back, the front being jammed between sheer granite walls from thirty-five hundred to four thousand feet high. It shows grandly from where it broke on our sight, sweeping boldly forward and downward in its majestic channel, swaying from side to side in graceful fluent lines around stern unflinching rocks. While I stood in the canoe making a sketch of it, several bergs came off with tremendous dashing and thunder, raising a cloud of ice-dust and spray to a height of a hundred feet or more.

"The ice-mountain is well disposed toward you," said Tyeen. "He is firing his big guns to welcome you."

After completing my sketch and entering a few notes, I directed the crew to pull around a lofty burnished rock on the west side of the channel, where, as I knew from the trend of the cañon, a large glacier once came in; and what was my delight to discover that the glacier was still there and still pouring its ice into a branch of the fiord. Even the Indians shared my joy and shouted with me. I expected only one first-class glacier here, and found two. They are only about two miles apart. How glorious a mansion that precious pair dwell in! After sunset we made haste to seek a camp-ground. I would fain have shared these upper chambers with the two glaciers, but there was no landing-place in sight, and we had to make our way back a few miles in the twilight to the mouth of a side cañon where we had seen timber on the way up. There seemed to be a good landing as we approached the shore, but, coming nearer, we found that the granite fell directly into deep water without leading any level margin, though the slope a short distance back was not very steep.

After narrowly scanning the various seams and steps that roughened the granite, we concluded to attempt a landing rather than grope our way farther down the fiord through the ice. And what a time we had climbing on hands and knees up the slippery glacier-polished rocks to a shelf some two hundred feet above the water and dragging provisions and blankets after us! But it proved to be a glorious place, the very best camp-ground of all the trip,—a perfect garden, ripe berries nodding from a fringe of bushes around its edges charmingly displayed in the light of our big fire. Close alongside there was a lofty mountain capped with ice, and from the blue edge of that ice-cap there were sixteen silvery cascades in a row, falling about four thousand feet, each one of the sixteen large enough to be heard at least two miles.

How beautiful was the firelight on the nearest larkspurs and geraniums and daisies of our garden! How hearty the wave greeting on the rocks below brought to us from the two glaciers! And how glorious a song the sixteen cascades sang!

The cascade songs made us sleep all the sounder, and we were so happy as to find in the morning that the berg waves had spared our canoe. We set off in high spirits down the fiord and across to the right side to explore a remarkably deep and narrow branch of the main fiord that I had noted on the way up, and that, from the magnitude of the glacial characters on the two colossal rocks that guard the entrance, promised a rich reward for our pains.

After we had sailed about three miles up this side fiord, we came to what seemed to be its head, for trees and rocks swept in a curve around from one side to the other without showing any opening, although the walls of the cañon were seen extending back indefinitely, one majestic brow beyond the other.

When we were tracing this curve, however, in a leisurely way, in search of a good landing, we were startled by Captain Tyeen shouting, "Skookum chuck! Skookum chuck!" (strong water, strong water), and found our canoe was being swept sideways by a powerful current, the roar of which we had mistaken for a waterfall. We barely escaped being carried over a rocky bar on the boiling flood, which, as we afterwards learned, would have been only a happy shove on our way. After we had made a landing a little distance back from the brow of the bar, we climbed the highest rock near the shore to seek a view of the channel beyond the inflowing tide rapids, to find out whether or not we could safely venture in. Up over rolling, mossy, bushy, burnished rock waves we scrambled for an hour or two, which resulted in a fair view of the deep-blue waters of the fiord stretching on and on along the feet of the most majestic Yosemite rocks we had yet seen. This determined our plan of shooting the rapids and exploring it to its farthest recesses. This novel interruption of the channel is a bar of exceedingly hard resisting granite, over which the great glacier that once occupied it swept, without degrading it to the general level, and over which tide-waters now rush in and out with the violence of a mountain torrent.

Returning to the canoe, we pushed off, and in a few moments were racing over the bar with lightning speed through hurrahing waves and eddies and sheets of foam, our little shell of a boat tossing lightly as a bubble. Then, rowing across a belt of back-flowing

water, we found ourselves on a smooth mirror reach between granite walls of the very wildest and most exciting description, surpassing in some ways those of the far-famed Yosemite Valley.

As we drifted silent and awe-stricken beneath the shadows of the
mighty cliffs, which, in their tremendous height and abruptness,
seemed to overhang at the top, the Indians gazing intently, as if
they, too, were impressed with the strange, awe-inspiring grandeur
that shut them in, one of them at length broke the silence by saying,
"This must be a good place for woodchucks; I hear them calling."

When I asked them, further on, how they thought this gorge was
made, they gave up the question, but offered an opinion as to the formation of rain and soil. The rain, they said, was produced by the
rapid whirling of the earth by a stout mythical being called Yek. The
water of the ocean was thus thrown up, to descend again in showers,
just as it is thrown off a wet grindstone. They did not, however, understand why the ocean water should be salt, while the rain from it is
fresh. The soil, they said, for the plants to grow on is formed by the
washing of the rain on the rocks and gradually accumulating. The
grinding action of ice in this connection they had not recognized.

Gliding on and on, the scenery seemed at every turn to become
more lavishly fruitful in forms as well as more sublime in dimensions—snowy falls booming in splendid dress; colossal domes and
battlements and sculptured arches of a fine neutral-gray tint, their
bases laved by the blue fiord water; green ferny dells; bits of flower-
bloom on ledges; fringes of willow and birch; and glaciers above all.
But when we approached the base of a majestic rock like the
Yosemite Half Dome at the head of the fiord, where two short
branches put out, and came in sight of another glacier of the first
order sending off bergs, our joy was complete. I had a most glorious
view of it, sweeping in grand majesty from high mountain fountains,
swaying around one mighty bastion after another, until it fell into
the fiord in shattered over-leaning fragments. When we had feasted
awhile on this unhoped-for treasure, I directed the Indians to pull to
the head of the left fork of the fiord, where we found a large cascade
with a volume of water great enough to be called a river, doubtless
the outlet of a receding glacier not in sight from the fiord.

This is in form and origin a typical Yosemite valley, though as yet its floor is covered with ice and water,—ice above and beneath, a noble mansion in which to spend a winter and a summer! It is about ten miles long, and from three quarters of a mile to one mile wide. It contains ten large falls and cascades, the finest one on the left side near the head. After coming in an admirable rush over a granite brow where it is first seen at a height of nine hundred or a thousand feet, it leaps a sheer precipice of about two hundred and fifty feet, then divides and reaches the tide-water in broken rapids over boulders. Another about a thousand feet high drops at once on to the margin of the glacier two miles back from the front. Several of the others are upwards of three thousand feet high, descending through narrow gorges as richly feathered with ferns as any channel that water ever flowed in, though tremendously abrupt and deep. A grander array of rocks and waterfalls I have never yet beheld in Alaska.

The amount of timber on the walls is about the same as that on the Yosemite walls, but owing to greater moisture, there is more small vegetation,—bushes, ferns, mosses, grasses, etc.; though by far the greater portion of the area of the wall-surface is bare and shining with the polish it received when occupied by the glacier that formed the fiord. The deep-green patches seen on the mountains back of the walls at the limits of vegetation are grass, where the wild goats, or chamois rather, roam and feed. The still greener and more luxuriant patches farther down in gullies and on slopes where the declivity is not excessive, are made up mostly of willows, birch, and huckleberry bushes, with a varying amount of prickly ribes and rubus and echinopanax. This growth, when approached, especially on the lower slopes near the level of the sea at the jaws of the great side cañons, is found to be the most impenetrable and tedious and toilsome combination of fighting bushes that the weary explorer ever fell into, incomparably more punishing than the buckthorn and manzanita tangles of the Sierra.

The cliff gardens of this hidden Yosemite are exceedingly rich in color. On almost every rift and bench, however small, as well as on the wider table-rocks where a little soil has lodged, we found gay multitudes of flowers, far more brilliantly colored than would be looked for in so cool and beclouded a region,—larkspurs, geraniums, painted-cups, bluebells, gentians, saxifrages, epilobiums, violets, parnassia, veratrum, spiranthes and other orchids, fritillaria, smilax, asters, daisies, bryanthus, cassiope, linnæa, and a great variety of flowering ribes and rubus and heathworts. Many of the above, though with soft stems and leaves, are yet as brightly painted as those of the warm sunlands of the south. The heathworts in particular are very abundant and beautiful, both in flower and fruit, making delicate green carpets for the rocks, flushed with pink bells, or dotted with red and blue berries. The tallest of the grasses have ribbon leaves well tempered and arched, and with no lack of bristly spikes and nodding purple panicles. The alpine grasses of the Sierra, making close carpets on the glacier meadows, I have not yet seen in Alaska.

The ferns are less numerous in species than in California, but about equal in the number of fronds. I have seen three aspidiums, two woodsias, a lomaria, polypodium, cheilanthes, and several species of pteris.

In this eastern arm of Sum Dum Bay and its Yosemite branch, I counted from my canoe, on my way up and down, thirty small glaciers back of the walls, and we saw three of the first order; also thirty-seven cascades and falls, counting only those large enough to make themselves heard several miles. The whole bay, with its rocks and woods and ice, reverberates with their roar. How many glaciers may be disclosed in the other great arm that I have not seen as yet, I cannot say, but, judging from the bergs it sends down, I guess not less than a hundred pour their turbid streams into the fiord, making about as many joyful, bouncing cataracts.

About noon we began to retrace our way back into the main fiord, and arrived at the gold-mine camp after dark, rich and weary.

On the morning of August 21 I set out with my three Indians to explore the right arm of this noble bay, Mr. Young having decided, on account of mission work, to remain at the gold-mine. So here is another fine lot of Sum Dum ice,—thirty-five or forty square miles of bergs, one great glacier of the first class descending into the fiord at the head, the fountain whence all these bergs were derived, and thirty-one smaller glaciers that do not reach tide-water; also nine cascades and falls, large size, and two rows of Yosemite rocks from three to four thousand feet high, each row about eighteen or twenty miles long, burnished and sculptured in the most telling glacier style, and well trimmed with spruce groves and flower gardens; a' that and more of a kind that cannot here be catalogued.

For the first five or six miles there is nothing excepting the ice-bergs that is very striking in the scenery as compared with that of the smooth unencumbered outside channels, where all is so evenly beautiful. The mountain-wall on the right as you go up is more precipitous than usual, and a series of small glaciers is seen along the top of it, extending their blue-crevassed fronts over the rims of pure-white snow fountains, and from the end of each front a hearty stream coming in a succession of falls and rapids over the terminal moraines, through patches of dwarf willows, and then through the spruce woods into the bay, singing and dancing all the way down. On the opposite side of the bay from here there is a small side bay about three miles deep, with a showy group of glacier-bearing mountains back of it. Everywhere else the view is bounded by comparatively low mountains densely forested to the very top.

After sailing about six miles from the mine, the experienced mountaineer could see some evidence of an opening from this wide lower portion, and on reaching it, it proved to be the continuation of the main west arm, contracted between stupendous walls of gray granite, and crowded with bergs from shore to shore, which seem to bar the way against everything but wings. Headland after headland, in most imposing array, was seen plunging sheer and bare from dizzy heights, and planting its feet in the ice-encumbered water without leaving a spot on which one could land from a boat, while no part of the great glacier that pours all these miles of ice into the fiord was visible. Pushing our way slowly through the packed bergs, and passing headland after headland, looking eagerly forward, the glacier and its fountain mountains were still beyond sight, cut off by other projecting headland capes, toward which I

urged my way, enjoying the extraordinary grandeur of the wild unfinished Yosemite. Domes swell against the sky in fine lines as lofty
and as perfect in form as those of the California valley, and rock-
fronts stand forward, as sheer and as nobly sculptured. No ice-work
that I have ever seen surpasses this, either in the magnitude of the
features or effectiveness of composition.

On some of the narrow benches and tables of the walls rows of
spruce trees and two-leaved pines were growing, and patches of
considerable size were found on the spreading bases of those
mountains that stand back inside the cañons, where the continuity
of the walls is broken. Some of these side cañons are cut down to
the level of the water and reach far back, opening views into groups
of glacier fountains that give rise to many a noble stream; while all
along the tops of the walls on both sides small glaciers are seen, still
busily engaged in the work of completing their sculpture. I counted
twenty-five from the canoe. Probably the drainage of fifty or more
pours into this fiord. The average elevation at which they melt is
about eighteen hundred feet above sea-level, and all of them are
residual branches of the grand trunk that filled the fiord and over-
flowed its walls when there was only one Sum Dum glacier.

The afternoon was wearing away as we pushed on and on
through the drifting bergs without our having obtained a single
glimpse of the great glacier. A Sum Dum seal-hunter, whom we
met groping his way deftly through the ice in a very small, un-
splitable cottonwood canoe, told us that the ice-mountain was yet
fifteen miles away. This was toward the middle of the afternoon,
and I gave up sketching and making notes and worked hard with
the Indians to reach it before dark. About seven o'clock we approached what seemed to be the extreme head of the fiord, and still
no great glacier in sight—only a small one, three or four miles long,
melting a thousand feet above the sea. Presently, a narrow side
opening appeared between tremendous cliffs sheer to a height of
four thousand feet or more, trending nearly at right angles to the
general trend of the fiord, and apparently terminated by a cliff,
scarcely less abrupt or high, at a distance of a mile or two. Up this
bend we toiled against wind and tide, creeping closely along the

wall on the right side, which, as we looked upward, seemed to be leaning over, while the waves beating against the bergs and rocks made a discouraging kind of music. At length, toward nine o'clock, just before the gray darkness of evening fell, a long, triumphant shout told that the glacier, so deeply and desperately hidden, was at last hunted back to its benmost bore. A short distance around a second bend in the cañon, I reached a point where I obtained a good view of it as it pours its deep, broad flood into the fiord in a majestic course from between the noble mountains, its tributaries, each of which would be regarded elsewhere as a grand glacier, converging from right and left from a fountain set far in the silent fastnesses of the mountains.

"There is your lost friend," said the Indians laughing; "he says, 'Sagh-a-ya' " (how do you do)? And while berg after berg was being born with thundering uproar, Tyeen said, "Your friend has klosh tumtum [good heart]. Hear! Like the other big-hearted one he is firing his guns in your honor."

I stayed only long enough to make an outline sketch, and then urged the Indians to hasten back some six miles to the mouth of a side cañon I had noted on the way up as a place where we might camp in case we should not find a better. After dark we had to move with great caution through the ice. One of the Indians was stationed in the bow with a pole to push aside the smaller fragments and look out for the most promising openings, through which he guided us, shouting, "Friday! Tucktay!" (shoreward, seaward) about ten times a minute. We reached this landing-place after ten o'clock, guided in the darkness by the roar of a glacier torrent. The ground was all boulders and it was hard to find a place among them, however small, to lie on. The Indians anchored the canoe well out from the shore and passed the night in it to guard against berg-waves and drifting waves, after assisting me to set my tent in some sort of way among the stones well back beyond the reach of the tide. I asked them as they were returning to the canoe if they were not going to eat something. They answered promptly:—

"We will sleep now, if your ice friend will let us. We will eat tomorrow, but we can find some bread for you if you want it."

"No," I said, "go to rest. I, too, will sleep now and eat tomorrow." Nothing was attempted in the way of light or fire. Camping that night was simply lying down. The boulders seemed to make a fair bed after finding the best place to take their pressure.

During the night I was awakened by the beating of the spent ends of berg-waves against the side of my tent, though I had fancied myself well beyond their reach. These special waves are not raised by wind or tide, but by the fall of large bergs from the snout of the glacier, or sometimes by the overturning or breaking of large bergs that may have long floated in perfect poise. The highest berg-waves oftentimes travel half a dozen miles or farther before they are much spent, producing a singularly impressive uproar in the far recesses of the mountains on calm dark nights when all beside is still. Far and near they tell the news that a berg is born, repeating their story again and again, compelling attention and reminding us of earthquake-waves that roll on for thousands of miles, taking their story from continent to continent.

When the Indians came ashore in the morning and saw the condition of my tent they laughed heartily and said, "Your friend [meaning the big glacier] sent you a good word last night, and his servant knocked at your tent and said, 'Sagh-a-ya, are you sleeping well?' "

I had fasted too long to be in very good order for hard work, but while the Indians were cooking, I made out to push my way up the cañon before breakfast to seek the glacier that once came into the fiord, knowing from the size and muddiness of the stream that drains it that it must be quite large and not far off. I came in sight of it after a hard scramble of two hours through thorny chaparral and across steep avalanche taluses of rocks and snow. The front reaches across the cañon from wall to wall, covered with rocky detritus, and looked dark and forbidding in the shadow cast by the cliffs, while from a low, cave-like hollow its draining stream breaks forth, a river in size, with a reverberating roar that stirs all the cañon. Beyond, in a cloudless blaze of sunshine, I saw many tributaries, pure and white as new-fallen snow, drawing their sources from clusters of peaks and sweeping down waving slopes to unite their crystal currents with the trunk glacier in the central cañon. This fine glacier reaches to within two hundred and fifty feet of the level of the sea, and would even yet reach the fiord and send off bergs but for the waste it suffers in flowing slowly through the trunk cañon, the declivity of which is very slight.

Returning, I reached camp and breakfast at ten o'clock; then had everything packed into the canoe, and set off leisurely across the fiord to the mouth of another wide and low cañon, whose lofty outer cliffs, facing the fiord, are telling glacial advertisements. Gladly I should have explored it all, traced its streams of water and streams of ice, and entered its highest chambers, the homes and fountains of the snow. But I had to wait. I only stopped an hour or two, and climbed to the top of a rock through the common underbrush, whence I had a good general view. The front of the main glacier is not far distant from the fiord, and sends off small bergs into a lake. The walls of its tributary cañons are remarkably jagged and high, cut in a red variegated rock, probably slate. On the way back to the canoe I gathered ripe salmon-berries an inch and a half in diameter, ripe huckleberries, too, in great abundance, and several interesting plants I had not before met in the Territory.

About noon, when the tide was in our favor, we set out on the return trip to the gold-mine camp. The sun shone free and warm. No wind stirred. The water spaces between the bergs were as smooth as glass, reflecting the unclouded sky, and doubling the ravishing beauty of the bergs as the sunlight streamed through their innumerable angles in rainbow colors.

Soon a light breeze sprang up, and dancing lily spangles on the water mingled their glory of light with that burning on the angles of the ice.

On days like this, true sun-days, some of the bergs show a purplish tinge, though most are white from the disintegrating of their weathered surfaces. Now and then a new-born one is met that is pure blue crystal throughout, freshly broken from the fountain or recently exposed to the air by turning over. But in all of them, old and new, there are azure caves and rifts of ineffable beauty, in which the purest tones of light pulse and shimmer, lovely and untainted as anything on earth or in the sky.

As we were passing the Indian village I presented a little tobacco to the headmen as an expression of regard, while they gave us a few smoked salmon, after putting many questions concerning my exploration of their bay and bluntly declaring their disbelief in the ice business.

About nine o'clock we arrived at the gold camp, where we found Mr. Young ready to go on with us the next morning, and thus ended two of the brightest and best of all my Alaska days.

CHAPTER XV

FROM TAKU RIVER TO TAYLOR BAY

I never saw Alaska looking better than it did when we bade farewell to Sum Dum on August 22 and pushed on northward up the coast toward Taku. The morning was clear, calm, bright—not a cloud in all the purple sky, nor wind, however gentle, to shake the slender spires of the spruces or dew-laden grass around the shores. Over the mountains and over the broad white bosoms of the glaciers the sunbeams poured, rosy as ever fell on fields of ripening wheat, drenching the forests and kindling the glassy waters and icebergs into a perfect blaze of colored light. Every living thing seemed joyful, and nature's work was going on in glowing enthusiasm, not less appreciable in the deep repose that brooded over every feature of the landscape, suggesting the coming fruitfulness of the icy land and showing the advance that has already been made from glacial winter to summer. The care-laden commercial lives we lead close our eyes to the operations of God as a workman, though openly carried on that all who will look may see. The scarred rocks here and the moraines make a vivid showing of the old winter-time of the glacial period, and mark the bounds of the *mer-de-glace* that once filled the bay and covered the surrounding mountains. Already that sea of ice is replaced by water, in which multitudes of fishes are fed, while the hundred glaciers lingering about the bay and the streams that pour from them are busy night and day bringing in sand and mud and stones, at the rate of tons every minute, to fill it up. Then, as the seasons grow warmer, there will be fields here for the plough.

Our Indians, exhilarated by the sunshine, were garrulous as the gulls and plovers, and pulled heartily at their oars, evidently glad to get out of the ice with a whole boat.

"Now for Taku," they said, as we glided over the shining water. "Good-bye, Ice-Mountains; good-bye, Sum Dum." Soon a light breeze came, and they unfurled the sail and laid away their oars and began, as usual in such free times, to put their goods in order, unpacking and sunning provisions, guns, ropes, clothing, etc. Joe has an old flintlock musket suggestive of Hudson's Bay times, which he wished to discharge and reload. So, stepping in front of the sail, he fired at a gull that was flying past before I could prevent him, and it fell slowly with outspread wings alongside the canoe, with blood dripping from its bill. I asked him why he had killed the bird, and followed the question by a severe reprimand for his stupid cruelty, to which he could offer no other excuse than that he had learned from the whites to be careless about taking life. Captain Tyeen denounced the deed as likely to bring bad luck.

Before the whites came most of the Thlinkits held, with Agassiz, that animals have souls, and that it was wrong and unlucky to even speak disrespectfully of the fishes or any of the animals that supplied them with food. A case illustrating their superstitious beliefs in this connection occurred at Fort Wrangell while I was there the year before. One of the sub-chiefs of the Stickeens had a little son five or six years old, to whom he was very much attached, always taking him with him in his short canoe-trips, and leading him by the hand while going about town. Last summer the boy was taken sick, and gradually grew weak and thin, whereupon his father became alarmed, and feared, as is usual in such obscure cases, that the boy had been bewitched. He first applied in his trouble to Dr. Carliss, one of the missionaries, who gave medicine, without effecting the immediate cure that the fond father demanded. He was, to some extent, a believer in the powers of missionaries, both as to material and spiritual affairs, but in so serious an exigency it was natural that he should go back to the faith of his fathers. Accordingly, he sent for one of the shamans, or medicine-men, of his tribe, and submitted the case to him, who, after going through the customary incantations, declared that he had discovered the cause of the difficulty.

"Your boy," he said, "has lost his soul, and this is the way it happened. He was playing among the stones down on the beach when he saw a crawfish in the water, and made fun of it, pointing his finger at it and saying, 'Oh, you crooked legs! Oh, you crooked legs! You can't walk straight; you go sidewise,' which made the crab so angry that he reached out his long nippers, seized the lad's soul, pulled it out of him and made off with it into deep water. And," continued the medicine-man, "unless his stolen soul is restored to him and put back in its place he will die. Your boy is really dead already; it is only his lonely, empty body that is living now, and though it may continue to live in this way for a year or two, the boy will never be of any account, not strong, nor wise, nor brave."

The father then inquired whether anything could be done about it; was the soul still in possession of the crab, and if so, could it be recovered and re-installed in his forlorn son? Yes, the doctor rather thought it might be charmed back and re-united, but the job would be a difficult one, and would probably cost about fifteen blankets.

After we were fairly out of the bay into Stephens Passage, the wind died away, and the Indians had to take to their oars again, which ended our talk. On we sped over the silvery level, close alongshore. The dark forests extending far and near, planted like a field of wheat, might seem monotonous in general views, but the appreciative observer, looking closely, will find no lack of interesting variety, however far he may go. The steep slopes on which they grow allow almost every individual tree, with its peculiarities of form and color, to be seen like an audience on seats rising above one another—the blue-green, sharply-tapered spires of the Menzies spruce, the warm yellow-green Mertens spruce with their finger-like tops all pointing in the same direction, or drooping gracefully like leaves of grass, and the airy, feathery, brownish-green Alaska cedar. The outer fringe of bushes along the shore and hanging over the brows of the cliffs, the white mountains above, the shining water beneath, the changing sky over all, form pictures of divine beauty in which no healthy eye may ever grow weary.

Toward evening at the head of a picturesque bay we came to a village belonging to the Taku tribe. We found it silent and deserted. Not a single shaman or policeman had been left to keep it. These people are so happily rich as to have but little of a perishable kind to keep, nothing worth fretting about. They were away catching salmon, our Indians said. All the Indian villages hereabout are thus abandoned at regular periods every year, just as a tent is left for a day, while they repair to fishing, berrying, and hunting stations, occupying each in succession for a week or two at a time, coming and going from the main, substantially built villages. Then, after their summer's work is done, the winter supply of salmon dried and packed, fish-oil and seal-oil stored in boxes, berries and spruce bark pressed into cakes, their trading-trips completed, and the year's stock of quarrels with the neighboring tribe patched up in some way, they devote themselves to feasting, dancing, and hootchenoo drinking. The Takus, once a powerful and war-like tribe, were at this time, like most of the neighboring tribes, whiskied nearly out of existence. They had a larger village on the Taku River, but, according to the census taken that year by the missionaries, they numbered only 269 in all,—109 men, 79 women, and 81 children, figures that show the vanishing condition of the tribe at a glance.

Our Indians wanted to camp for the night in one of the deserted houses, but I urged them on into the clean wilderness until dark, when we landed on a rocky beach fringed with devil's-clubs, greatly to the disgust of our crew. We had to make the best of it, however, as it was too dark to seek farther. After supper was accomplished among the boulders, they retired to the canoe, which they anchored a little way out, beyond low tide, while Mr. Young and I at the expense of a good deal of scrambling and panax stinging, discovered a spot on which we managed to sleep.

The next morning, about two hours after leaving our thorny camp, we rounded a great mountain rock nearly a mile in height and entered the Taku fiord. It is about eighteen miles long and from three to five miles wide, and extends directly back into the heart of the mountains, draining hundreds of glaciers and streams. The ancient glacier that formed it was far too deep and broad and too little concentrated to erode one of those narrow cañons, usually so impressive in sculpture and architecture, but it is all the more interesting on this account when the grandeur of the ice-work accomplished is recognized. This fiord, more than any other I have examined, explains the formation of the wonderful system of channels extending along the coast from Puget Sound to about latitude 59 degrees, for it is a marked portion of the system,—a branch of Stephens Passage. Its trends and general sculpture are as distinctly glacial as those of the narrowest fiord, while the largest tributaries of the great glacier that occupied it are still in existence. I counted some forty-five altogether, big and little, in sight from the canoe in sailing up the middle of the fiord. Three of them, drawing their sources from magnificent groups of snowy mountains, came down to the level of the sea and formed a glorious spectacle. The middle one of the three belongs to the first class, pouring its majestic flood, shattered and crevassed, directly into the fiord, and crowding about twenty-five square miles of it with bergs. The next below it also sends off bergs occasionally, though a narrow strip of glacial detritus separates it from the tide-water. That forenoon a large mass fell from it, damming its draining stream, which at length broke the dam, and the resulting flood swept forward thousands of small bergs across the mud-flat into the fiord. In a short time all was quiet again; the flood-waters receded, leaving only a large blue scar on the front of the glacier and stranded bergs on the moraine flat to tell the tale.

These two glaciers are about equal in size—two miles wide—and their fronts are only about a mile and a half apart. While I sat sketching them from a point among the drifting icebergs where I could see far back into the heart of their distant fountains, two

Taku seal-hunters, father and son, came gliding toward us in an extremely small canoe. Coming alongside with a goodnatured "Sagh-a-ya," they inquired who we were, our objects, etc., and gave us information about the river, their village, and two other large glaciers that descend nearly to the sea-level a few miles up the river cañon. Crouching in their little shell of a boat among the great bergs, with paddle and barbed spear, they formed a picture as arctic and remote from anything to be found in civilization as ever was sketched for us by the explorers of the Far North.

Making our way through the crowded bergs to the extreme head of the fiord, we entered the mouth of the river, but were soon compelled to turn back on account of the strength of the current. The Taku River is a large stream, nearly a mile wide at the mouth, and, like the Stickeen, Chilcat, and Chilcoot, draws its sources from far inland, crossing the mountain-chain from the interior through a majestic cañon, and draining a multitude of glaciers on its way.

The Taku Indians, like the Chilcats, with a keen appreciation of the advantages of their position for trade, hold possession of the river and compel the Indians of the interior to accept their services as middle-men, instead of allowing them to trade directly with the whites.

When we were baffled in our attempt to ascend the river, the day was nearly done, and we began to seek a camp-ground. After sailing two or three miles along the left side of the fiord, we were so fortunate as to find a small nook described by the two Indians, where firewood was abundant, and where we could drag our canoe up the bank beyond reach of the berg-waves. Here we were safe, with a fine outlook across the fiord to the great glaciers and near enough to see the birth of the icebergs and the wonderful commotion they make, and hear their wild, roaring rejoicing. The sunset sky seemed to have been painted for this one mountain mansion, fitting it like a ceiling. After the fiord was in shadow the level sunbeams continued to pour through the miles of bergs with ravishing beauty, reflecting and refracting the purple light like cut crystal. Then all save the tips of the highest became dead white. These, too, were speedily quenched, the glowing points vanishing like stars sinking beneath the horizon. And after the shadows had crept higher, submerging the glaciers and the ridges between them, the divine alpenglow still lingered on their highest fountain peaks as they stood transfigured in glorious array. Now the last of the twilight purple has vanished, the stars begin to shine, and all trace of the day is gone. Looking across the fiord the water seems perfectly black, and the two great glaciers are seen stretching dim and ghostly into the shadowy mountains now darkly massed against the starry sky.

Next morning it was raining hard, everything looked dismal, and on the way down the fiord a growling head wind battered the rain in our faces, but we held doggedly on and by 10 A.M. got out of the fiord into Stephens Passage. A breeze sprung up in our favor that swept us bravely on across the passage and around the end of Admiralty Island by dark. We camped in a boggy hollow on a bluff among scraggy, usnea-bearded spruces. The rain, bitterly cold and driven by a stormy wind, thrashed us well while we floundered in the stumpy bog trying to make a fire and supper.

When daylight came we found our camp-ground a very savage place. How we reached it and established ourselves in the thick darkness it would be difficult to tell. We crept along the shore a few miles against strong head winds, then hoisted sail and steered straight across Lynn Canal to the mainland, which we followed without great difficulty, the wind having moderated toward evening. Near the entrance to Icy Strait we met a Hoona who had seen us last year and who seemed glad to see us. He gave us two salmon, and we made him happy with tobacco and then pushed on and camped near Sitka Jack's deserted village.

Though the wind was still ahead next morning, we made about twenty miles before sundown and camped on the west end of Farewell Island. We bumped against a hidden rock and sprung a small leak that was easily stopped with resin. The salmon-berries were ripe. While climbing a bluff for a view of our course, I discovered moneses, one of my favorites, and saw many well-traveled deer-trails, though the island is cut off from the mainland and other islands by at least five or six miles of icy, berg-encumbered water.

We got under way early next day,—a gray, cloudy morning with rain and wind. Fair and head winds were about evenly balanced throughout the day. Tides run fast here, like great rivers. We rowed and paddled around Point Wimbledon against both wind and tide, creeping close to the feet of the huge, bold rocks of the north wall of Cross Sound, which here were very steep and awe-inspiring as the heavy swells from the open sea coming in past Cape Spencer dashed white against them, tossing our frail canoe up and down lightly as a feather. The point reached by vegetation shows that the surf dashes up to a height of about seventy-five or a hundred feet. We were awe-stricken and began to fear that we might be upset should the ocean waves rise still higher. But little Stickeen seemed to enjoy the storm, and gazed at the foam-wreathed cliffs like a dreamy, comfortable tourist admiring a sunset. We reached the mouth of Taylor Bay about two or three o'clock in the afternoon, when we had a view of the open ocean before we entered the bay. Many large bergs from Glacier Bay were seen drifting out to sea past Cape Spencer. We reached the head of the fiord now called Taylor Bay at five o'clock and camped near an immense glacier with a front about three miles wide stretching across from wall to wall. No icebergs are discharged from it, as it is separated from the water of the fiord at high tide by a low, smooth mass of outspread, overswept moraine material, netted with torrents and small shallow rills from the glacier-front, with here and there a lakelet, and patches of yellow mosses and garden spots bright with epilobium, saxifrage, grass-tufts, sedges, and creeping willows on the higher ground. But only the mosses were sufficiently abundant to make conspicuous masses of color to relieve the dull slaty gray of the glacial mud and gravel. The front of the glacier, like all those which do not discharge icebergs, is rounded like a brow, smooth-looking in general views, but cleft and furrowed, nevertheless, with chasms and grooves in which the light glows and shimmers in glorious beauty. The granite walls of the fiord, though very high, are not deeply sculptured. Only a few deep side cañons with trees, bushes, grassy and flowery spots interrupt their massive simplicity, leaving but few of the cliffs absolutely sheer and bare like those of

Yosemite, Sum Dum, or Taku. One of the side cañons is on the left side of the fiord, the other on the right, the tributaries of the former leading over by a narrow tide-channel to the bay next to the eastward, and by a short portage over into a lake into which pours a branch glacier from the great glacier. Still another branch from the main glacier turns to the right. Counting all three of these separate fronts, the width of this great Taylor Bay Glacier must be about seven or eight miles.

While camp was being made, Hunter Joe climbed the eastern wall in search of wild mutton, but found none. He fell in with a brown bear, however, and got a shot at it, but nothing more. Mr. Young and I crossed the moraine slope, splashing through pools and streams up to the ice-wall, and made the interesting discovery that the glacier had been advancing of late years, ploughing up and shoving forward moraine soil that had been deposited long ago, and overwhelming and grinding and carrying away the forests on the sides and front of the glacier. Though not now sending off icebergs, the front is probably far below sea-level at the bottom, thrust forward beneath its wave-washed moraine.

Along the base of the mountain-wall we found an abundance of salmon-berries, the largest measuring an inch and a half in diameter. Strawberries, too, are found hereabouts. Some which visiting Indians brought us were as fine in size and color and flavor as any I ever saw anywhere. After wandering and wondering an hour or two, admiring the magnificent rock and crystal scenery about us, we returned to camp at sundown, planning a grand excursion for the morrow.

I set off early the morning of August 30 before any one else in camp had stirred, not waiting for breakfast, but only eating a piece of bread. I had intended getting a cup of coffee, but a wild storm was blowing and calling, and I could not wait. Running out against the rain-laden gale and turning to catch my breath, I saw that the minister's little dog had left his bed in the tent and was coming boring through the storm, evidently determined to follow me. I told him to go back, that such a day as this had nothing for him.

"Go back," I shouted, "and get your breakfast." But he simply stood with his head down, and when I began to urge my way again, looking around, I saw he was still following me. So I at last told him to come on if he must and gave him a piece of the bread I had in my pocket.

Instead of falling, the rain, mixed with misty shreds of clouds, was flying in level sheets, and the wind was roaring as I had never heard wind roar before. Over the icy levels and over the woods, on the mountains, over the jagged rocks and spires and chasms of the glacier it boomed and moaned and roared, filling the fiord in even, gray, structureless gloom, inspiring and awful. I first struggled up in the face of the blast to the east end of the ice-wall, where a patch of forest had been carried away by the glacier when it was advancing. I noticed a few stumps well out on the moraine flat, showing that its present bare, raw condition was not the condition of fifty or a hundred years ago. In front of this part of the glacier there is a small moraine lake about half a mile in length, around the margin of which are a considerable number of trees standing knee-deep, and of course dead. This also is a result of the recent advance of the ice.

Pushing up through the ragged edge of the woods on the left margin of the glacier, the storm seemed to increase in violence, so that it was difficult to draw breath in facing it; therefore I took shelter back of a tree to enjoy it and wait, hoping that it would at last somewhat abate. Here the glacier, descending over an abrupt rock, falls forward in grand cascades, while a stream swollen by the rain was now a torrent,—wind, rain, ice-torrent, and water-torrent in one grand symphony.

At length the storm seemed to abate somewhat, and I took off my heavy rubber boots, with which I had waded the glacial streams on the flat, and laid them with my overcoat on a log, where I might find them on my way back, knowing I would be drenched anyhow, and firmly tied my mountain shoes, tightened my belt, shouldered my ice-axe, and, thus free and ready for rough work, pushed on, regardless as possible of mere rain. Making my way up a steep granite slope, its projecting polished bosses encumbered here and there by boulders and the ground and bruised ruins of the ragged edge of the forest that had been uprooted by the glacier during its recent advance, I traced the side of the glacier for two or three miles, finding everywhere evidence of its having encroached on the woods, which here run back along its edge for fifteen or twenty miles. Under the projecting edge of this vast ice-river I could see down beneath it to a depth of fifty feet or so in some places, where logs and branches were being crushed to pulp, some of it almost fine enough for paper, though most of it stringy and coarse.

After thus tracing the margin of the glacier for three or four miles, I chopped steps and climbed to the top, and as far as the eye could reach, the nearly level glacier stretched indefinitely away in the gray cloudy sky, a prairie of ice. The wind was now almost moderate, though rain continued to fall, which I did not mind, but a tendency to mist in the drooping draggled clouds made me hesitate about attempting to cross to the opposite shore. Although the distance was only six or seven miles, no traces at this time could be seen of the mountains on the other side, and in case the sky should grow darker, as it seemed inclined to do, I feared that when I got out of sight of land and perhaps into a maze of crevasses I might find difficulty in winning a way back.

Lingering a while and sauntering about in sight of the shore, I found this eastern side of the glacier remarkably free from large crevasses. Nearly all I met were so narrow I could step across them almost anywhere, while the few wide ones were easily avoided by going up or down along their sides to where they narrowed. The dismal cloud ceiling showed rifts here and there, and, thus encouraged, I struck out for the west shore, aiming to strike it five or six miles above the front wall, cautiously taking compass bearings at short intervals to enable me to find my way back should the weather darken again with mist or rain or snow. The structure lines of the glacier itself were, however, my main guide. All went well. I came to a deeply furrowed section about two miles in width where I had to zigzag in long, tedious tacks and make narrow doublings, tracing the edges of wide longitudinal furrows and chasms until I could find a bridge connecting their sides, oftentimes making the direct distance ten times over. The walking was good of its kind, however, and by dint of patient doubling and axe-work on dangerous places, I gained the opposite shore in about three hours, the width of the glacier at this point being about seven miles. Occasionally, while making my way, the clouds lifted a little, revealing a few bald, rough mountains sunk to the throat in the broad, icy sea which encompassed them on all sides, sweeping on forever and forever as we count time, wearing them away, giving them the shape they are destined to take when in the fullness of time they shall be parts of new landscapes.

Ere I lost sight of the east-side mountains, those on the west came in sight, so that holding my course was easy, and, though making haste, I halted for a moment to gaze down into the beautiful pure blue crevasses and to drink at the lovely blue wells, the most beautiful of all Nature's water-basins, or at the rills and streams outspread over the ice-land prairie, never ceasing to admire their lovely color and music as they glided and swirled in their blue crystal channels and pot-holes, and the rumbling of the moulins, or mills, where streams poured into blue-walled pits of unknown depth, some of them as regularly circular as if bored with augers. Interesting, too, were the cascades over blue cliffs, where streams fell into crevasses or slid almost noiselessly down slopes so smooth and frictionless their motion was concealed. The round or oval wells, however, from one to ten feet wide, and from one to twenty or thirty feet deep, were perhaps the most beautiful of all, the water so pure as to be almost invisible. My widest views did not probably exceed fifteen miles, the rain and mist making distances seem greater.

On reaching the farther shore and tracing it a few miles to northward, I found a large portion of the glacier-current sweeping out westward in a bold and beautiful curve around the shoulder of a mountain as if going direct to the open sea. Leaving the main trunk, it breaks into a magnificent uproar of pinnacles and spires and up-heaving, splashing wave-shaped masses, a crystal cataract incomparably greater and wilder than a score of Niagaras.

Tracing its channel three or four miles, I found that it fell into a lake, which it fills with bergs. The front of this branch of the glacier is about three miles wide. I first took the lake to be the head of an arm of the sea, but, going down to its shore and tasting it, I found it

fresh, and by my aneroid perhaps less than a hundred feet above
sea-level. It is probably separated from the sea only by a moraine
dam. I had not time to go around its shores, as it was now near five
o'clock and I was about fifteen miles from camp, and I had to make
haste to recross the glacier before dark, which would come on
about eight o'clock. I therefore made haste up to the main glacier,
and, shaping my course by compass and the structure lines of the
ice, set off from the land out on to the grand crystal prairie again.
All was so silent and so concentrated, owing to the low dragging
mist, the beauty close about me was all the more keenly felt, though
tinged with a dim sense of danger, as if coming events were casting
shadows. I was soon out of sight of land, and the evening dusk that
on cloudy days precedes the real night gloom came stealing on and
only ice was in sight, and the only sounds, save the low rumbling of
the mills and the rattle of falling stones at long intervals, were the
low, terribly earnest moanings of the wind or distant waterfalls
coming through the thickening gloom. After two hours of hard
work I came to a maze of crevasses of appalling depth and width
which could not be passed apparently either up or down. I traced
them with firm nerve developed by the danger, making wide jumps,
poising cautiously on dizzy edges after cutting footholds, taking
wide crevasses at a grand leap at once frightful and inspiring. Many
a mile was thus traveled, mostly up and down the glacier, making
but little real headway, running much of the time as the danger of
having to pass the night on the ice became more and more immi-
nent. This I could do, though with the weather and my rain-soaked
condition it would be trying at best. In treading the mazes of this
crevassed section I had frequently to cross bridges that were only
knife-edges for twenty or thirty feet, cutting off the sharp tops and
leaving them flat so that little Stickeen could follow me. These I
had to straddle, cutting off the top as I progressed and hitching
gradually ahead like a boy riding a rail fence. All this time the little
dog followed me bravely, never hesitating on the brink of any
crevasse that I had jumped, but now that it was becoming dark and
the crevasses became more troublesome, he followed close at my
heels instead of scampering far and wide, where the ice was at all

smooth, as he had in the forenoon. No land was now in sight. The mist fell lower and darker and snow began to fly. I could not see far enough up and down the glacier to judge how best to work out of the bewildering labyrinth, and how hard I tried while there was yet hope of reaching camp that night! a hope which was fast growing dim like the sky. After dark, on such ground, to keep from freezing, I could only jump up and down until morning on a piece of flat ice between the crevasses, dance to the boding music of the winds and waters, and as I was already tired and hungry I would be in bad condition for such ice work. Many times I was put to my mettle, but with a firm-braced nerve, all the more unflinching as the dangers thickened, I worked out of that terrible ice-web, and with blood fairly up Stickeen and I ran over common danger without fatigue. Our very hardest trial was in getting across the very last of the sliver bridges. After examining the first of the two widest crevasses, I followed its edge half a mile or so up and down and discovered that its narrowest spot was about eight feet wide, which was the limit of what I was able to jump. Moreover, the side I was on—that is, the west side—was about a foot higher than the other, and I feared that in case I should be stopped by a still wider impassable crevasse ahead that I would hardly be able to take back that jump from its lower side. The ice beyond, however, as far as I could see it, looked temptingly smooth. Therefore, after carefully making a socket for my foot on the rounded brink, I jumped, but found that I had nothing to spare and more than ever dreaded having to retrace my way. Little Stickeen jumped this, however, without apparently taking a second look at it, and we ran ahead joyfully over smooth, level ice, hoping we were now leaving all danger behind us. But hardly had we gone a hundred or two yards when to our dismay we found ourselves on the very widest of all the longitudinal crevasses we had yet encountered. It was about forty feet wide. I ran anxiously up the side of it to northward, eagerly hoping that I could get around its head, but my worst fears were realized when at a distance of about a mile or less it ran into the crevasse that I had just jumped. I then ran down the edge for a mile or more below the point where I had first met it, and found that its lower end also united with the crevasse I had jumped, showing dismally that we were on an island two or three hundred yards wide and about two miles long and the only way of escape from this island was by turning back and jumping again that crevasse which I dreaded, or venturing ahead across the giant crevasse by the very worst of the sliver bridges I had ever seen. It was so badly weathered and melted down that it formed a knife-edge, and extended across from side to side in a low, drooping curve like that made by a loose rope attached at each end at the same height. But the worst difficulty was that the ends of the down-curving sliver were attached to the sides at a depth of about eight or ten feet below the surface of the glacier. Getting down to the end of the bridge, and then after crossing it getting up the other side, seemed hardly possible. However, I decided to dare the dangers of the fearful sliver rather than to attempt to retrace my steps. Accordingly I dug a low groove in the rounded edge for my knees to rest in and, leaning over, began to cut a narrow foothold on the steep, smooth side. When I was doing this, Stickeen came up behind me, pushed his head over my shoulder, looked into the crevasses and along the narrow knife-edge, then turned and looked in my face, muttering and whining as if trying to say, "Surely you are not going down there." I said, "Yes, Stickeen, this is the only way." He then began to cry and ran wildly along the rim of the crevasse, searching for a better way, then, returning baffled, of course, he came behind me and lay down and cried louder and louder.

After getting down one step I cautiously stooped and cut another and another in succession until I reached the point where the sliver was attached to the wall. There, cautiously balancing, I chipped down the upcurved end of the bridge until I had formed a small level platform about a foot wide, then, bending forward, got astride of the end of the sliver, steadied myself with my knees, then cut off the top of the sliver, hitching myself forward an inch or two at a time, leaving it about four inches wide for Stickeen. Arrived at the farther end of the sliver, which was about seventy-five feet long, I chipped another little platform on its upcurved end, cautiously rose to my feet, and with infinite pains cut narrow notch steps and finger-holds in the wall and finally got safely across. All this dreadful time poor little Stickeen was crying as if his heart was broken, and when I called to him in as reassuring a voice as I could muster, he only cried the louder, as if trying to say that he never, never could get down there—the only time that the brave little fellow appeared to know what danger was. After going away as if I was leaving him, he still howled and cried without venturing to try to follow me. Returning to the edge of the crevasse, I told him that I must go, that he could come if he only tried, and finally in despair he hushed his cries, slid his little feet slowly down into my footsteps out on the big sliver, walked slowly and cautiously along the sliver as if holding his breath, while the snow was falling and the wind was moaning and threatening to blow him off. When he arrived at the foot of the slope below me, I was kneeling on the brink ready to assist him in case he should be unable to reach the top. He looked up along the row of notched steps I had made, as if fixing them in his mind, then with a nervous spring he whizzed up and passed me out on to the level ice, and ran and cried and barked and rolled about fairly hysterical in the sudden revulsion from the depth of despair to triumphant joy. I tried to catch him and pet him and tell him how good and brave he was, but he would not be caught. He ran round and round, swirling like autumn leaves in an eddy, lay down and rolled head over heels. I told him we still had far to go and that we must now stop all nonsense and get off the ice before dark. I knew by the ice-lines that every step was now taking me nearer the shore and soon it came in sight. The headland four or five miles back from the front, covered with spruce trees, loomed faintly but surely through the mist and light fall of snow not more than two miles away. The ice now proved good all the way across, and we reached the lateral moraine just at dusk, then with trembling limbs, now that the danger was over, we staggered and stumbled down the bouldery edge of the glacier and got over the dangerous rocks by the cascades while yet a faint light lingered. We were safe, and then, too, came limp weariness such as no ordinary work ever produces, however hard it may be. Wearily we stumbled down through the woods, over logs and brush and roots, devil's-clubs pricking us at every faint blundering tumble. At last we got out on the smooth mud slope with only a mile of slow but sure dragging of weary limbs to camp. The Indians had been firing guns to guide me and had a fine supper and fire ready, though fearing they would be compelled to seek us in the morning, a care not often applied to me. Stickeen and I were too tired to eat much, and, strange to say, too tired to sleep. Both of us, springing up in the night again and again, fancied we were still on that dreadful ice bridge in the shadow of death.

Nevertheless, we arose next morning in newness of life. Never before had rocks and ice and trees seemed so beautiful and wonderful, even the cold, biting rainstorm that was blowing seemed full of loving-kindness, wonderful compensation for all that we had endured, and we sailed down the bay through the gray, driving rain rejoicing.

CHAPTER XVI

GLACIER BAY

While Stickeen and I were away, a Hoona, one of the head men of the tribe, paid Mr. Young a visit, and presented him with porpoise-meat and berries and much interesting information. He naturally expected a return visit, and when we called at his house, a mile or two down the fiord, he said his wives were out in the rain gathering fresh berries to complete a feast prepared for us. We remained, however, only a few minutes, for I was not aware of this arrangement or of Mr. Young's promise until after leaving the house. Anxiety to get around Cape Wimbelton was the cause of my haste, fearing the storm might increase. On account of this ignorance, no apologies were offered him, and the upshot was that the good Hoona became very angry. We succeeded, however, in the evening of the same day, in explaining our haste, and by sincere apologies and presents made peace.

After a hard struggle we got around stormy Wimbelton and into the next fiord to the northward (Klunastucksana—Dundas Bay). A cold, drenching rain was falling, darkening but not altogether hiding its extraordinary beauty, made up of lovely reaches and side fiords, feathery headlands and islands, beautiful every one and charmingly collocated. But how it rained, and how cold it was, and how weary we were pulling most of the time against the wind! The branches of this bay are so deep and so numerous that, with the rain and low clouds concealing the mountain landmarks, we could hardly make out the main trends. While groping and gazing among the islands through the misty rain and clouds, we discovered wisps of smoke at the foot of a sheltering rock in front of a mountain, where a choir of cascades were chanting their rain songs. Gladly we made for this camp, which proved to belong to a rare old Hoona sub-chief, so tall and wide and dignified in demeanor he looked grand even in the sloppy weather, and every inch a chief in spite of his bare legs and the old shirt and draggled, ragged blanket in which he was dressed. He was given to much handshaking, gripping hard, holding on and looking you gravely in the face while most emphatically speaking in Thlinkit, not a word of which we understood until interpreter John came to our help. He turned from one to the other of us, declaring, as John interpreted, that our presence did him good like food and fire, that he would welcome white men, especially teachers, and that he and all his people compared to ourselves were only children. When Mr. Young informed him that a missionary was about to be sent to his people, he said he would call them all together four times and explain that a teacher and preacher were coming and that they therefore must put away all foolishness and prepare their hearts to receive them and their words. He then introduced his three children, one a naked lad five or six years old who, as he fondly assured us, would soon be a chief, and later to his wife, an intelligent-looking woman of whom he seemed proud. When we arrived she was out at the foot of the cascade mountain gathering salmon-berries. She came in dripping and loaded. A few of the fine berries saved for the children she presented, proudly and fondly beginning with the youngest, whose only clothing was a nose-ring and a string of beads. She was lightly appareled in a cotton gown and bit of blanket, thoroughly bedraggled, but after unloading her berries she retired with a dry calico gown around the corner of a rock and soon returned fresh as a daisy and with becoming dignity took her place by the fireside. Soon two other berry-laden women came in, seemingly enjoying the rain like the bushes and trees. They put on little clothing so that they may be the more easily dried, and as for the children, a thin shirt of sheeting is the most they encumber themselves with, and get wet and half dry without seeming to notice it while we shiver with two or three dry coats. They seem to prefer being naked. The men also wear but little in wet weather. When they go out for all day they put on a single blanket, but in choring around camp, getting firewood, cooking, or looking after their precious canvas, they seldom wear anything, braving wind and rain in utter nakedness to avoid the bother of drying clothes. It is a rare sight to see the children bringing in big chunks of firewood on their shoulders, balancing in crossing boulders with firmly set bow-legs and bulging back muscles.

We gave Ka-hood-oo-shough, the old chief, some tobacco and rice and coffee, and pitched our tent near his hut among tall grass. Soon after our arrival the Taylor Bay sub-chief came in from the opposite direction from ours, telling us that he came through a cut-off passage not on our chart. As stated above, we took pains to conciliate him and soothe his hurt feelings. Our words and gifts, he said, had warmed his sore heart and made him glad and comfortable.

The view down the bay among the islands was, I thought, the finest of this kind of scenery that I had yet observed.

The weather continued cold and rainy. Nevertheless Mr. Young and I and our crew, together with one of the Hoonas, an old man who acted as guide, left camp to explore one of the upper arms of the bay, where we were told there was a large glacier. We managed to push the canoe several miles up the stream that drains the glacier to a point where the swift current was divided among rocks and the banks were overhung with alders and willows. I left the canoe and pushed up the right bank past a magnificent waterfall some twelve hundred feet high, and over the shoulder of a mountain, until I secured a good view of the lower part of the glacier. It is probably a lobe of the Taylor Bay or Brady Glacier.

On our return to camp, thoroughly drenched and cold, the old chief came to visit us, apparently as wet and cold as ourselves.

"I have been thinking of you all day," he said, "and pitying you, knowing how miserable you were, and as soon as I saw your canoe coming back I was ashamed to think that I had been sitting warm and dry at my fire while you were out in the storm; therefore I made haste to strip off my dry clothing and put on these wet rags to share your misery and show how much I love you."

I had another long talk with Ka-hood-oo-shough the next day.

"I am not able," he said, "to tell you how much good your words have done me. Your words are good, and they are strong words. Some of my people are foolish, and when they make their salmon-traps they do not take care to tie the poles firmly together, and when the big rain-floods come the traps break and are washed away because the people who made them are foolish people. But your words are strong words and when storms come to try them they will stand the storms."

There was much handshaking as we took our leave and assurances of eternal friendship. The grand old man stood on the shore watching us and waving farewell until we were out of sight.

We now steered for the Muir Glacier and arrived at the front on the east side the evening of the third, and camped on the end of the moraine, where there was a small stream. Captain Tyeen was inclined to keep at a safe distance from the tremendous threatening cliffs of the discharging wall. After a good deal of urging he ventured within half a mile of them, on the east side of the fiord, where with Mr. Young I went ashore to seek a camp-ground on the moraine, leaving the Indians in the canoe. In a few minutes after we landed a huge berg sprung aloft with awful commotion, and the frightened Indians incontinently fled down the fiord, plying their paddles with admirable energy in the tossing waves until a safe harbor was reached around the south end of the moraine. I found a good place for a camp in a slight hollow where a few spruce stumps afforded firewood. But all efforts to get Tyeen out of his harbor failed. "Nobody knew," he said, "how far the angry ice-mountain could throw waves to break his canoe." Therefore I had my bedding and some provisions carried to my stump camp, where I could watch the bergs as they were discharged and get night views of the brow of the glacier and its sheer jagged face all the way across from side to side of the channel. One night the water was luminous and the surge from discharging icebergs churned the water into silver fire, a glorious sight in the darkness. I also went back up the east side of the glacier five or six miles and ascended a mountain between its first two eastern tributaries, which, though covered with grass near the top, was exceedingly steep and difficult. A bulging ridge near the top I discovered was formed of ice, a remnant of the glacier when it stood at this elevation which had been preserved by moraine material and later by a thatch of dwarf bushes and grass.

Next morning at daybreak I pushed eagerly back over the comparatively smooth eastern margin of the glacier to see as much as possible of the upper fountain region. About five miles back from the front I climbed a mountain twenty-five hundred feet high, from the flowery summit of which, the day being clear, the vast glacier and its principal branches were displayed in one magnificent view. Instead of a stream of ice winding down a mountain-walled valley like the largest of the Swiss glaciers, the Muir looks like a broad undulating prairie streaked with medial moraines and gashed with crevasses, surrounded by numberless mountains from which flow its many tributary glaciers. There are seven main tributaries from ten to twenty miles long and from two to six miles wide where they enter the trunk, each of them fed by many secondary tributaries; so that the whole number of branches, great and small, pouring from the mountain fountains perhaps number upward of two hundred, not counting the smallest. The area drained by this one grand glacier can hardly be less than seven or eight hundred miles, and probably contains as much ice as all the eleven hundred Swiss glaciers combined. Its length from the frontal wall back to the head of its farthest fountain seemed to be about forty or fifty miles, and the width just below the confluence of the main tributaries about twenty-five miles. Though apparently motionless as the mountains, it flows on forever, the speed varying in every part with the seasons, but mostly with the depth of the current, and the declivity, smoothness and directness of the different portions of the basin. The flow of the central cascading portion near the front, as determined by Professor Reid, is at the rate of from two and a half to five inches an hour, or from five to ten feet a day. A strip of the main trunk about a mile in width, extending along the eastern margin about fourteen miles to a lake filled with bergs, has so little motion and is so little interrupted by crevasses, a hundred horsemen might ride abreast over it without encountering very much difficulty.

But by far the greater portion of the vast expanse looking smooth in the distance is torn and crumpled into a bewildering network of hummocky ridges and blades, separated by yawning gulfs and crevasses, so that the explorer, crossing it from shore to shore, must always have a hard time. In hollow spots here and there in the heart of the icy wilderness are small lakelets fed by swift-glancing streams that flow without friction in blue shining channels, making delightful melody, singing and ringing in silvery tones of peculiar sweetness, radiant crystals like flowers ineffably fine growing in dazzling beauty along their banks. Few, however, will be likely to enjoy them. Fortunately to most travelers the thundering ice-wall, while comfortably accessible, is also the most strikingly interesting portion of the glacier.

The mountains about the great glacier were also seen from this standpoint in exceedingly grand and telling views, ranged and grouped in glorious array. Along the valleys of the main tributaries to the northwestward I saw far into their shadowy depths, one noble peak in its snowy robes appearing beyond another in fine perspective. One of the most remarkable of them, fashioned like a superb crown with delicately fluted sides, stands in the middle of the second main tributary, counting from left to right. To the westward the magnificent Fairweather Range is displayed in all its glory, lifting its peaks and glaciers into the blue sky. Mt. Fairweather, though not the highest, is the noblest and most majestic in port and architecture of all the sky-dwelling company. La Pérouse, at the south end of the range, is also a magnificent mountain, symmetrically peaked and sculptured, and wears its robes of snow and glaciers in noble style. Lituya, as seen from here, is an immense tower, severely plain and massive. It makes a fine and terrible and lonely impression. Crillon, though the loftiest of all (being nearly sixteen thousand feet high), presents no well-marked features. Its ponderous glaciers have ground it away into long, curling ridges until, from this point of view, it resembles a huge twisted shell. The lower summits about the Muir Glacier, like this one, the first that I climbed, are richly adorned and enlivened with flowers, though they make but a faint show in general views. Lines and dashes of bright green appear on the lower slopes as one approaches them from the glacier, and a fainter green tinge may be noticed on the subordinate summits at a height of two thousand or three thousand feet. The lower are mostly alder bushes and the top-most a lavish profusion of flowering plants, chiefly cassiope, vaccinium, pyrola, erigeron, gentiana, campanula, anemone, larkspur, and columbine, with a few grasses and ferns. Of these cassiope is at once the commonest and the most beautiful and influential. In some places its delicate stems make mattresses more than a foot thick over several acres, while the bloom is so abundant that a single handful plucked at random contains hundreds of its pale pink bells. The very thought of this Alaska garden is a joyful exhilaration. Though the storm-beaten ground it is growing on is nearly half a mile high, the glacier centuries ago flowed over it as a river flows over a boulder; but out of all the cold darkness and glacial crushing and grinding comes this warm, abounding beauty and life to teach us that what we in our faithless ignorance and fear call destruction is creation finer and finer.

When night was approaching I scrambled down out of my blessed garden to the glacier, and returned to my lonely camp, and, getting some coffee and bread, again went up the moraine to the east end of the great ice-wall. It is about three miles long, but the length of the jagged, berg-producing portion that stretches across the fiord from side to side like a huge green-and-blue barrier is only about two miles and rises above the water to a height of from two hundred and fifty to three hundred feet. Soundings made by Captain Carroll show that seven hundred and twenty feet of the wall is below the surface, and a third unmeasured portion is buried beneath the moraine detritus deposited at the foot of it. Therefore, were the water and rocky detritus cleared away, a sheer precipice of ice would be presented nearly two miles long and more than a thousand feet high. Seen from a distance, as you come up the fiord, it seems comparatively regular in form, but it is far otherwise; bold, jagged capes jut forward into the fiord, alternating with deep reëntering angles and craggy hollows with plain bastions, while the top is roughened with innumerable spires and pyramids and sharp hacked blades leaning and toppling or cutting straight into the sky.

The number of bergs given off varies somewhat with the weather and the tides, the average being about one every five or six minutes, counting only those that roar loud enough to make themselves heard at a distance of two or three miles. The very largest, however, may under favorable conditions be heard ten miles or even farther. When a large mass sinks from the upper fissured portion of the wall, there is first a keen, prolonged, thundering roar, which slowly subsides into a low muttering growl, followed by numerous smaller grating clashing sounds from the agitated bergs that dance in the waves about the newcomer as if in welcome; and these again are followed by the swash and roar of the waves that are raised and hurled up the beach against the moraines. But the largest and most beautiful of the bergs, instead of thus falling from the upper weathered portion of the wall, rise from the submerged portion with a still grander commotion, springing with tremendous voice and gestures nearly to the top of the wall, tons of water streaming like hair down their sides, plunging and rising again and again before they finally settle in perfect poise, free at last, after having formed part of the slow-crawling glacier for centuries. And as we contemplate their history, as they sail calmly away down the fiord to the sea, how wonderful it seems that ice formed from pressed snow on the far-off mountains two or three hundred years ago should still be pure and lovely in color after all its travel and toil in the rough mountain quarries, grinding and fashioning the features of predestined landscapes.

When sunshine is sifting through the midst of the multitude of icebergs that fill the fiord and through the jets of radiant spray ever rising from the tremendous dashing and splashing of the falling and upspringing bergs, the effect is indescribably glorious. Glorious, too, are the shows they make in the night when the moon and stars are shining. The berg-thunder seems far louder than by day, and the projecting buttresses seem higher as they stand forward in the pale light, relieved by gloomy hollows, while the new-born bergs are dimly seen, crowned with faint lunar rainbows in the up-dashing spray. But it is in the darkest nights when storms are blowing and the waves are phosphorescent that the most impressive displays are made. Then the long range of ice-bluffs is plainly seen stretching through the gloom in weird, unearthly splendor, luminous wave foam dashing against every bluff and drifting berg; and ever and anon amid all this wild auroral splendor some huge new-born berg dashes the living water into yet brighter foam, and the streaming torrents pouring from its sides are worn as robes of light, while they roar in awful accord with the winds and waves, deep calling unto deep, glacier to glacier, from fiord to fiord over all the wonderful bay.

After spending a few days here, we struck across to the main Hoona village on the south side of Icy Strait, thence by a long cut-off with one short portage to Chatham Strait, and thence down through Peril Strait, sailing all night, hoping to catch the mail steamer at Sitka. We arrived at the head of the strait about day-break. The tide was falling, and rushing down with the swift current as if descending a majestic cataract was a memorable experience. We reached Sitka the same night, and there I paid and discharged my crew, making allowance for a couple of days or so for the journey back home to Fort Wrangell, while I boarded the steamer for Portland and thus ended my explorations for this season.

PART THREE

THE TRIP OF
1890

CHAPTER XVII

In Camp at Glacier Bay

I left San Francisco for Glacier Bay on the steamer City of Pueblo, June 14, 1890, at 10 A.M., this being my third trip to southeastern Alaska and fourth to Alaska, including northern and western Alaska as far as Unalaska and Pt. Barrow and the northeastern coast of Siberia. The bar at the Golden Gate was smooth, the weather cool and pleasant. The redwoods in sheltered coves approach the shore closely, their dwarfed and shorn tops appearing here and there in ravines along the coast up to Oregon. The wind-swept hills, beaten with scud, are of course bare of trees. Along the Oregon and Washington coast the trees get nearer the sea, for spruce and contorted pine endure the briny winds better than the redwoods. We took the inside passage between the shore and Race Rocks, a long range of islets on which many a good ship has been wrecked. The breakers from the deep Pacific, driven by the gale, made a glorious display of foam on the bald islet rocks, sending spray over the tops of some of them a hundred feet high or more in sublime, curving, jagged-edged and flame-shaped sheets. The gestures of these upspringing, purple-tinged waves as they dashed and broke were sublime and serene, combining displays of graceful beauty of motion and form with tremendous power—a truly glori-

ous show. I noticed several small villages on the green slopes between the timbered mountains and the shore. Long Branch made
quite a display of new houses along the beach, north of the mouth
of the Columbia.

I had pleasant company on the Pueblo and sat at the chief engineer's table, who was a good and merry talker. An old San Francisco
lawyer, rather stiff and dignified, knew my father-in-law, Dr.
Strentzel. Three ladies, opposed to the pitching of the ship, were
absent from table the greater part of the way. My best talker was an
old Scandinavian sea-captain, who was having a new bark built at
Port Blakely,—an interesting old salt, every sentence of his conversation flavored with sea-brine, bluff and hearty as a sea-wave,
keen-eyed, courageous, self-reliant, and so stubbornly skeptical he
refused to believe even in glaciers.

"After you see your bark," I said, "and find everything being done
to your mind, you had better go on to Alaska and see the glaciers."

"Oh, I haf seen many glaciers already."

"But are you sure that you know what a glacier is?" I asked.

"Vell, a glacier is a big mountain all covered up with ice."

"Then a river," said I, "must be a big mountain all covered
with water."

I explained what a glacier was and succeeded in exciting his interest. I told him he must reform, for a man who neither believed in
God nor glaciers must be very bad, indeed the worst of all unbe-
lievers.

At Port Townsend I met Mr. Loomis, who had agreed to go with
me as far as the Muir Glacier. We sailed from here on the steamer
Queen. We touched again at Victoria, and I took a short walk into
the adjacent woods and gardens and found the flowery vegetation
in its glory, especially the large wild rose for which the region is famous, and the spiræa and English honeysuckle of the gardens.

JUNE 18. We sailed from Victoria on the Queen at 10.30 A.M. The
weather all the way to Fort Wrangell was cloudy and rainy, but the
scenery is delightful even in the dullest weather. The marvelous
wealth of forests, islands, and waterfalls, the cloud-wreathed

heights, the many avalanche slopes and slips, the pearl-gray tones of the sky, the browns of the woods, their purple flower edges and mist fringes, the endless combinations of water and land and ever-shifting clouds—none of these greatly interest the tourists. I noticed one of the small whales that frequent these channels and mentioned the fact, then called attention to a charming group of islands, but they turned their eyes from the islands, saying, "Yes, yes, they are very fine, but where did you see the whale?"

The timber is larger and apparently better every way as you go north from Victoria, that is on the islands, perhaps on account of fires from less rain to the southward. All the islands have been overswept by the ice-sheet and are but little changed as yet, save a few of the highest summits which have been sculptured by local residual glaciers. All have approximately the form of greatest strength with reference to the overflow of an ice-sheet, excepting those mentioned above, which have been more or less eroded by local residual glaciers. Every channel also has the form of greatest strength with reference to ice-action. Islands, as we have seen, are still being born in Glacier Bay and elsewhere to the northward.

I found many pleasant people aboard, but strangely ignorant on the subject of earth-sculpture and landscape-making. Professor Niles, of the Boston Institute of Technology, is aboard; also Mr. Russell and Mr. Kerr of the Geological Survey, who are now on their way to Mt. St. Elias, hoping to reach the summit; and a granddaughter of Peter Burnett, the first governor of California.

We arrived at Wrangell in the rain at 10.30 P.M. There was a grand rush on shore to buy curiosities and see totem poles. The shops were jammed and mobbed, high prices paid for shabby stuff manufactured expressly for tourist trade. Silver bracelets hammered out of dollars and half dollars by Indian smiths are the most popular articles, then baskets, yellow cedar toy canoes, paddles, etc. Most people who travel look only at what they are directed to look at. Great is the power of the guidebook-maker, however ignorant. I inquired for my old friends Tyeen and Shakes, who were both absent.

JUNE 20. We left Wrangell early this morning and passed through the Wrangell Narrows at high tide. I noticed a few bergs near Cape Fanshawe from Wrangell Glacier. The water ten miles from Wrangell is colored with particles derived mostly from the Stickeen River glaciers and Le Conte Glacier. All the waters of the channels north of Wrangell are green or yellowish from glacier erosion. We had a good view of the glaciers all the way to Juneau, but not of their high, cloud-veiled fountains. The stranded bergs on the moraine bar at the mouth of Sum Dum Bay looked just as they did when I first saw them ten years ago.

Before reaching Juneau, the Queen proceeded up the Taku Inlet that the passengers might see the fine glacier at its head, and ventured to within half a mile of the berg-discharging front, which is about three quarters of a mile wide. Bergs fell but seldom, perhaps one in half an hour. The glacier makes a rapid descent near the front. The inlet, therefore, will not be much extended beyond its present limit by the recession of the glacier. The grand rocks on either side of its channel show ice-action in telling style. The Norris Glacier, about two miles below the Taku, is a good example of a glacier in the first stage of decadence. The Taku River enters the head of the inlet a little to the east of the glaciers, coming from beyond the main coast range. All the tourists are delighted at seeing a grand glacier in the flesh. The scenery is very fine here and in the channel at Juneau. On Douglas Island there is a large mill of 240 stamps, all run by one small water-wheel, which, however, is acted on by water at enormous pressure. The forests around the mill are being rapidly nibbled away. Wind is here said to be very violent at times, blowing away people and houses and sweeping scud far up the mountain-side. Winter snow is seldom more than a foot or two deep.

JUNE 21. We arrived at Douglas Island at five in the afternoon and went sight-seeing through the mill. Six hundred tons of low-grade quartz are crushed per day. Juneau, on the mainland opposite the Douglas Island mills, is quite a village, well supplied with stores, churches, etc. A dance-house in which Indians are supposed to show native dances of all sorts is perhaps the best-patronized of all the places of amusement. A Mr. Brooks, who prints a paper here, gave us some information on Mt. St. Elias, Mt. Wrangell, and the Cook Inlet and Prince William Sound region. He told Russell that he would never reach the summit of St. Elias, that it was inaccessible. He saw no glaciers that discharged bergs into the sea at Cook Inlet, but many in Prince William Sound.

JUNE 22. Leaving Juneau at noon, we had a good view of the Auk Glacier at the mouth of the channel between Douglas Island and the mainland, and of Eagle Glacier a few miles north of the Auk on the east side of Lynn Canal. Then the Davidson Glacier came in sight, finely curved, striped with medial moraines, and girdled in front by its magnificent tree-fringed terminal moraine; and besides these many others of every size and pattern on the mountains bounding Lynn Canal, most of them comparatively small, completing their sculpture. The mountains on either hand and at the head of the canal are strikingly beautiful at any time of the year. The sky to-day is mostly clear, with just clouds enough hovering about the mountains to show them to best advantage as they stretch onward in sustained grandeur like two separate and distinct ranges, each mountain with its glaciers and clouds and fine sculpture glowing bright in smooth, graded light. Only a few of them exceed five thousand feet in height; but as one naturally associates great height with ice-and-snow-laden mountains and with glacial sculpture so pronounced, they seem much higher. There are now two canneries at the head of Lynn Canal. The Indians furnish some of the salmon at ten cents each. Everybody sits up to see the midnight sky. At this time of the year there is no night here, though the sun drops a degree or two below the horizon. One may read at twelve o'clock San Francisco time.

JUNE 23. Early this morning we arrived in Glacier Bay. We passed through crowds of bergs at the mouth of the bay, though, owing to wind and tide, there were but few at the front of Muir Glacier. A fine, bright day, the last of a group of a week or two, as shown by the dryness of the sand along the shore and on the moraine—rare weather hereabouts. Most of the passengers went ashore and climbed the moraine on the east side to get a view of the glacier from a point a little higher than the top of the front wall. A few ventured on a mile or two farther. The day was delightful, and our one hundred and eighty passengers were happy, gazing at the beautiful blue of the bergs and the shattered pinnacled crystal wall, awed by the thunder and commotion of the falling and rising ice-bergs, which ever and anon sent spray flying several hundred feet into the air and raised swells that set all the fleet of bergs in motion and roared up the beach, telling the story of the birth of every ice-berg far and near. The number discharged varies much, influenced in part no doubt by the tides and weather and seasons, sometimes one every five minutes for half a day at a time on the average, though intervals of twenty or thirty minutes may occur without any considerable fall, then three or four immense discharges will take place in as many minutes. The sound they make is like heavy thunder, with a prolonged roar after deep thudding sounds—a per-petual thunderstorm easily heard three or four miles away. The roar in our tent and the shaking of the ground one or two miles dis-tant from points of discharge seems startlingly near.

I had to look after camp-supplies and left the ship late this morning, going with a crowd to the glacier; then, taking advantage of the fine weather, I pushed off alone into the silent icy prairie to the east, to Nunatak Island, about five hundred feet above the ice. I discovered a small lake on the larger of the two islands, and many battered and ground fragments of fossil wood, large and small. They seem to have come from trees that grew on the island perhaps centuries ago. I mean to use this island as a station in setting out stakes to measure the glacial flow. The top of Mt. Fairweather is in sight at a distance of perhaps thirty miles, the ice all smooth on the eastern border, wildly broken in the central portion. I reached the ship at 2.30 P.M. I had intended getting back at noon and sending letters and bidding friends good-bye, but could not resist this gla-cier saunter. The ship moved off as soon as I was seen on the moraine bluff, and Loomis and I waved our hats in farewell to the many wav-ings of handkerchiefs of acquaintances we had made on the trip.

Our goods—blankets, provisions, tent, etc.—lay in a rocky moraine hollow within a mile of the great terminal wall of the glacier, and the discharge of the rising and falling icebergs kept up an almost continuous thundering and echoing, while a few gulls flew about on easy wing or stood like specks of foam on the shore. These were our neighbors.

After my twelve-mile walk, I ate a cracker and planned the camp. I found that one of my boxes had been left on the steamer, but still we have more than enough of everything. We obtained two cords of dry wood at Juneau which Captain Carroll kindly had his men carry up the moraine to our camp-ground. We piled the wood as a wind-break, then laid a floor of lumber brought from Seattle for a square tent, nine feet by nine. We set the tent, stored our provisions in it, and made our beds. This work was done by 11.30 P.M., good daylight lasting to this time. We slept well in our roomy cotton house, dreaming of California home nests in the wilderness of ice.

JUNE 25. A rainy day. For a few hours I kept count of the number of bergs discharged, then sauntered along the beach to the end of the crystal wall. A portion of the way is dangerous, the moraine bluff being capped by an overlying lobe of the glacier, which as it melts sends down boulders and fragments of ice, while the strip of sandy shore at high tide is only a few rods wide, leaving but little room to escape from the falling moraine material and the berg-waves. The view of the ice-cliffs, pinnacles, spires and ridges was very telling, a magnificent picture of nature's power and industry and love of beauty. About a hundred or a hundred and fifty feet from the shore a large stream issues from an arched, tunnel-like channel in the wall of the glacier, the blue of the ice hall being of an exquisite tone, contrasting with the strange, sooty, smoky, brown-colored stream. The front wall of the Muir Glacier is about two and a half or three miles wide. Only the central portion about two miles wide discharges icebergs. The two wings advanced over the washed and stratified moraine deposits have little or no motion, melting and receding as fast, or perhaps faster, than it advances. They have been advanced at least a mile over the old re-formed moraines, as is shown by the overlying, angular, recent moraine deposits, now being laid down, which are continuous with the medial moraines of the glacier.

In the old stratified moraine banks, trunks and branches of trees showing but little sign of decay occur at a height of about a hundred feet above tide-water. I have not yet compared this fossil wood with that of the opposite shore deposits. That the glacier was once withdrawn considerably back of its present limit seems plain. Immense torrents of water had filled in the inlet with stratified moraine material, and for centuries favorable climatic conditions allowed forests to grow upon it. At length the glacier advanced, probably three or four miles, uprooting and burying the trees which had grown undisturbed for centuries. Then came a great thaw, which produced the flood that deposited the uprooted trees. Also the trees which grew around the shores above the reach of floods were shed off, perhaps by the thawing of the soil that was resting on the buried margin of the glacier, left on its retreat and protected by a covering of moraine material from melting as fast as the exposed surface of the glacier. What appear to be remnants of the margin of the glacier when it stood at a much higher level still exist on the left side and probably all along its banks on both sides just below its present terminus.

JUNE 26. We fixed a mark on the left wing to measure the motion if any. It rained all day, but I had a grand tramp over mud, ice, and rock to the east wall of the inlet. Brown metamorphic slate, close-grained in places, dips away from the inlet, presenting edges to ice-action, which has given rise to a singularly beautiful and striking surface, polished and grooved and fluted.

All the next day it rained. The mountains were smothered in dull-colored mist and fog, the great glacier looming through the gloomy gray fog fringes with wonderful effect. The thunder of bergs booms and rumbles through the foggy atmosphere. It is bad weather for exploring but delightful nevertheless, making all the strange, mysterious region yet stranger and more mysterious.

JUNE 28. A light rain. We were visited by two parties of Indians. A man from each canoe came ashore, leaving the women in the canoe to guard against the berg-waves. I tried my Chinook and made out to say that I wanted to hire two of them in a few days to go a little way back on the glacier and around the bay. They are seal-hunters and promised to come again with "Charley," who "hi yu kumtux wawa Boston"—knew well how to speak English.

I saw three huge bergs born. Spray rose about two hundred feet. Lovely reflections showed of the pale-blue tones of the ice-wall and mountains in the calm water. Mirages are common, making the stranded bergs along the shore look like the sheer frontal wall of the glacier from which they were discharged.

I am watching the ice-wall, berg life and behavior, etc. Yesterday and to-day a solitary small flycatcher was feeding about camp. A sandpiper on the shore, loons, ducks, gulls, and crows, a few of each, and a bald eagle are all the birds I have noticed thus far. The glacier is thundering gloriously.

JUNE 30. Clearing clouds and sunshine. In less than a minute I saw three large bergs born. First there is usually a preliminary thundering of comparatively small masses as the large mass begins to fall, then the grand crash and boom and reverberating roaring. Oftentimes three or four heavy main throbbing thuds and booming explosions are heard as the main mass falls in several pieces, and also secondary thuds and thunderings as the mass or masses plunge and rise again and again ere they come to rest. Seldom, if ever, do the towers, battlements, and pinnacles into which the front of the glacier is broken fall forward head-long from their bases like falling trees at the water-level or above or below it. They mostly sink vertically or nearly so, as if undermined by the melting action of the water of the inlet, occasionally maintaining their upright position after sinking far below the level of the water, and rising again a hundred feet or more into the air with water streaming like hair down their sides from their crowns, then launch forward and fall flat with yet another thundering report, raising spray in magnificent, flame-like, radiating jets and sheets, occasionally to the very top of the front wall. Illumined by the sun, the spray and angular crystal masses are indescribably beautiful. Some of the discharges pour in fragments from clefts in the wall like waterfalls, white and mealy-looking, even dusty with minute swirling ice-particles, followed by a rushing succession of thunder-tones combining into a huge, blunt, solemn roar. Most of these crumbling discharges are from the excessively shattered central part of the ice-wall; the solid deep-blue masses from the ends of the wall forming the large bergs rise from the bottom of the glacier.

Many lesser reports are heard at a distance of a mile or more from the fall of pinnacles into crevasses or from the opening of new crevasses. The berg discharges are very irregular, from three to twenty-two an hour. On one rising tide, six hours, there were sixty bergs discharged, large enough to thunder and be heard at distances of from three quarters to one and a half miles; and on one succeeding falling tide, six hours, sixty-nine were discharged.

JULY 1. We were awakened at four o'clock this morning by the whistle of the steamer George W. Elder. I went out on the moraine and waved my hand in salute and was answered by a toot from the whistle. Soon a party came ashore and asked if I was Professor Muir. The leader, Professor Harry Fielding Reid of Cleveland, Ohio, introduced himself and his companion, Mr. Cushing, also of Cleveland, and six or eight young students who had come well provided with instruments to study the glacier. They landed seven or eight tons of freight and pitched camp beside ours. I am delighted to have companions so congenial—we have now a village.

As I set out to climb the second mountain, three thousand feet high, on the east side of the glacier, I met many tourists returning from a walk on the smooth east margin of the glacier, and had to answer many questions. I had a hard climb, but wonderful views were developed and I sketched the glacier from this high point and most of its upper fountains.

Many fine alpine plants grew here, an anemone on the summit, two species of cassiope in shaggy mats, three or four dwarf willows, large blue hairy lupines eighteen inches high, parnassia, phlox, solidago, dandelion, white-flowered bryanthus, daisy, pedicularis, epilobium, etc., with grasses, sedges, mosses, and lichens, forming a delightful deep spongy sod. Woodchucks stood erect and piped dolefully for an hour "Chee-chee!" with jaws absurdly stretched to emit so thin a note—rusty-looking, seedy fellows, also a smaller striped species which stood erect and cheeped and whistled like a Douglas squirrel. I saw three or four species of birds. A finch flew from her nest at my feet; and I almost stepped on a family of young ptarmigan ere they scattered, little bunches of downy brown silk, small but able to run well. They scattered along a snow-bank, over boulders, through willows, grass, and flowers, while the mother, very lame, tumbled and sprawled at my feet. I stood still until the little ones began to peep; the mother answered "Too-too-too" and showed admirable judgment and devotion. She was in brown plumage with white on the wing primaries. She had fine grounds on which to lead and feed her young.

Not a cloud in the sky to-day; a faint film to the north vanished by noon, leaving all the sky full of soft, hazy light. The magnificent mountains around the widespread tributaries of the glacier; the great, gently undulating, prairie-like expanse of the main trunk, bluish on the east, pure white on the west and north; its trains of moraines in magnificent curving lines and many colors—black, gray, red, and brown; the stormy, cataract-like, crevassed sections; the hundred fountains; the lofty, pure white Fairweather Range; the thunder of the plunging bergs; the fleet of bergs sailing tranquilly in the inlet—formed a glowing picture of nature's beauty and power.

JULY 2. I crossed the inlet with Mr. Reid and Mr. Adams to-day. The stratified drift on the west side all the way from top to base contains fossil wood. On the east side, as far as I have seen it, the wood occurs only in one stratum at a height of about a hundred and twenty feet in sand and clay. Some in a bank of the west side are rooted in clay soil. I noticed a large grove of stumps in a washed-out channel near the glacier-front but had no time to examine closely. Evidently a flood carrying great quantities of sand and gravel had overwhelmed and broken off these trees, leaving high stumps. The deposit, about a hundred feet or more above them, had been recently washed out by one of the draining streams of the glacier, exposing a part of the old forest floor certainly two or three centuries old.

I climbed along the right bank of the lowest of the tributaries and set a signal flag on a ridge fourteen hundred feet high. This tributary is about one and a fourth or one and a half miles wide and has four secondary tributaries. It reaches tide-water but gives off no bergs. Later I climbed the large Nunatak Island, seven thousand feet high, near the west margin of the glacier. It is composed of crumbling granite draggled with washed boulders, but has some enduring bosses which on sides and top are polished and scored rigidly, showing that it had been heavily overswept by the glacier when it was thousands of feet deeper than now, like a submerged boulder in a river-channel. This island is very irregular in form, owing to the variations in the structure joints of the granite. It has several small lakelets and has been loaded with glacial drift, but by the melting of the ice about its flanks is shedding it off, together with some of its own crumbling surface. I descended a deep rock gully on the north side, the rawest, dirtiest, dustiest, most dangerous that I have seen hereabouts. There is also a large quantity of fossil wood scattered on this island, especially on the north side, that on the south side having been cleared off and carried away by the first tributary glacier, which, being lower and melting earlier, has allowed the soil of the moraine material to fall, together with its forest, and be carried off. That on the north side is now being carried off or buried. The last of the main ice foundation is melting and the moraine material re-formed over and over again, and the fallen tree-trunks, decayed or half decayed or in a fair state of preservation, are also unburied and buried again or carried off to the terminal or lateral moraine.

I found three small seedling Sitka spruces, feeble beginnings of a new forest. The circumference of the island is about seven miles. I arrived at camp about midnight, tired and cold. Sailing across the inlet in a cranky rotten boat through the midst of icebergs was dangerous, and I was glad to get ashore.

JULY 4. I climbed the east wall to the summit, about thirty-one hundred feet or so, by the northern-most ravine next to the yellow ridge, finding about a mile of snow in the upper portion of the ravine and patches on the summit. A few of the patches probably lie all the year, the ground beneath them is so plantless. On the edge of some of the snow-banks I noticed cassiope. The thin, green, moss-like patches seen from camp are composed of a rich, shaggy growth of cassiope, white-flowered bryanthus, dwarf vaccinium with bright pink flowers, saxifrages, anemones, bluebells, gentians, small erigeron, pedicularis, dwarf willow and a few species of grasses. Of these, *Cassiope tetragona* is far the most influential and beautiful. Here it forms mats a foot thick and an acre or more in area, the sections being measured by the size and drainage of the soil-patches. I saw a few plants anchored in the less crumbling parts of the steep-faced bosses and steps—parnassia, potentilla, hedysarum, lutkea, etc. The lower, rough-looking patches half way up the mountain are mostly alder bushes ten or fifteen feet high. I had a fine view of the top of the mountain-mass which forms the boundary wall of the upper portion of the inlet on the west side, and of several glaciers, tributary to the first of the eastern tributaries of the main Muir Glacier. Five or six of these tributaries were seen, most of them now melted off from the trunk and independent. The highest peak to the eastward has an elevation of about five thousand feet or a little less. I also had glorious views of the Fairweather Range, La Pérouse, Crillon, Lituya, and Fairweather. Mt. Fairweather is the most beautiful of all the giants that stand guard about Glacier Bay. When the sun is shining on it from the east or south its magnificent glaciers and colors are brought out in most telling display. In the late afternoon its features become less distinct. The atmosphere seems pale and hazy, though around to the north and northeastward of Fairweather innumerable white peaks are displayed, the highest fountain-heads of the Muir Glacier crowded together in bewildering array, most exciting and inviting to the mountaineer. Altogether I have had a delightful day, a truly glorious celebration of the fourth.

JULY 6. I sailed three or four miles down the east coast of the inlet with the Reid party's cook, who is supposed to be an experienced camper and prospector, and landed at a stratified moraine-bank. It was here that I camped in 1880, a point at that time less than half a mile from the front of the glacier, now one and a half miles. I found my Indian's old camp made just ten years ago, and Professor Wright's of five years ago. Their alder-bough beds and fireplace were still marked and but little decayed. I found thirty-three species of plants in flower, not counting willows—a showy garden on the shore only a few feet above high tide, watered by a fine stream. Lutkea, hedysarum, parnassia, epilobium, bluebell, solidago, habenaria, strawberry with fruit half grown, arctostaphylos, mertensia, erigeron, willows, tall grasses and alder are the principal species. There are many butterflies in this garden. Gulls are breeding near here. I saw young in the water to-day.

On my way back to camp I discovered a group of monumental stumps in a washed-out valley of the moraine and went ashore to observe them. They are in the dry course of a flood-channel about eighty feet above mean tide and four or five hundred yards back from the shore, where they have been pounded and battered by boulders rolling against them and over them, making them look like gigantic shaving-brushes. The largest is about three feet in diameter and probably three hundred years old. I mean to return and examine them at leisure. A smaller stump, still firmly rooted, is standing astride of an old crumbling trunk, showing that at least two generations of trees flourished here undisturbed by the advance or retreat of the glacier or by its draining stream-floods. They are Sitka spruces and the wood is mostly in a good state of preservation. How these trees were broken off without being uprooted is dark to me at present. Perhaps most of their companions were uprooted and carried away.

JULY 7. Another fine day; scarce a cloud in the sky. The icebergs in the bay are miraged in the distance to look like the frontal wall of

Ruins of Buried Forest, East Side of Muir Glacier

a great glacier. I am writing letters in anticipation of the next steamer, the Queen.

She arrived about 2.30 P.M. with two hundred and thirty tourists. What a show they made with their ribbons and kodaks! All seemed happy and enthusiastic, though it was curious to see how promptly all of them ceased gazing when the dinner-bell rang, and how many turned from the great thundering crystal world of ice to look curiously at the Indians that came alongside to sell trinkets, and how our little camp and kitchen arrangements excited so many to loiter and waste their precious time prying into our poor hut.

JULY 8. A fine clear day. I went up the glacier to observe stakes and found that a marked point near the middle of the current had flowed about a hundred feet in eight days. On the medial moraine one mile from the front there was no measureable displacement. I found a raven devouring a tom-cod that was alive on a shallow at the mouth of the creek. It had probably been wounded by a seal or eagle.

JULY 10. I have been getting acquainted with the main features of the glacier and its fountain mountains with reference to an exploration of its main tributaries and the upper part of its prairie-like trunk, a trip I have long had in mind. I have been building a sled and must now get fully ready to start without reference to the weather. Yesterday evening I saw a large blue berg just as it was detached sliding down from the front. Two of Professor Reid's party rowed out to it as it sailed past the camp, estimating it to be two hundred and forty feet in length and one hundred feet high.

CHAPTER XVIII

My Sled-Trip on the Muir Glacier

I started off the morning of July 11 on my memorable sled-trip to obtain general views of the main upper part of the Muir Glacier and its seven principal tributaries, feeling sure that I would learn something and at the same time get rid of a severe bronchial cough that followed an attack of the grippe and had troubled me for three months. I intended to camp on the glacier every night, and did so, and my throat grew better every day until it was well, for no lowland microbe could stand such a trip. My sled was about three feet long and made as light as possible. A sack of hardtack, a little tea and sugar, and a sleeping-bag were firmly lashed on it so that nothing could drop off however much it might be jarred and dangled in crossing crevasses.

Two Indians carried the baggage over the rocky moraine to the clear glacier at the side of one of the eastern Nunatak Islands. Mr. Loomis accompanied me to this first camp and assisted in dragging the empty sled over the moraine. We arrived at the middle Nunatak Island about nine o'clock. Here I sent back my Indian carriers, and Mr. Loomis assisted me the first day in hauling the loaded sled to my second camp at the foot of Hemlock Mountain, returning the next morning.

JULY 13. I skirted the mountain to eastward a few miles and was delighted to discover a group of trees high up on its ragged rocky side, the first trees I had seen on the shores of Glacier Bay or on those of any of its glaciers. I left my sled on the ice and climbed the mountain to see what I might learn. I found that all the trees were mountain hemlock (*Tsuga mertensiana*), and were evidently the remnant of an old well-established forest, standing on the only ground that was stable, all the rest of the forest below it having been sloughed off with the soil from the disintegrating slate bed rock. The lowest of the trees stood at an elevation of about two thousand feet above the sea, the highest at about three thousand feet or a little higher. Nothing could be more striking than the contrast between the raw, crumbling, deforested portions of the mountain, looking like a quarry that was being worked, and the forested part with its rich, shaggy beds of cassiope and bryanthus in full bloom, and its sumptuous cushions of flower-enameled mosses. These garden-patches are full of gay colors of gentian, erigeron, anemone, larkspur, and columbine, and are enlivened with happy birds and bees and marmots. Climbing to an elevation of twenty-five hundred feet, which is about fifteen hundred feet above the level of the glacier at this point, I saw and heard a few marmots, and three ptarmigans that were as tame as barnyard fowls. The sod is sloughing off on the edges, keeping it ragged. The trees are storm-bent from the southeast. A few are standing at an elevation of nearly three thousand feet; at twenty-five hundred feet, pyrola, veratrum, vaccinium, fine grasses, sedges, willows, mountain-ash, buttercups, and acres of the most luxuriant cassiope are in bloom.

A lake encumbered with icebergs lies at the end of Divide Glacier. A spacious, level-floored valley beyond it, eight or ten miles long, with forested mountains on its west side, perhaps discharges to the southeastward into Lynn Canal. The divide of the glacier is about opposite the third of the eastern tributaries. Another berg-dotted lake into which the drainage of the Braided Glacier flows, lies a few miles to the westward and is one and a half miles long. Berg Lake is next to the remarkable Girdled Glacier to the southeastward.

When the ice-period was in its prime, much of the Muir Glacier that now flows northward into Howling Valley flowed southward into Glacier Bay as a tributary of the Muir. All the rock contours show this, and so do the medial moraines. Berg Lake is crowded with bergs because they have no outlet and melt slowly. I heard none discharged. I had a hard time crossing the Divide Glacier, on which I camped. Half a mile back from the lake I gleaned a little fossil wood and made a fire on moraine boulders for tea. I slept fairly well on the sled. I heard the roar of four cascades on a shaggy green mountain on the west side of Howling Valley and saw three wild goats fifteen hundred feet up in the steep grassy pastures.

JULY 14. I rose at four o'clock this cloudy and dismal morning and looked for my goats, but saw only one. I thought there must be wolves where there were goats, and in a few minutes heard their low, dismal, far-reaching howling. One of them sounded very near and came nearer until it seemed to be less than a quarter of a mile away on the edge of the glacier. They had evidently seen me, and one or more had come down to observe me, but I was unable to catch sight of any of them. About half an hour later, while I was eating breakfast, they began howling again, so near I began to fear they had a mind to attack me, and I made haste to the shelter of a big square boulder, where, though I had no gun, I might be able to defend myself from a front attack with my alpenstock. After waiting half an hour or so to see what these wild dogs meant to do, I ventured to proceed on my journey to the foot of Snow Dome, where I camped for the night.

There are six tributaries on the northwest side of Divide arm, counting to the Gray Glacier, next after Granite Cañon Glacier going northwest. Next is Dirt Glacier, which is dead. I saw bergs on the edge of the main glacier a mile back from here which seem to have been left by the draining of a pool in a sunken hollow. A circling rim of driftwood, back twenty rods on the glacier, marks the edge of the lakelet shore where the bergs lie scattered and stranded. It is now half past ten o'clock and getting dusk as I sit by my little fossil-wood fire writing these notes. A strange bird is calling and complaining. A stream is rushing into a glacier well on the edge of which I am camped, back a few yards from the base of the mountain for fear of falling stones. A few small ones are rattling down the steep slope. I must go to bed.

JULY 15. I climbed the dome to plan a way, scan the glacier, and take bearings, etc., in case of storms. The main divide is about fifteen hundred feet; the second divide, about fifteen hundred also, is about one and one half miles southeastward. The flow of water on the glacier noticeably diminished last night though there was no frost. It is now already increasing. Stones begin to roll into the crevasses and into new positions, sliding against each other, half turning over or falling on moraine ridges. Mud pellets with small pebbles slip and roll slowly from ice-hummocks again and again. How often and by how many ways are boulders finished and finally brought to anything like permanent form and place in beds for farms and fields, forests and gardens. Into crevasses and out again, into moraines, shifted and reinforced and re-formed by avalanches, melting from pedestals, etc. Rain, frost, and dew help in the work; they are swept in rills, caught and ground in pot-hole mills. Moraines of washed pebbles, like those on glacier margins, are formed by snow avalanches deposited in crevasses, then weathered out and projected on the ice as shallow raised moraines. There is one such at this camp.

A ptarmigan is on a rock twenty yards distant, as if on show. It has red over the eye, a white line, not conspicuous, over the red, belly white, white markings over the upper parts on ground of brown and black wings, mostly white as seen when flying, but the coverts the same as the rest of the body. Only about three inches of the folded primaries show white. The breast seems to have golden iridescent colors, white under the wings. It allowed me to approach within twenty feet. It walked down a sixty degree slope of the rock, took flight with a few whirring wingbeats, then sailed with wings perfectly motionless four hundred yards down a gentle grade, and vanished over the brow of a cliff. Ten days ago Loomis told me that he found a nest with nine eggs. On the way down to my sled I saw four more ptarmigans. They utter harsh notes when alarmed. "Crack, chuck, crack," with the *r* rolled and prolonged. I also saw fresh and old goat-tracks and some bones that suggest wolves.

There is a pass through the mountains at the head of the third glacier. Fine mountains stand at the head on each side. The one on the northeast side is the higher and finer every way. It has three glaciers, tributary to the third. The third glacier has altogether ten tributaries, five on each side. The mountain on the left side of White Glacier is about six thousand feet high. The moraines of Girdled Glacier seem scarce to run anywhere. Only a little material is carried to Berg Lake. Most of it seems to be at rest as a terminal on the main glacier-field, which here has little motion. The curves of these last as seen from this mountain-top are very beautiful.

It has been a glorious day, all pure sunshine. An hour or more before sunset the distant mountains, a vast host, seemed more softly ethereal than ever, pale blue, ineffably fine, all angles and harshness melted off in the soft evening light. Even the snow and the grinding, cascading glaciers became divinely tender and fine in this celestial amethystine light. I got back to camp at 7.15, not tired. After my hardtack supper I could have climbed the mountain again and got back before sunrise, but dragging the sled tires me. I have been out on the glacier examining a moraine-like mass about a third of a mile from camp. It is perhaps a mile long, a hundred yards wide, and is thickly strewn with wood. I think that it has been brought down the mountain by a heavy snow avalanche, loaded on the ice, then carried away from the shore in the direction of the flow of the glacier. This explains detached moraine-masses. This one seems to have been derived from a big roomy cirque or amphitheatre on the northwest side of this Snow Dome Mountain.

To shorten the return journey I was tempted to glissade down what appeared to be a snow-filled ravine, which was very steep. All went well until I reached a bluish spot which proved to be ice, on which I lost control of myself and rolled into a gravel talus at the foot without a scratch. Just as I got up and was getting myself orientated, I heard a loud fierce scream, uttered in an exulting, diabolical tone of voice which startled me, as if an enemy, having seen me fall, was glorying in my death. Then suddenly two ravens came swooping from the sky and alighted on the jag of a rock within a few feet of me, evidently hoping that I had been maimed and that they were going to have a feast. But as they stared at me, studying my condition, impatiently waiting for bone-picking time, I saw what they were up to and shouted, "Not yet, not yet!"

JULY 16. At 7 A.M. I left camp to cross the main glacier. Six ravens came to the camp as soon as I left. What wonderful eyes they must have! Nothing that moves in all this icy wilderness escapes the eyes of these brave birds. This is one of the loveliest mornings I ever saw in Alaska; not a cloud or faintest hint of one in all the wide sky. There is a yellowish haze in the east, white in the west, mild and mellow as a Wisconsin Indian Summer, but finer, more ethereal, God's holy light making all divine.

In an hour or so I came to the confluence of the first of the seven grand tributaries of the main Muir Glacier and had a glorious view of it as it comes sweeping down in wild cascades from its magnificent, pure white, mountain-girt basin to join the main crystal sea, its many fountain peaks, clustered and crowded, all pouring forth their tribute to swell its grand current. I crossed its front a little below its confluence, where its shattered current, about two or three miles wide, is reunited, and many rills and good-sized brooks glide gurgling and ringing in pure blue channels, giving delightful animation to the icy solitude.

Most of the ice-surface crossed to-day has been very uneven, and hauling the sled and finding a way over hummocks has been fatiguing. At times I had to lift the sled bodily and to cross many narrow, nerve-trying, ice-sliver bridges, balancing astride of them, and cautiously shoving the sled ahead of me with tremendous chasms on either side. I had made perhaps not more than six or eight miles in a straight line by six o'clock this evening when I reached ice so hummocky and tedious I concluded to camp and not try to take the sled any farther. I intend to leave it here in the middle of the basin and carry my sleeping-bag and provisions the rest of the way across to the west side. I am cozy and comfortable here resting in the midst of glorious icy scenery, though very tired. I made out to get a cup of tea by means of a few shavings and splinters whittled from the bottom board of my sled, and made a fire in a little can, a small camp-fire, the smallest I ever made or saw, yet it answered well enough as far as tea was concerned. I crept into my sack before eight o'clock as the wind was cold and my feet wet. One of my shoes is about worn out. I may have to put on a wooden sole. This day has been cloudless throughout, with lovely sunshine, a purple evening and morning. The circumference of mountains beheld from the midst of this world of ice is marvelous, the vast plain reposing in such soft tender light, the fountain mountains so clearly cut, holding themselves aloft with their loads of ice in supreme strength and beauty of architecture. I found a skull and most of the other bones of a goat on the glacier about two miles from the nearest land. It had probably been chased out of its mountain home by wolves and devoured here. I carried its horns with me. I saw many considerable depressions in the glacial surface, also a pit-like hole, irregular, not like the ordinary wells along the slope of the many small dirt-clad hillocks, faced to the south. Now the sun is down and the sky is saffron yellow, blending and fading into purple around to the south and north. It is a curious experience to be lying in bed writing these notes, hummock waves rising in every direction, their edges marking a multitude of crevasses and pits, while all around the horizon rise peaks innumerable of most intricate style of architecture. Solemnly growling and grinding moulins contrast with the sweet low-voiced whispering and warbling of a network of rills, singing like water-ouzels, glinting, gliding with indescribable softness and sweetness of voice. They are all around, one within a few feet of my hard sled bed.

JULY 17. Another glorious cloudless day is dawning in yellow and purple and soon the sun over the eastern peak will blot out the blue peak shadows and make all the vast white ice prairie sparkle. I slept well last night in the middle of the icy sea. The wind was cold but my sleeping-bag enabled me to lie neither warm nor intolerably cold. My three-months' cough is gone. Strange that with such work and exposure one should know nothing of sore throats and of what are called colds. My heavy, thick-soled shoes, resoled just before starting on the trip six days ago, are about worn out and my feet have been wet every night. But no harm comes of it, nothing but good. I succeeded in getting a warm breakfast in bed. I reached over the edge of my sled, got hold of a small cedar stick that I had been carrying, whittled a lot of thin shavings from it, stored them on my breast, then set fire to a piece of paper in a shallow tin can, added a pinch of shavings, held the cup of water that always stood at my bedside over the tiny blaze with one hand, and fed the fire by adding little pinches of shavings until the water boiled, then pulling my bread sack within reach, made a good warm breakfast, cooked and eaten in bed. Thus refreshed, I surveyed the wilderness of crevassed, hummocky ice and concluded to try to drag my little sled a mile or two farther, then, finding encouragement, persevered, getting it across innumerable crevasses and streams and around several lakes and over and through the midst of hummocks, and at length reached the western shore between five and six o'clock this evening, extremely fatigued. This I consider a hard job well done, crossing so wildly broken a glacier, fifteen miles of it from Snow Dome Mountain, in two days with a sled weighing altogether not less than a hundred pounds. I found innumerable crevasses, some of them brimful of water. I crossed in most places just where the ice was close pressed and welded after descending cascades and was being shoved over an upward slope, thus closing the crevasses at the bottom, leaving only the upper sun-melted beveled portion open for water to collect in.

Vast must be the drainage from this great basin. The waste in sunshine must be enormous, while in dark weather rains and winds also melt the ice and add to the volume produced by the rain itself. The winds also, though in temperature they may be only a degree or two above freezing-point, dissolve the ice as fast, or perhaps faster, than clear sunshine. Much of the water caught in tight crevasses doubtless freezes during the winter and gives rise to many of the irregular veins seen in the structure of the glacier. Saturated snow also freezes at times and is incorporated with the ice, as only from the lower part of the glacier is the snow melted during the summer. I have noticed many traces of this action. One of the most beautiful things to be seen on the glacier is the myriads of minute and intensely brilliant radiant lights burning in rows on the banks of streams and pools and lakelets from the tips of crystals melting in the sun, making them look as if bordered with diamonds. These gems are rayed like stars and twinkle; no diamond radiates keener or more brilliant light. It was perfectly glorious to think of this divine light burning over all this vast crystal sea in such ineffably fine effulgence, and over how many other of icy Alaska's glaciers where nobody sees it. To produce these effects I fancy the ice must be melting rapidly, as it was being melted to-day. The ice in these pools does not melt with anything like an even surface, but in long branches and leaves, making fairy forests of points, while minute bubbles of air are constantly being set free. I am camped to-night on what I call Quarry Mountain from its raw, loose, plantless condition, seven or eight miles above the front of the glacier. I found enough fossil wood for tea. Glorious is the view to the eastward from this camp. The sun has set, a few clouds appear, and a torrent rushing down a gully and under the edge of the glacier is making a solemn roaring. No tinkling, whistling rills this night. Ever and anon I hear a falling boulder. I have had a glorious and instructive day, but am excessively weary and to bed I go.

JULY 18. I felt tired this morning and meant to rest to-day. But after breakfast at 8 A.M. I felt I must be up and doing, climbing, sketching new views up the great tributaries from the top of Quarry Mountain. Weariness vanished and I could have climbed, I think, five thousand feet. Anything seems easy after sled-dragging over hummocks and crevasses, and the constant nerve-strain in jumping crevasses so as not to slip in making the spring. Quarry Mountain is the barest I have seen, a raw quarry with infinite abundance of loose decaying granite all on the go. Its slopes are excessively steep. A few patches of epilobium make gay purple spots of color. Its seeds fly everywhere seeking homes. Quarry Mountain is cut across into a series of parallel ridges by oversweeping ice. It is still overswept in three places by glacial flows a half to three quarters of a mile wide, finely arched at the top of the divides. I have been sketching, though my eyes are much inflamed and I can scarce see. All the lines I make appear double. I fear I shall not be able to make the few more sketches I want to-morrow, but must try. The day has been gloriously sunful, the glacier pale yellow toward five o'clock. The hazy air, white with a yellow tinge, gives an Indiansummerish effect. Now the blue evening shadows are creeping out over the icy plain, some ten miles long, with sunny yellow belts between them. Boulders fall now and again with dull, blunt booming, and the gravel pebbles rattle.

JULY 19. Nearly blind. The light is intolerable and I fear I may be long unfitted for work. I have been lying on my back all day with a snow poultice bound over my eyes. Every object I try to look at seems double; even the distant mountain-ranges are doubled, the upper an exact copy of the lower, though somewhat faint. This is the first time in Alaska that I have had too much sunshine. About four o'clock this afternoon, when I was waiting for the evening shadows to enable me to get nearer the main camp, where I could be more easily found in case my eyes should become still more inflamed and I should be unable to travel, thin clouds cast a grateful shade over all the glowing landscape. I gladly took advantage of these kindly clouds to make an effort to cross the few miles of the glacier that lay between me and the shore of the inlet. I made a pair of goggles but am afraid to wear them. Fortunately the ice here is but little broken, therefore I pulled my cap well down and set off about five o'clock. I got on pretty well and camped on the glacier in sight of the main camp, which from here in a straight line is only five or six miles away. I went ashore on Granite Island and gleaned a little fossil wood with which I made tea on the ice.

JULY 20. I kept wet bandages on my eyes last night as long as I could, and feel better this morning, but all the mountains still seem to have double summits, giving a curiously unreal aspect to the landscape. I packed everything on the sled and moved three miles farther down the glacier, where I want to make measurements. Twice to-day I was visited on the ice by a hummingbird, attracted by the red lining of the bear-skin sleeping-bag.

I have gained some light on the formation of gravel-beds along the inlet. The material is mostly sifted and sorted by successive rollings and washings along the margins of the glacier-tributaries, where the supply is abundant beyond anything I ever saw elsewhere. The lowering of the surface of a glacier when its walls are not too steep leaves a part of the margin dead and buried and protected from the wasting sunshine beneath the lateral moraines. Thus a marginal valley is formed, clear ice on one side, or nearly so, buried ice on the other. As melting goes on, the marginal trough, or valley, grows deeper and wider, since both sides are being melted, the land side slower. The dead, protected ice in melting first sheds off the large boulders, as they are not able to lie on slopes where smaller ones can. Then the next larger ones are rolled off, and pebbles and sand in succession. Meanwhile this material is subjected to torrent-action, as if it were cast into a trough. When floods come it is carried forward and stratified, according to the force of the current, sand, mud, or larger material. This exposes fresh surfaces of ice and melting goes on again, until enough material has been undermined to form a veil in front; then follows another washing and carrying-away and depositing where the current is allowed to spread. In melting, protected margin terraces are oftentimes formed. Perhaps these terraces mark successive heights of the glacial surface. From terrace to terrace the grist of stone is rolled and sifted. Some, meeting only feeble streams, have only the fine particles carried away and deposited in smooth beds; others, coarser, from swifter streams, overspread the fine beds, while many of the large boulders no doubt roll back upon the glacier to go on their travels again.

It has been cloudy mostly to-day, though sunny in the afternoon, and my eyes are getting better. The steamer Queen is expected in a day or two, so I must try to get down to the inlet to-morrow and make signal to have some of the Reid party ferry me over. I must hear from home, write letters, get rest and more to eat.

Near the front of the glacier the ice was perfectly free, apparently, of anything like a crevasse, and in walking almost carelessly down it I stopped opposite the large granite Nunatak Island, thinking that I would there be partly sheltered from the wind. I had not gone a dozen steps toward the island when I suddenly dropped into a concealed water-filled crevasse, which on the surface showed not the slightest sign of its existence. This crevasse like many others was being used as the channel of a stream, and at some narrow point the small cubical masses of ice into which the glacier surface disintegrates were jammed and extended back farther and farther till they completely covered and concealed the water. Into this I suddenly plunged, after crossing thousands of really dangerous crevasses, but never before had I encountered a danger so completely concealed. Down I plunged over head and ears, but of course bobbed up again, and after a hard struggle succeeded in dragging myself out over the farther side. Then I pulled my sled over close to Nunatak cliff, made haste to strip off my clothing, threw it in a sloppy heap and crept into my sleeping-bag to shiver away the night as best I could.

JULY 21. Dressing this rainy morning was a miserable job, but might have been worse. After wringing my sloppy underclothing, getting it on was far from pleasant. My eyes are better and I feel no bad effect from my icy bath. The last trace of my three months' cough is gone. No lowland grippe microbe could survive such experiences.

I have had a fine telling day examining the ruins of the old forest of Sitka spruce that no great time ago grew in a shallow mud-filled basin near the southwest corner of the glacier. The trees were protected by a spur of the mountain that puts out here, and when the glacier advanced they were simply flooded with fine sand and overborne. Stumps by the hundred, three to fifteen feet high, rooted in a stream of fine blue mud on cobbles, still have their bark on. A stratum of decomposed bark, leaves, cones, and old trunks is still in place. Some of the stumps are on rocky ridges of gravelly soil about one hundred and twenty-five feet above the sea. The valley has been washed out by the stream now occupying it, one of the glacier's draining streams a mile long or more and an eighth of a mile wide.

I got supper early and was just going to bed, when I was startled by seeing a man coming across the moraine, Professor Reid, who had seen me from the main camp and who came with Mr. Loomis and the cook in their boat to ferry me over. I had not intended making signals for them until to-morrow but was glad to go. I had been seen also by Mr. Case and one of his companions, who were on the western mountain-side above the fossil forest, shooting ptarmigans. I had a good rest and sleep and leisure to find out how rich I was in new facts and pictures and how tired and hungry I was.

CHAPTER XIX

Auroras

A few days later I set out with Professor Reid's party to visit some of the other large glaciers that flow into the bay, to observe what changes have taken place in them since October, 1879, when I first visited and sketched them. We found the upper half of the bay closely choked with bergs, through which it was exceedingly difficult to force a way. After slowly struggling a few miles up the east side, we dragged the whale-boat and canoe over rough rocks into a fine garden and comfortably camped for the night.

The next day was spent in cautiously picking a way across to the west side of the bay; and as the strangely scanty stock of provisions was already about done, and the ice-jam to the northward seemed impenetrable, the party decided to return to the main camp by a comparatively open, roundabout way to the southward, while with the canoe and a handful of food-scraps I pushed on northward. After a hard, anxious struggle, I reached the mouth of the Hugh Miller fiord about sundown, and tried to find a camp-spot on its steep, boulder-bound shore. But no landing-place where it seemed possible to drag the canoe above high-tide mark was discovered after examining a mile or more of this dreary, forbidding barrier, and as night was closing down, I decided to try to grope my way across the mouth of the fiord in the starlight to an open sandy spot on which I had camped in October, 1879, a distance of about three or four miles.

With the utmost caution I picked my way through the sparkling bergs, and after an hour or two of this nerve-trying work, when I was perhaps less than halfway across and dreading the loss of the frail canoe which would include the loss of myself, I came to a pack of very large bergs which loomed threateningly, offering no visible thoroughfare. Paddling and pushing to right and left, I at last discovered a sheer-walled opening about four feet wide and perhaps two hundred feet long, formed apparently by the splitting of a huge iceberg. I hesitated to enter this passage, fearing that the slightest change in the tide-current might close it, but ventured nevertheless, judging that the dangers ahead might not be greater than those I had already passed. When I had got about a third of the way in, I suddenly discovered that the smooth-walled ice-lane was growing narrower, and with desperate haste backed out. Just as the bow of the canoe cleared the sheer walls they came together with a growling crunch. Terror-stricken, I turned back, and in an anxious hour or two gladly reached the rock-bound shore that had at first repelled me, determined to stay on guard all night in the canoe or find some place where with the strength that comes in a fight for life I could drag it up the boulder wall beyond ice danger. This at last was happily done about midnight, and with no thought of sleep I went to bed rejoicing.

My bed was two boulders, and as I lay wedged and bent on their up-bulging sides, beguiling the hard, cold time in gazing into the starry sky and across the sparkling bay, magnificent upright bars of light in bright prismatic colors suddenly appeared, marching swiftly in close succession along the northern horizon from west to east as if in diligent haste, an auroral display very different from any I had ever before beheld. Once long ago in Wisconsin I saw the heavens draped in rich purple auroral clouds fringed and folded in most magnificent forms; but in this glory of light, so pure, so bright, so enthusiastic in motion, there was nothing in the least cloud-like. The short color-bars, apparently about two degrees in height,

Floating Iceberg, Taku Inlet

though blending, seemed to be as well defined as those of the solar spectrum.

How long these glad, eager soldiers of light held on their way I cannot tell; for sense of time was charmed out of mind and the blessed night circled away in measureless rejoicing enthusiasm.

In the early morning after so inspiring a night I launched my canoe feeling able for anything, crossed the mouth of the Hugh Miller fiord, and forced a way three or four miles along the shore of the bay, hoping to reach the Grand Pacific Glacier in front of Mt. Fairweather. But the farther I went, the ice-pack, instead of showing inviting little open streaks here and there, became so much harder jammed that on some parts of the shore the bergs, drifting south with the tide, were shoving one another out of the water beyond high-tide line. Farther progress to northward was thus rigidly stopped, and now I had to fight for a way back to my cabin, hoping that by good tide luck I might reach it before dark. But at sundown I was less than half-way home, and though very hungry was glad to land on a little rock island with a smooth beach for the canoe and a thicket of alder bushes for fire and bed and a little sleep. But shortly after sundown, while these arrangements were being made, lo and behold another aurora enriching the heavens! and though it proved to be one of the ordinary almost colorless kind, thrusting long, quivering lances toward the zenith from a dark cloud-like base, after last night's wonderful display one's expectations might well be extravagant and I lay wide awake watching.

On the third night I reached my cabin and food. Professor Reid and his party came in to talk over the results of our excursions, and just as the last one of the visitors opened the door after bidding good-night, he shouted, "Muir, come look here. Here's something fine."

I ran out in auroral excitement, and sure enough here was another aurora, as novel and wonderful as the marching rainbow-colored columns—a glowing silver bow spanning the Muir Inlet in a magnificent arch right under the zenith, or a little to the south of it, the ends resting on the top of the mountain-walls. And though colorless and steadfast, its intense, solid, white splendor, noble proportions, and fineness of finish excited boundless admiration. In form and proportion it was like a rainbow, a bridge of one span five miles wide; and so brilliant, so fine and solid and homogeneous in every part, I fancy that if all the stars were raked together into one windrow, fused and welded and run through some celestial rolling-mill, all would be required to make this one glowing white colossal bridge.

After my last visitor went to bed, I lay down on the moraine in front of the cabin and gazed and watched. Hour after hour the wonderful arch stood perfectly motionless, sharply defined and substantial-looking as if it were a permanent addition to the furniture of the sky. At length while it yet spanned the inlet in serene unchanging splendor, a band of fluffy, pale gray, quivering ringlets came suddenly all in a row over the eastern mountain-top, glided in nervous haste up and down the under side of the bow and over the western mountain-wall. They were about one and a half times the apparent diameter of the bow in length, maintained a vertical posture all the way across, and slipped swiftly along as if they were suspended like a curtain on rings. Had these lively auroral fairies marched across the fiord on the top of the bow instead of shuffling along the under side of it, one might have fancied they were a happy band of spirit people on a journey making use of the splendid bow for a bridge. There must have been hundreds of miles of them; for the time required for each to cross from one end of the bridge to the other seemed only a minute or less, while nearly an hour elapsed from their first appearance until the last of the rushing throng vanished behind the western mountain, leaving the bridge as bright and solid and steadfast as before they arrived. But later, half an hour or so, it began to fade. Fissures or cracks crossed it diagonally through which a few stars were seen, and gradually it became thin and nebulous until it looked like the Milky Way, and at last vanished, leaving no visible monument of any sort to mark its place.

I now returned to my cabin, replenished the fire, warmed myself, and prepared to go to bed, though too aurorally rich and happy to go to sleep. But just as I was about to retire, I thought I had better take another look at the sky, to make sure that the glorious show was over; and, contrary to all reasonable expectations, I found that the pale foundation for another bow was being laid right overhead like the first. Then losing all thought of sleep, I ran back to my cabin, carried out blankets and lay down on the moraine to keep watch until daybreak, that none of the sky wonders of the glorious night within reach of my eyes might be lost.

I had seen the first bow when it stood complete in full splendor, and its gradual fading decay. Now I was to see the building of a new one from the beginning. Perhaps in less than half an hour the silvery material was gathered, condensed, and welded into a glowing, evenly proportioned arc like the first and in the same part of the sky. Then in due time over the eastern mountain-wall came another throng of restless electric auroral fairies, the infinitely fine pale-gray garments of each lightly touching those of their neighbors as they swept swiftly along the under side of the bridge and down over the western mountain like the merry band that had gone the same way before them, all keeping quivery step and time to music too fine for mortal ears.

While the gay throng was gliding swiftly along, I watched the bridge for any change they might make upon it, but not the slightest could I detect. They left no visible track, and after all had passed the glowing arc stood firm and apparently immutable, but at last faded slowly away like its glorious predecessor.

Excepting only the vast purple aurora mentioned above, said to have been visible over nearly all the continent, these two silver bows in supreme, serene, supernal beauty surpassed everything auroral I ever beheld.

Glossary of Words in the Chinook Jargon

Boston: English.

Chuck: Water, stream.

Delait: Very, *or* very good.

Friday: Shoreward.

Hi yu: A great quantity of, plenty of.

Hootchenoo: A native liquor. *See page* 152.

Hyas: Big, very.

Klosh: Good.

Kumtux: Know, understand.

Mika: You, your (*singular*).

Muck-a-muck: Food.

Poogh: Shoot, shooting.

Sagh-a-ya: How do you do?

Skookum: Strong.

Skookum-house: Jail.

Tillicum: Friend.

Tola: Lead (*verb*).

Tucktay: Seaward.

Tumtum: Mind, heart.

Wawa: Talk (*noun or verb*).

INDEX

A Note on the Type

The principal text of this Modern Library edition
was set in a digitized version of Janson,
a typeface that dates from about 1690 and was cut by Nicholas Kis,
a Hungarian working in Amsterdam. The original matrices have
survived and are held by the Stempel foundry in Germany.
Hermann Zapf redesigned some of the weights and sizes for Stempel,
basing his revisions on the original design.

MODERN LIBRARY IS ONLINE AT WWW.MODERNLIBRARY.COM

MODERN LIBRARY ONLINE IS YOUR GUIDE TO CLASSIC LITERATURE ON THE WEB

THE MODERN LIBRARY E-NEWSLETTER

Our free e-mail newsletter is sent to subscribers, and features sample chapters, interviews with and essays by our authors, upcoming books, special promotions, announcements, and news.

To subscribe to the Modern Library e-newsletter, send a blank e-mail to: sub_modernlibrary@info.randomhouse.com or visit www.modernlibrary.com

THE MODERN LIBRARY WEBSITE

Check out the Modern Library website at
www.modernlibrary.com for:

- The Modern Library e-newsletter
- A list of our current and upcoming titles and series
- Reading Group Guides and exclusive author spotlights
- Special features with information on the classics and other paperback series
- Excerpts from new releases and other titles
- A list of our e-books and information on where to buy them
- The Modern Library Editorial Board's 100 Best Novels and 100 Best Nonfiction Books of the Twentieth Century written in the English language
- News and announcements

Questions? E-mail us at modernlibrary@randomhouse.com.
For questions about examination or desk copies, please visit
the Random House Academic Resources site at
www.randomhouse.com/academic